CHE

"An [...] being fair, shrew [...] rystal clarity that Rowan h[...] ristlike, form of 'leadership'. Among his astonishing array of accomplishments, that may be the most important."
Professor Tom Wright, former Bishop of Durham

"Here in this wonderful book you are given the opportunity to see a true living saint, scholar, and servant of God. I will never forget the day when I took my curate from Baghdad to meet with the archbishop. As we prepared to leave the archbishop got down on his knees and said to my curate 'Will you bless me before you leave?' This was the grace, peace and humility of our primate that we see so clearly in this book."
Canon Andrew White, author of *The Vicar of Baghdad*

"Early assessments are risky, but this one takes that risk with a commitment to fairness, and to affirmation as much as critique. Future commentary on this remarkable archbishop will be able to build on this picture, but this is a very helpful beginning to our understanding of the gifts we have received from Rowan Williams."
Peter Selby, former Bishop of Worcester

"Andrew is highly skilled as a writer and a theologian, which makes him an excellent person to paint this clear and fascinating portrait of Rowan Williams. It's a timely book for anyone wanting a deeper look at Rowan's legacy. I thoroughly enjoyed it and recommend it to you."
Vicky Beeching, theologian, ethicist, writer, and broadcaster

"Frank and perceptive, Goddard draws together a wealth of reflections on Rowan Williams, as well as a remarkable collection of the archbishop's own writings and comments, giving us a deep and fresh insight into Williams' humanity and theology."
Christina Rees, member of the General Synod, a broadcaster and writer

"Rowan Williams' tenure as Archbishop of Canterbury provided the scope for considerable intellect and graciousness during a very demanding decade of spiritual leadership. This biography introduces us more closely to the man behind the ministry."
Joel Edwards, international director of Micah Challenge

With thanks to God for my fellowship and friendship with those in Fulcrum and the Anglican Communion Institute

ROWAN WILLIAMS

His Legacy

ANDREW
GODDARD

LION

Published by Lion Books
an imprint of
Lion Hudson plc
Wilkinson House, Jordan Hill Road,
Oxford OX2 8DR, England
www.lionhudson.com/lion

ISBN 978 0 7459 5602 2
e-ISBN 978 0 7459 5762 3

First edition 2013

Every effort has been made to trace the original copyright holders where required. In some cases this has proved impossible. We shall be happy to correct any such omissions in future editions. pp. 29–30: Extracts from *The Body's Grace* by Rowan Williams copyright © Rowan Williams, 2002. Reprinted by permission of Lesbian and Gay Christian Movement; pp. 35–36: Extracts from "Our differences need not destroy us" in *The Tablet* copyright © The Tablet, 2000. Reprinted by permission of The Tablet; pp. 40–41: Extracts from *Rowan's Rule: The Biography of the Archbishop* by Rupert Shortt copyright © Rupert Shortt, 2009. Published by Hodder and Stoughton; p. 139: Extracts from "The Structures of Unity" in *New Directions* magazine copyright © New Directions, 2004. Reprinted by permission of New Directions; pp. 176, 202–203: Extracts from *The Ecumenical Relationship* by Mark Langham copyright © Mark Langham, 2012. Reprinted by permission of Mark Langham; pp. 242, 244: Extracts from BBC ... ed by permission of BBC;

Scripture quotation taken from the Holy Bible, New International Version, copyright © 1973, 1978, 1984 International Bible Society. Used by permission of Hodder & Stoughton, a member of the Hodder Headline Group. All rights reserved. 'NIV' is a trademark of International Bible Society. UK trademark number 1448790.

A catalogue record for this book is available from the British Library

Printed and bound in Great Britain, December 2012, LH26

Contents

Preface

The ten years of Rowan Williams' primacy as Archbishop of Canterbury from 2002 to 2012 have seen major change and turmoil in the life of the Church of England and the wider Anglican Communion. It has not been an easy time to lead the church, and he was clear that he hoped his successor would have "the constitution of an ox and the skin of a rhinoceros".

The playwright David Hare recalled a conversation with him in the BBC make-up room before they appeared together on *Newsnight* in September 2009. Hare was writing his diary and when Rowan asked him about its contents he "admitted it was the usual unattractive mix of whingeing and self-pity". He suggested that Rowan's own diary as archbishop would be far more interesting and asked him if he kept one. Rowan explained that he didn't but he feared that if he had it would have been pretty much like Hare's. One of the antidotes to self-pity was remarked upon when he preached in Oxford to mark the 450th anniversary of the martyrdom of Thomas Cranmer in 2006, only a month after commemorating the centenary of the birth of twentieth-century martyr, Dietrich Bonhoeffer. In conversation with a former colleague, Rowan remarked that one of the benefits of such events is that when things were tough they reminded him how easy his calling was compared to that of some of his predecessors as archbishop and other Christian leaders.

It would, however, be wrong to focus solely on the negative and tragic features as under Rowan there has also been much to celebrate. The chapters that follow seek to paint a rounded portrait of Rowan as archbishop, provide an account of his ministry and the theological vision that shaped it, and put forward some initial, tentative assessments of both its highs and lows and the legacy he leaves the church and his successor. The opening chapter offers a biographical sketch of Rowan which highlights those elements that proved most decisive in shaping his time as archbishop. Here I am particularly grateful to Rupert Shortt for his biography which has proved an invaluable guide. Following an account of his messy appointment to lead a messy church and a reminder of his initial vision and commitments (Chapter 2), the book begins its journey through his primacy with a focus on his ministry within the Church of England. Rather than open with the internal politics that so often dominate the media, it starts by looking out in terms of the church's mission (Chapters 3–5) and only then turning to the hot topics of sexuality (Chapter 6) and women bishops (Chapter 7). The next three chapters (Chapters 8–10) try to chart a path through the turmoil within the wider Anglican Communion. There follow accounts of his relations with other churches (Chapter 11) and his contributions to interfaith relationships (Chapter 12) and issues in wider society (Chapters 13–14). The book concludes by stepping back from such piece-by-piece examinations of different areas to offer an interpretative sketch of the hallmarks of his ministry as priest and bishop (Chapter 15), perhaps his most obvious and immediate legacy.

Throughout the book, but particularly in that final chapter, I am greatly indebted to the many people who spoke or wrote to me and provided material, reflections, and expertise as I wrote the book. A few asked not to be named but I am glad to be able to thank the following publicly for their input in various forms: Francis Bridger, Mark Broomhead, Malcolm Brown, Colin Buchanan, Andrew Burnham, Paul Butler, Brett Cane, George Carey, John Chane, Jonathan Chaplin, Mark Chapman, John Clark, Jonathan Clatworthy, Colin Coward, Graham

Cray, Louie Crew, Steven Croft, Alastair Cutting, Tim Dakin, Martin Davie, Ian Douglas, Colin Fletcher, Philip Giddings, Giles Goddard, Jonathan Goodall, Michael Green, Jon Groves, Phil Groves, Tudor Griffiths, Ben Guyer, Richard Harries, Clare Herbert, Mike Higton, David Hilborn, Mike Hill, John Hind, Bob Hopkins, Mary Hopkins, David Houlding, Rachel Jordan, Kenneth Kearon, Christopher Landau, Mark Langham, Andy Lines, David Marshall, Mark McCall, Marilyn McCord Adams, Martyn Minns, Roger Paul, Colin Podmore, Michael Poon, Ephraim Radner, John Rees, Geoffrey Rowell, Chris Rowland, Sarah Rowland Jones, Mark Russell, Michael Scott-Joynt, Christopher Seitz, Peter Selby, Keith Sinclair, Richard Sudworth, Rod Symmons, Graham Tomlin, Nick Townsend, Philip Turner, Craig Uffmann, Dominic Walker, Justin Welby, Christopher Wells, Meurig Williams, Stephen Williams, Tom Wright.

Alongside their reflections the most valuable resource has been the excellent website of the archbishop (http://www.archbishopofcanterbury.org). I thought I had a fairly good sense of what Rowan had said and done over the last ten years until I began exploring the website more fully and discovered the astonishing range of his activities through the material gathered there. As I hope to enable people to understand something of what Rowan thought he was doing and see how his actions are integrated into his theological vision and reflection, I quote extensively from the site. My publishers and I gratefully acknowledge Archbishop Williams' generous permission to quote this website so liberally; the copyright in all that material remains his. Thanks are also due to Robin Baird-Smith and Bloomsbury Publishing for their kind permission to quote from the archbishop's lectures and speeches that were recently gathered and published under the title *Faith in the Public Square*. It is planned that other major pieces by the archbishop in various subject areas will be gathered and published in this way. The articles in *Faith in the Public Square* are especially relevant to Chapters 12 to 14 of the present book.

Attempting to produce this sort of book while Rowan still has a number of months to serve sadly makes it guilty of some of the failings of our culture which he rightly critiqued, including an impatient unwillingness to take time and a hurried rush to judgment. I suspect his own approach would be closer to that of church historians who, when asked to offer an assessment of the Reformation on the life of the church and whether it was "a good thing", warn you that it is too soon to make such judgments. The speed of production also means that there are inevitably going to be some errors of fact as well as of interpretation in the pages which follow and I apologize for these. If you spot any, or have additional material you would like to provide for any possible further editions or writing on Rowan, please write to me at rowanslegacy@gmail.com.

To keep notes to a minimum, only quotations from personal interviews and emails, quotations heading chapters and sections, and longer, indented quotations are referenced in the Notes section at the end of the book.

A short commentary may be necessary on nomenclature. Although it would have been possible to refer to "Dr Williams" or "Williams" or "Archbishop Rowan", one of the distinctive features of his primacy is that Rowan Williams is almost universally referred to in the church simply as "Rowan" and so, following the precedent set in Rupert Shortt's biography, that is the style adopted here.

I am grateful to Ali Hull at Lion Hudson for approaching me last June with the idea of this book and thankful to her and all the others who provided support and help throughout the pressured production process, particularly Jessica Tinker, Lawrence Osborn, Margaret Milton, and Miranda Lever. Less than four months is rather a short time in which to research and write and my wife Lis and children, Jonathan and Nell, have been an incredible support and encouragement, even tolerating me reading more Rowan Williams than I should have done during our summer holiday. I am particularly grateful to Nell who also read and commented honestly on a first draft and who will make a great editor. I am sorry, Nell, that the more eye-catching title you wanted was never going to happen!

Serving as a Church of England priest throughout Rowan's time as archbishop I've been involved to varying degrees in areas discussed in this book – particularly those relating to the Reading crisis, sexuality debates, and the Anglican Communion – and through this have been enriched by fellowship with many fellow Anglicans. Two particular sets of relationships were first formed around the time Rowan's appointment was announced, and they have been especially sustaining and significant throughout the last ten years. I am therefore pleased to dedicate this book to my friends and colleagues in Fulcrum and the Anglican Communion Institute.

Back in 2004, when asked by Mary Ann Sieghart how he would like to be judged at the end of his tenure, Rowan laughed and answered with one word: "Mercifully!" A similar note was struck in 2007 when he was asked, "When your tenure of office is over, when you have gone to retirement, how would you like the world to remember you?" He replied "I would like the world to remember me mercifully, and I hope, as somebody who tried to serve the body of Christ." My hope and prayer is that the account and judgments that follow are fair and merciful and that they honour Rowan as a servant of Christ and of the body of Christ.

1

The Making of an Archbishop

On Thursday 23 July 2002 it was officially announced that Rowan Douglas Williams, the Archbishop of the Church in Wales, was to be the 104th Archbishop of Canterbury. The news, by then, surprised no one, even though Rowan admitted that it was "still something of a shock to find myself here". Ever since George Carey's announcement in early January that he would be stepping down in October, Rowan's name had been at the forefront of speculation. By the time of this formal confirmation it was the worst-kept secret in Christendom.

A consistent hallmark of almost all the profiles of Rowan Williams that appeared prior to his appointment is reference to his spirituality and acknowledgment of his personal relationship with, and transformation by, God. Mary Ann Sieghart wrote that "it is hard to describe what makes a man holy – a combination of wisdom, compassion, intelligence and humility perhaps – but it is not hard to see that Rowan Williams possesses the quality of holiness in abundance". In addition to this, four other aspects of his story particularly shaped him and his subsequent pattern of ministry and legacy:

- he was not English and came from a non-English diocese with no experience of senior leadership in the Church of England;

- he was a world-renowned academic theologian, teacher, and intellectual;

- he was, partly because of his academic calling, associated with controversy;

- he was already a serving Primate of the Anglican Communion.

Rather than attempting a chronological account, what follows tells the story of Rowan's formation up to his appointment through each of these four lenses.

A Bishop from Wales

Given the growing international role of the Archbishop of Canterbury, it was fitting that George Carey's successor should not be English. Rowan was a permanent reminder to English Anglicans that they are no longer at the centre of Anglicanism and the Anglican Communion is not simply an ecclesial remnant of Britain's imperial past.

Rowan Williams was born in Swansea in South Wales on 14 June 1950 (making him, at just fifty-two, much younger at appointment than any recent archbishop). His parents – Aneurin and Delphine – had married two years earlier and Rowan would be their only child. His early life was marked by ill health. In February 1952, he contracted a rare form of meningitis which left him with a limp and permanent deafness in his left ear. This, in the words of one friend, "is quite significant... if somebody lives with deafness from childhood they are not uninfluenced by that". After his recovery, in 1953, the family moved to Cardiff and he began his formal education at Lamorna, a fee-paying primary school, before the family returned to Swansea in 1960 where he attended Dynevor Grammar School until 1968.

In Cardiff the family worshipped at Park End Chapel, a Presbyterian church, the first of many non-Anglican influences on the future archbishop. Rowan has often spoken warmly of the influence of the minister there, Geraint Nantlais Williams (the son of William Nantlais Williams, prominent during the Welsh Revival of 1904). His theological sympathies were less overtly evangelical than his famous father's but lay with that tradition, and his preaching had a major impact on the young Rowan who would himself become a powerful preacher. He recalls his preaching was marked by "enormous fervour and intelligence" and this, together with the hymns and lessons, "made me feel, yes, there's reality here".[1]

On returning to Swansea, Rowan quickly became captured by and committed to the Anglican worship, shaped by Prayer Book Catholicism, of his Church in Wales parish, All Saints, Oystermouth. This shift would be decisive, moving him into the more Anglo-Catholic tradition within Anglicanism with which he would remain identified. All Saints' vicar, Eddie Hughes (incumbent, 1946–80) and curate Huw Thomas (from 1965 to 1968) were important influences on both the intellectual and spiritual formation of (in Rupert Shortt's words) this "unusually churchy" youngster. Indeed, it appears, he was even described as a future Archbishop of Canterbury aged twelve. He was already displaying some of the characteristics that would draw comment during his archiepiscopacy: shy, quiet, academically brilliant and, as one teacher said, a lover of seclusion. His interest in history, politics, community service, and drama grew, and he developed his gifts as a poet and translator.

Rowan's life and faith were, therefore, shaped by the culture and church of Wales, with little or no connection to English Anglicanism until he moved to study at Cambridge in 1968. Although for a time he seriously considered becoming a Roman Catholic and was strongly drawn to Eastern Orthodoxy, he committed himself to the Church of England, being ordained a deacon in 1977, after earlier exploring but deciding against becoming a monk. His training and ordained ministry in the Church of England were, however, very different from most Anglican clergy. He never trained as an ordinand in a theological college nor served a traditional curacy in a title parish. Instead he moved from teaching at one theological college – the Community of the Resurrection in Mirfield – to being lecturer at another, Westcott House in Cambridge (1977–80) where he was ordained and served as chaplain. He gained parish experience as honorary curate at St George's, Chesterton from 1980 to 1983 before becoming Dean of Clare College, Cambridge (1984–86).

In Cambridge, after an earlier broken engagement with a Lutheran ordinand, Rowan met Jane Paul, and they married in Bradford on 4 July 1981. A graduate at Clare College, studying theology, she would also become a gifted theologian, teacher, and writer. Born in India, she was one of five daughters of Geoffrey Paul, Bishop of Hull (1977–81) and then Bishop of Bradford until his death in 1983. Bishop Paul, associated with the more evangelical traditions of the Church of England, was a powerful influence and model for Rowan who described him as "one of the greatest Christians I have been privileged to know. He was not only a scholar and bishop of unusual stature, but a man who commanded love and loyalty in a rare degree, from the most diverse souls."

Leaving Cambridge in 1986, Rowan spent the next six years in Oxford as Lady Margaret Professor of Divinity and as a canon of Christ Church. For the first fifteen years of his ordained ministry, therefore, his experience of the Church of England was focused on, though by no means restricted to, the Oxbridge interface between church and academy. Then, after nearly quarter of a century, he returned to his homeland and full-time episcopal ministry. In 1992 he became Bishop of Monmouth, the first of two dioceses created after the Church in Wales left the Church of England on disestablishment in 1920.

Rowan spent ten years as Bishop of Monmouth, also serving as Archbishop of Wales from 1999. A number of features of his ministry are worth noting for the insight they give. He quickly established himself as a respected chief pastor who, in the words of his successor, Dominic Walker, "was much loved in the diocese",[2] committed to the care of his clergy and offering support in regular parish visits. Some, however, commented on the perhaps excessive time he devoted to those struggling and wished it could be given to other clergy. Questions were also raised about the wisdom of some of his choices and appointments (he tended to see the best in people even when there was contrary evidence that should have raised alarms). He was thought to be administratively challenged and generally eschewed ideas of strategic planning and management (although he did develop a process for local permanent deacons). Despite his consensual impulses, he was not a notable team player. Richard Tarran (diocesan secretary, 1995–2009), reflecting on his time with Rowan, said he had learnt "so much from him spiritually" but added that his successor "brought about significant and welcome changes in leadership styles which have become more inclusive".

As bishop, Rowan was respected by Anglicans from across different traditions including the relatively small number of evangelicals. They particularly welcomed his concern for mission and evangelism (he was the only Welsh bishop to sponsor Good News in Wales) and his support for various initiatives in church planting and new forms of church. He had appointed Tudor Griffiths as diocesan missioner in 1995 because, in Rowan's words to him, "evangelicals know what mission is".[3] When he asked Rowan whether he should concentrate on building on strength or addressing weaknesses in the diocese, Rowan thought a while and said, "It's rather Thatcherite of me, I know, but I want you to concentrate on building strength."[4] The need to turn things around was clear. The diocese was in rapid numerical decline, with the job description for a new diocesan secretary in 2009 admitting that "church attendance has been in decline for many years and the statistics for Monmouth Diocese in the 1990s were depressing". In 1999, Rowan established the training of evangelists to be licensed in the diocese and also commissioned a diocesan mission team to establish and lead certain mission initiatives. In November 1999, Bob and Mary Hopkins, recognized leaders in church-planting initiatives, spent ten days reviewing eleven missional initiatives Rowan had identified. They recall how "in two of the projects we reviewed we loved how Rowan was combining traditional forms with creative innovation in his formal recognition of two of the church plants as Orders – the Order of Jacobs Well and Living Proof".[5]

Outside Monmouth, Rowan played a prominent role, including in contentious issues. In April 1993 he seconded the motion in favour of women priests in Wales. This was lost and so, despite his strong commitment to the cause, he refused invitations to preach at ordinations in England where women were being ordained from 1994. Despite his support for women's ordination, when this was approved in 1997, he was then the strongest advocate among the bishops for episcopal provision for those opposed.

Demonstrating the wide esteem in which he was held, he was elected as Archbishop of Wales (a post not tied to a particular diocese but elected by the six bishops from among themselves) on 7 December 1999, at the end of a difficult year in which he suffered the death of both his parents within two weeks of each other.

As bishop, and then archbishop, Williams continued to write and to speak as a theologian. His remarkable gifting as a speaker and a lecturer – used to the full at Canterbury – is illustrated by a change that had to occur under his successor, Bishop Dominic Walker. After arriving he raised with the bishop's secretary his concern about the need for more time for preparation, reasonably pointing out a coming week with three major speaking engagements and no time set aside to prepare for them. The response was, "We're not really used to that. What we're used to is Rowan going out of the door saying, 'Just what was the title of the lecture I'm going to give?'"

By the time the vacancy at Canterbury was announced, Rowan had thus served for nearly ten years as a diocesan bishop but his experience was very different from someone with that level of episcopal experience within the Church of England. The Church in Wales is a small church, with bishops and the national church having limited administrative support staff, certainly nothing comparable to either Church House or the Lambeth Palace staff. The administrative burden on bishops was also small compared to almost all English dioceses, allowing more time for the hands-on pastoral ministry which Rowan enjoyed. Asked eighteen months in about the new job he tellingly commented that a key difference from Wales was, "moving from a context where the basic stuff, day by day and week by week, was pastoral work in the parishes of the diocese to a situation where that's not the primary thing, in terms of time consumption, anyway". Such a transition would not have been as stark for most English diocesans. The Church in Wales is also intimate and familial so the clergy and many leading lay people know practically everyone else in the church's leadership across the divisions of geography and churchmanship.

Appointing someone with no experience as a bishop in England was a major innovation which raised potential problems. In his relatively few comments about the vacancy, Rowan explicitly drew attention to some of these: "It would be extremely unusual for the Crown to look beyond the ranks of English bishops, given the need to understand the workings of the Church of England, the House of Lords and so on."

There was, then, to be a steep learning curve on appointment to Canterbury, and his inexperience may have helped create the major Reading crisis that engulfed him within his first year. His non-English upbringing and ecclesial experience remained a cause of concern among those for whom the distinctively English character of the church is of great importance. Tom Sutcliffe, reflecting on Rowan's time in office, said:

> His biggest failing has been his poorly communicated
> and perhaps inarticulate vision of what he senses really
> matters about the Church of England as an English
> institution. Anglicanism in its English heartland is as
> much our national heritage as Shakespeare… There was
> never before an Archbishop of Canterbury who seemed
> not to believe in that in his bones and in his heart. But
> Rowan is a Welshman and an intellectual, and believes
> in the Church of England as merely a part of a much
> larger historical accident.[6]

Or, even more importantly, Rowan is simply first and foremost a catholic Christian who believes, in "one, holy, catholic and apostolic church" rather than any particular national church.

An Academic Theologian and Intellectual

The period just described was also marked by Rowan establishing his reputation as an academic. He initially left Wales in 1968 for Cambridge University to study theology. His first-choice college – St John's – turned him down, but he gained a scholarship at Christ's College. Even as an undergraduate his intellect and breadth of knowledge was such that he did not have to face the shock many Oxbridge students have to negotiate when they cease to be a big fish in a small pond and enter the elite world of gifted academics. One close college friend jokes that Rowan as a student seemed to know "as much aged eighteen as I know now in my sixties". Rupert Shortt recounts how Barbara Dancy, a mature student, missed a lecture and asked Rowan if she could borrow his notes, to be informed that she could but she might have a bit of trouble because he had written them in Latin. Unsurprisingly, he gained a First in his initial exams and a starred First in his final exams in 1971.

Among his tutors and lecturers was Donald MacKinnon (Norris-Hulse Professor of Divinity, 1960–78) whom Rowan described in 2010 as, "one of the most overwhelming influences on my thinking". Many themes within Rowan's thought that shaped his ministry as archbishop – the interrelationship of theology and philosophy, the place of the tragic and the experience of suffering, the questioning nature of revelation and hence of proper theology, and the importance of self-emptying (*kenosis*) – can be traced back to MacKinnon's influence. They also share a similar approach to the theological task. The opening words of the *Independent*'s 1994 obituary of MacKinnon captures a quality also evident in Rowan's academic career and episcopal ministry: "His greatest strength was the breadth of human experience and learning which he brought to bear on deep, intractable problems which others tried to tame by isolating monodimensional aspects of them for minute analysis."

It was clear Rowan would pursue doctoral research but its focus was not obvious. He left Cambridge to study in Oxford (first at Christ Church and then at Wadham) and turned his mind, in what he describes as a "rather deliberate counter-cultural move", to Eastern Orthodoxy. Supervised by Donald Allchin, he completed his thesis, entitled "The Theology of Vladimir Nikolaevich Lossky: An Exposition and Critique" and was awarded his doctorate in early 1975. This deep intellectual and spiritual engagement with Lossky (1903–58) and Russian Orthodoxy more widely moulded his life and thought. Among the key influences are the interconnections between doctrine, worship, and spirituality, which would be a hallmark of his writing and ministry from the start. Perhaps even more important was his immersion in the apophatic tradition of Christian theology. This emphasizes the limits and failings of all of our attempts to speak of God and, in Rowan's words, "says you will never get it wrapped up, you will never have it completely sorted". Lossky also solidified Williams' constant and emphatic focus on God as Trinity and the scandalous humiliation of the cross as the revelation of God's personal being. This leads to the centrality of *kenosis* as the heart of the divine life which in turn reveals what we are called to in our lives. As Williams wrote in 1979, in words which capture a hallmark of his ministry as archbishop, "the renunciation of existing-for-oneself is man's most authentically personal act and so also man's most *Godlike* act". Lossky showed him that the Christian dogma of the Trinity "is 'a cross for human ways of thought' because it demands a belief that the abnegation of self and the absence of self-assertive, self-interested 'individualism' are the fundamental notes of personal existence at its source, in God".

On completing his doctorate, Rowan applied for but was not appointed to a post at Durham University. In April 1975 he was left deeply scarred by the tragic suicide of his friend Hilary

Watson. Later that year he took up his first teaching post, at the Community of the Resurrection in Mirfield, West Yorkshire, a monastic community and theological college in the Anglo-Catholic tradition of Anglicanism. His published work during these years was limited but his lectures were being shaped into his first book, *The Wound of Knowledge*. In both method and content, the book sows seeds that would continue to flower throughout his later academic work and his time at Canterbury. It weaves together history and theology in its exploration of Christian spirituality from the New Testament through the Desert Fathers and often ignored medieval writers before finally reaching Luther and St John of the Cross. A recurring theme is that of encountering the questioning God whom we cannot control but who is at work, often in and through the suffering and contradictions of life, graciously creating a new transformed and transforming community around Christ.

Alongside his extensive reading in, and interpretation of, the history of theology, Williams was also mastering the world of modern doctrine. Among the key thinkers were the Protestant theologian, Karl Barth (he published a major article on Barth's Trinitarian theology in 1979, before he turned thirty) and the Roman Catholic theologian, Hans Urs von Balthasar (he was later involved in translating three volumes of his theological aesthetics). Another theological giant, Dietrich Bonhoeffer, executed by the Nazi regime, was the person he named when asked in March 2012 whom he would like to sit down for dinner with if he could choose anyone in the last 100 years.

It was clear Rowan would soon land a full academic post. After returning to Cambridge to teach at Westcott House in 1977 he became a Cambridge University lecturer in 1980 and Dean of Clare College in 1984. Although his rise was seen by many as unimpeded and meteoric, it was not without its disappointments in the competitive academic world. He failed to get a professorship at King's College, London and was unsuccessful when he signalled his calling to be a theologian for the church by applying to be Principal of St Stephen's House, the traditional Anglo-Catholic training college in Oxford.

His profile in the wider church was raised by his study *Resurrection* (1982) based on talks to East London clergy and by the Archbishop of Canterbury's Lent Book for 1983, *The Truce of God*. This, revised and reissued when archbishop, addressed the highly contentious issue of nuclear weapons and peace during the Cold War. His more left-wing political views were also evident in his involvement with *Essays Catholic and Radical* (1983), co-edited with Kenneth Leech as a Jubilee Group publication, the movement he had helped found with Leech back in 1974.

Through the early 1980s Rowan worked on his most substantial single volume of scholarly theological writing: a study of the fourth-century heretic Arius, condemned by the Council of Nicaea (325) for denial of Christ's full divinity. Much in his analysis of early church political and theological feuding shaped him for his own subsequent experience of such conflicts. His choice of epigraph from Alasdair MacIntyre – "traditions, when vital, embody continuities of conflict" – captures a key understanding of his reading of the life of the church both past and present.

As Lady Margaret Professor of Divinity at Oxford University (1986–92) Rowan established himself as a popular lecturer who set his teaching in the context of prayer and whose pastoral gifts were evident in the "at homes" which he and Jane opened up to undergraduates as well as graduate students. He accrued a large number of gifted graduate students studying a remarkable range of subjects. According to Oliver O'Donovan, they were guaranteed inspiring personal one-to-one supervision as with both students and fellow dons "his ability to grasp where someone was coming from, to enthuse about any positive features he could identify and then to add just a nuance of his own that opened up new possibilities, was always evident – one of the gifts that have since made him a superb bishop". These Oxford years saw the publication of a significant number of dense, heavyweight journal articles on a range of theological themes. Many of these were then collected together in *On Christian Theology* (2000). Apart from *Arius*, the only book-length study in this period was his writing on the sixteenth-century mystic Teresa of Avila, although he also translated parts of von Balthasar's *The Glory of the Lord*.

When he moved to Monmouth, Williams was taken out of the academy but it proved impossible to take the academy out of him. He continued to write, alongside his other episcopal duties and his family responsibilities (their daughter Rhiannon had been born in 1988 while in Oxford and their son Pip was born in 1996). A book of sermons and addresses in 1994 (*Open to Judgment*) and his *Christ on Trial* (2000) provide two of the most accessible ways into central themes in his thinking. More heavily academic tomes included revisiting Russian Orthodoxy by editing and translating works relating to Bulgakov's political theology (1999) and his social commentary and critique in *Lost Icons* (2000). In addition to bringing together earlier articles in *On Christian Theology*, he produced the anthology *Love's Redeeming Work: The Anglican Quest for Holiness* (2001) with fellow bishops Geoffrey Rowell and Kenneth Stevenson. Rowan oversaw the selection of writings for the opening period from 1530 to 1650 but also recommended contributors such as William Stringfellow to his fellow editors. That same year, following his experience of being close to the Twin Towers on 9/11, he also wrote *Writing in the Dust: Reflections on 11th September and its Aftermath*, which appeared during 2002. In addition to these works, he began publishing his poetry and translations of other (particularly Welsh and Russian) poets.

These academic qualities in Rowan led to him being a leading public intellectual as archbishop. The academic world also strengthened aspects of his character and patterns of relating. Bishop Geoffrey Rowell (who first knew him in the early 1970s when they were part of a small Oxford group seeking to renew theology and challenge the dominance of theological liberalism) refers to how most people have a "default" pattern of relating and that for Rowan this has remained that of "the don".[7] His approach to issues and debates often had the feel of a contribution to a Senior Common Room discussion or the reflections of the chair of a graduate seminar. Finally, and most importantly, these features also made his actions and pronouncements much more self-consciously theologically driven and shaped and so only understandable in relation to his theology.

Rowan's freedom as an academic and intellectual and the range of issues he addressed both as a professor and, to a lesser extent, as bishop in Monmouth also meant he came to Canterbury as a controversial figure.

A Controversial Figure

Much of the controversy surrounding Rowan Williams at his appointment related to misunderstandings of his theological position and the erroneous portrayal of him as a "liberal". Many thus grouped him with people such as Maurice Wiles, a colleague at Oxford, Bishop Jack Spong in America, and Don Cupitt in Cambridge. In fact, he was a known and robust critic of their approaches, strongly committed to orthodox Christian faith as expressed in the catholic creeds. There were, however, areas where his views and actions were controversial. This gave basis for concerns – generally held by those who did not know him – that he would be a provocative and divisive archbishop in the church and wider society.

Politically, he was on record describing himself as a "hairy leftie" and was associated with radical and socialist Christian movements, including the Jubilee Group. One area of concern was his generally critical stance towards military action and long-standing opposition to nuclear weapons. On Ash Wednesday 1985 he had been forced to phone and excuse himself from Evensong duties as Dean of Clare College because he was spending a few hours in the cells having been arrested for scaling a fence at a nearby RAF base and then sitting singing psalms on a runway during an anti-nuclear protest. O'Donovan recounts how he had remarked to John Macquarrie that Rowan looked a worthy successor as Lady Margaret Professor and received the response, "Ay, it will be fine if only he's out of jail at the time!"

In 1998, Rowan had been an early critic of Tony Blair's New Labour and its concern with presentation and spin. Five months earlier, just prior to his appointment, polemical clergyman Peter Mullen launched a strident attack. Highly selective in quoting Rowan's writing about 9/11 and the military action that followed, this concluded with the warning that

> He is an old-fashioned class warrior, a typical bien-pensant despiser of Western capitalism and the way of life that goes with it… when the future of Western civilization itself is under threat, such posturing is suicidal. What havoc this man might wreak from the throne of Canterbury.[8]

One controversial area was Rowan's view on establishment. He arrived at Canterbury with a clear critical stance towards the traditional pattern of church–state relationships. This was due to various factors: he came from the disestablished Church in Wales and believed strongly in the church's distinctive identity as Christ's body, called to question and challenge the world, particularly those with power. At the Greenbelt Festival in 2000, he had said:

> The state link as it exists at the moment is not good for the Church. I think it encourages a level of self-deception in the church about how important it is, which in the long run may raise some sort of issue about credibility and integrity... I also think that the notion of the Monarch as Supreme Governor has outlived its usefulness.[9]

Such sentiments might be acceptable and reasonably uncontroversial from an academic theologian or even the Primate of Wales, but any English bishop who had spoken in such terms only eighteen months before a vacancy at Canterbury would probably have thereby ruled themselves out of the running. He was, to be fair, more cautious about how the relationship would change, speaking of "disestablishment by a thousand cuts" but still predicted that "at least within the next 15 years the Church of England will look a lot more like the Church of Scotland". Even after his appointment, he admitted he expected change. Tony Benn bumped into him at a Welsh train station in October 2002 and recorded in his diary, "I said, 'When will disestablishment come?' 'Well, it will,' he said, 'but it will take a bit of time.'" Despite these strongly stated views, Rowan would not push them on the church as archbishop.

Within the church, other aspects of his past meant he arrived at Canterbury with something of a reputation. At Oxford he had become closely identified with a particular grouping within the Church of England: Affirming Catholicism. This attracted those in the more "high church" or catholic traditions of the Church of England who were concerned that the dominant perception of their tradition was now one of sometimes angular traditionalism and in particular opposition to the ordination of women. They looked to Rowan for support, and at their first conference (June 1990) he was their main speaker. Along with Jeffrey John and Richard Holloway he was a founding trustee, only resigning shortly before taking up his position as Archbishop of Canterbury. By playing such a prominent role in launching and leading a new controversial political movement, Rowan was marked out in the eyes of many as strongly identified with one particular grouping and in particular its stance on the two most divisive issues within the church.

Affirming Catholicism was strongly supportive of women's ordination, which the General Synod approved in 1992. Rowan adopted that position around 1977 having held more traditional catholic views. As would become clear in Wales, and even more obvious in Canterbury, his commitment was not just a "liberal" embracing of new intellectual or cultural developments. His stance was also resolutely "catholic". This led him to support the church developing new structures to enable those unable to receive the ordained ministry of women priests (and bishops) to remain within the church.

The other issue with which Affirming Catholicism soon became identified was the one that caused Rowan constant problems from the start: same-sex partnerships. Given the significance of this area and people's reactions to his views, more detail is needed about his actions before he became archbishop.

Rowan moved towards acceptance of loving same-sex relationships as a result of the Church of England's 1979 Gloucester Report. This questioned the traditional unqualified prohibition on homosexual activity. In the following years, through friendships and providing pastoral care and spiritual guidance to gay and lesbian Christians, Rowan's concerns increased. He became convinced that the biblical texts, as traditionally interpreted, did not answer the questions faced today in relation to loving, committed same-sex unions and that the church's approach to the question was seriously flawed.

His main response was intellectual but initially, and surprisingly, polemical and political. In 1987 the General Synod passed a motion known as the Higton motion. This restated traditional Christian teaching that, as sexual intercourse belongs within marriage, not only fornication and adultery but "homosexual genital acts also fall short of this ideal, and are likewise to be met by a call to repentance and the exercise of compassion". In the introduction to a 1988 Jubilee Group pamphlet, Rowan was uncharacteristically acerbic, describing how "it has often been difficult to believe that it is possible to be an Anglican with integrity" due to self-destructive inner conflicts and "a degree of collective neurosis on the subject of sexuality that is really quite astounding in this century and this culture". He accused the church of collusion with populist homophobia and attacked bishops who described the motion as "representing the 'mind' of the Church" and accorded it "something like legislative force". Justice, he argued, was not divisible and "if we have no integrity here, we cannot expect to carry conviction elsewhere" and so "many people currently feel ashamed of our Church's public voice on this issue". He also condemned legal action to remove the Lesbian and Gay Christian Movement (LGCM) from London church premises. This was "scandalous for the Church" in its "deliberate will to humiliate".[10]

These pungent critiques explain the invitation to give the tenth Michael Harding Memorial Address for LGCM in 1989: "The Body's Grace".[11] His fullest discussion of the subject, it explores why sex matters and what it has to do with God. He does so through a discussion of grace, the Trinity, and the calling of the church. He identifies the key moral question as "how much we want our sexual activity to communicate, how much we want it to display a breadth of human possibility and a sense of the body's capacity to heal and enlarge the life of other subjects". This leads to reflections on sexual faithfulness and blessing sexual unions and the claim that it is "unreal and silly" to insist that "every sexual partnership must conform to the pattern of commitment or else have the nature of sin *and nothing else*". Turning to same-sex relationships, he rejects "the extraordinary idea that sexual orientation is an automatic pointer to the celibate life" and suggests our anxiety about such relationships may be because, as non-procreative, they oblige us to think *directly* about questions of bodiliness and sexuality, desire, joy, and grace.

A biblical sexual ethic would, he claims "steer us away from assuming that reproductive sex is a norm" and, given acceptance of contraception, absolute condemnation of intimate same-sex relations must rely on "an abstract fundamentalist deployment of a number of very ambiguous texts" or "a problematic and non-scriptural theory about natural complementarity, applied narrowly and crudely to physical differentiation without regard to psychological structures". Urging "a fuller exploration of the sexual metaphors of the Bible" rather than "flat citation of isolated texts", he concludes that "A theology of the body's grace which can do justice to the experience, the pain and the variety, of concrete sexual discovery is not, I believe, a marginal eccentricity in the doctrinal spectrum." In fact it leads back to and depends on God's triune life. His fundamental appeal was, and remains, for a fresh *theological* engagement with these issues and he continued to work for this in various ways. During a semester in Yale in 1990, he shared the lecture with Eugene Rogers who built on it in his own subsequent theological defence of same-sex unions and described it as "the best 10 pages written about sexuality in the twentieth century". Rowan also helped found LGCM's Institute for the Study of Christianity and Sexuality and its journal *Theology and Sexuality* (1994–), which by the time of his appointment as archbishop was publishing material that was used by opponents to raise questions about his judgment given he remained on its editorial board.

Rowan was invited by the English House of Bishops to join the group working in this area in the hope he would bring both academic rigour and a more questioning and critical stance to their work. He attended only a couple of meetings before resigning as it was clear their final report, *Issues in Human Sexuality* (which was released in December 1991 and made church policy under George Carey), would be too conservative. He was part of an Affirming Catholicism group, including Jeffrey John, who met with George Carey shortly after he became archbishop to express unhappiness with the Church of England's position.

In Wales, Rowan's engagement with the sexuality debates continued but was never as significant as it had been briefly in the late 1980s. Evangelical colleagues from Oxford were key players in a theological contribution to the debate issued as the St Andrew's Day Statement in 1995, and he entered into dialogue, writing the most thoughtful critical response published in *The Way Forward?* (1997). Expressing "unqualified agreement" with its principles, he questioned their application arguing that "a long job of cultural discernment" was necessary in relation to the significance of sexual orientation and our identity in Christ (is it more like race or class?). He also questioned whether homosexual inclinations are in some way rooted in spiritual confusion or error. Highlighting the fact that many gay Christians would not understand their experience as that described in the key biblical text of Romans 1, he asked how the traditional position proclaims good news to them as they seek a pattern of life which is costly and shows Christ to the world. This, he suggests, can be done by living "under promise" so that "the partnership of two persons of the same sex is in some way 'showing' what marriage shows of the God who promises and who remains faithful". A central concern is his plea for recognition that a view which holds "sexual expression" to be legitimate for those with homosexual inclination may "be trying to find a way of being faithful and obedient to the givens of revelation".

Prior to the 1998 Lambeth Conference, Rowan wrote a short foreword to a book of personal stories produced by Changing Attitude, a recently formed Anglican group headed by Colin Coward. This reveals central themes in his thinking: the importance of personal testimonies demonstrating "the cost and the integrity" of gay and lesbian people "struggling to be loyal to the Christian tradition and the Christian community". The question it posed "gently but urgently" was another recurring theme in Rowan's understanding of the church: "Can this seriousness be received as a gift in our Church?"

In 1998 Rowan almost became a bishop in the Church of England and his views on sexuality played a (subsequently much exaggerated) role in preventing this. The diocese of Southwark was vacant and many in the diocese lobbied for his appointment. The diocesan representatives on the Crown Appointments Commission (including Colin Slee, the dean) failed to persuade the majority who supported Tom Butler. There were rumours that the prime minister, Tony Blair, also wanted Rowan. George Carey met with Rowan to discuss both his own situation and the needs of Southwark diocese. Rowan made clear his continued disagreement with *Issues in Human Sexuality* but also his belief that Monmouth was where he should continue in episcopal ministry and so Butler was appointed to Southwark.

Later in 1998, at the Lambeth Conference, Rowan gave a plenary address on "Making Moral Decisions". This signalled, by discussion of how we live with different Christian attitudes to nuclear weapons, his own hope there would be a more respectful mutual recognition of, and a deeper theological conversation about, the range of responses to same-sex partnerships held among Christians. He did not contribute to the plenary debate on sexuality and he abstained on the final conservative resolution (I.10) which was overwhelmingly passed and would prove so determinative for his primacy. His immediate reaction is telling. Peter Selby, Bishop of Worcester, a friend who had voted against, walked out of the room next to him and recalls Rowan saying to him, "Well, I suppose that is where the Communion is."[12] He signalled his hope this would not be where the Communion remained by being one of 185 bishops (including 9 serving primates) who signed "A Pastoral Statement to Lesbian and Gay Anglicans from Some Member Bishops of the Lambeth Conference". Two years later, in a foreword to Bishop Michael Doe's book *Seeking the Truth in Love: The Church and Homosexuality* he questioned why "for a significant number of Anglicans, this has come to be the acid test of whether you are inside or outside the pale of authentic orthodoxy" and typically indicated that "there are a few questions we ought all to be putting to ourselves before turning on each other". Hoping the subject could prove "an area in which Christians might just possibly disagree without fracturing the reality of a common language", he called for "a more patient and (dare I say?) a more adult discussion than we have sometimes had of late". Finally, Rowan served on the International Anglican Conversations on Human Sexuality which reported in 2002, although he only attended the second of its three meetings, a poor attendance record matched by only one other participant.

By the time the succession for Canterbury was being considered, he was questioned about his views on sexuality during a trip to Uganda and responded honestly, making what would become an important distinction between his views as a theologian and the church's teaching:

> I wish I could say more wholeheartedly that I accept
> every aspect of the traditional teaching and that I accept
> personally every aspect of what the majority of people
> in my Church believe. I can't say that in conscience…
> So my hope is not to impose a view from America or
> Britain or anywhere else on any other province, but to
> see if we can go on talking prayerfully with each other,
> reading the Bible together with each other, to see what
> we can learn.[13]

Then, in June 2002, fresh controversy arose in relation to his actions as a bishop. In an interview from the Diocese of Sydney he confirmed he had ordained someone he knew had a homosexual partner in the background because he was sure the candidate would not flaunt it or cause a scandal. Asked whether the ordination vow to conform one's life and that of one's household didn't mean "giving up a homosexual lifestyle" he was clear:

> This is where I recognise I am in the minority, so I am
> cautious of making this a great campaigning issue. I am
> not convinced that a homosexual has to be celibate in
> every imaginable circumstance. But if that were the case
> I would also want to be sure that their attitude to their
> sexual habits is a responsible, prayerful and theologically
> informed one.[14]

To give such clear and honest answers to provocative questions intended for a theologically hostile audience was typical. Some might think it even a late attempt to prevent being called to Canterbury. Instead, this most recent statement would be used against him to ensure he would be viewed as a controversial figure from the start.

A Communion Primate

Rowan Williams was, finally, the first Archbishop of Canterbury who was already a Primate of the Anglican Communion when he was appointed. He was, therefore, in the intriguing, unprecedented position of never having been a member of the Church of England's House of Bishops or General Synod but having been a member of the Primates' Meeting. This perhaps contributed to him giving such value and so much time and energy to the Communion and its unity during his primacy.

His first Primates' Meeting in late March 2000 faced the initial impact on the Communion of the American church's divisions over sexuality. Two priests in the American province (then known as The Episcopal Church, USA [ECUSA] and subsequently as The Episcopal Church [TEC]; it will be referred to here as ECUSA/TEC), had been consecrated by two primates to serve as "missionary bishops". Rowan wrote up reflections which showed the feel he was already getting for a body whose meetings would be so important during his time at Canterbury. The major issue underlying the meeting was "how far can the Anglican Communion survive without some mechanism of authority more robust than currently exists?"[15] Two problems were identified. First, unprecedented breaches of Communion order by consecrating bishops for another province and paying no attention to the counsel of the Archbishop of Canterbury. Second, divisions in the American church, which led people to ask "Has North American Anglicanism no means at all… of reining in pluralism? And if it hasn't, are its structures at all trustworthy?"

Rowan observed primates wanting a final warning and supported by "a visible penumbra… of American conservatives, aiming to strengthen the resolve of traditionalist primates, hanging around in doorways and lobbies". However, many primates "can see the risks of the Communion either becoming completely mired in this question for years or breaking up over it" and wanted neither. The outcome was a careful reminder of the consequences of actions in the wider Communion but there was "no appetite for denunciation, or even direct appeal to the United States for a moratorium on gay ordinations". He identified the basis for this more measured response as "the clear statement that a province only excludes itself from the Anglican Communion by public and formal rejection of any aspect of what is familiarly called the 'Lambeth Quadrilateral'". Although debates would continue about actions implicitly denying the Quadrilateral and some provinces would be divided from others, "the debate on sexuality is clearly seen as one which… does not necessitate decisions about whether a local church is or is not in communion with the Archbishop of Canterbury, and so formally part of the Anglican family".

The next two Primates' Meetings in 2001 (in the US) and 2002 (at Canterbury) were much less dominated by these divisions but some significant seeds were sown. In 2001, Norman Doe spoke on canon law and floated the idea of a possible concordat between provinces, a precursor of the later Anglican Communion Covenant. In 2002, attention was again given to canon law, and Rowan and the Canadian primate read "stimulating papers" which "broke fresh ground in relation to the possibility of developing new ecclesial structures so as to free the Churches of the Communion for more effective mission in the context of a rapidly changing world". The statement also referred to the possibility of non-geographical networks within dioceses and "perhaps even transcending diocesan boundaries along the lines of the work of religious orders with specific ministry commitments".

These meetings enabled primates to recognize Rowan's spiritual discipline and depth, respect his contributions to the common life of the meeting, and value the personal relationships he built up. Asked before his move to Canterbury what benefit he derived from the meetings, he spoke of it being "enormously helpful to sit informally with the primates from other provinces, especially the ones from places such as Sudan, Tanzania and South East Asia. The building up of those friendships is a huge part of what the meetings are for." Being personally known and widely respected by fellow primates, in a way that would have been impossible for any other candidate, is a rarely noted but significant feature of what he brought to being Archbishop of Canterbury and helps explain why his views on sexuality were not quite as damaging as some expected within the Communion when his appointment was announced.

2

A New Archbishop of Canterbury

Recent months and recent weeks have been a strange time; it is a curious experience to have your future discussed, your personality, childhood influences and facial hair solemnly examined in the media, and opinions you didn't know you held expounded on your behalf. (July 2002)[1]

In the immediate aftermath of George Carey's announcement that he would be retiring, Rowan Williams told the BBC that it was an "intimidating and enormous" task and "it would be a very foolish man who thought he was adequate to its demands". He then kept a relatively low profile. A week later it was being reported that "Rowan Williams speaks seven languages but was saying nothing in any of them about the top job in the Church of England." Others, however, were not shy in speaking of his qualities. The *Guardian* offered four names with the list headed by Rowan:

A former Oxford theology professor, probably the
most charismatic and intellectual of the candidates.
A leading Anglo-Catholic but also a supporter of the
Alpha evangelical church courses. Would inspire huge
devotion but may be too outspoken for New Labour
and too hirsute and Guardianesque for the control freak
tendency. An appointment from outside the Church of
England would be a bit daring too.[2]

By mid-January, Rowan, labelled "the liberal candidate", was
reportedly the clear choice of the members of General Synod and
in the months that followed a number of often embarrassingly
glowing press profiles appeared. A significant body of opinion
within the Church of England shared the view of Peter Selby,
Bishop of Worcester. He said he was clear in 2002 that "there was
only one candidate and if we did not appoint this person we would
be judged by future generations to have been overcome by timidity
or foolishness or something like that; I've not changed my mind!"[3]

Although the official announcement of Rowan's appointment
did not happen until July, on 20 June there was an unprecedented
leak to Ruth Gledhill of *The Times*. Rowan learned that the
church was calling him to be archbishop when his chaplain
had to wake him after an early-morning call from the media
with news of the leak. Gledhill claimed that "the support for
Dr Williams at almost every level of the church and society has
been almost unprecedented", but it soon became clear that this
genuine widespread enthusiasm was not universal. Speculation
that evangelicals were strongly opposed to Rowan in large part
because of his previously published views on homosexuality was
confirmed when, the next day, leading conservative evangelicals
sent an open letter the prime minister. Referring to Rowan's
stated views and admitted actions over same-sex partnerships,

it signalled what would become a constant refrain in the years to come. It warned that "his actions and views fly in the face of the clear teaching of the Holy Scriptures and the resolutions of the Lambeth Conference 1998" and he "would not have the confidence of the vast majority of Anglicans in the world" so his appointment "would lead to a major split in the Anglican Communion (including the Church of England)". That there were other evangelical views was shown by a letter to *The Times* on 25 June from Rowan's former Oxford colleague, Oliver O'Donovan. He noted that Rowan's capacity for "subtle orthodoxy" should not be underestimated and that, if he became archbishop, the consensus on homosexuality would be "safe in his stewardship".

The big challenge lay with the wider Communion and whether, if appointed, Rowan would have their confidence. Anglicans from around the Communion were attending a conference at Wycliffe Hall, an evangelical Anglican theological college in Oxford. Some shared the open letter's concerns, in part because the diocesan synod of New Westminster in Canada had recently asked the bishop to authorize a rite of blessing of same-sex unions prompting a walkout from representatives of eight parishes. Aware that the conference risked fomenting division but also held potential for increased understanding, O'Donovan wined, dined, and conversed confidentially at Christ Church with three key conservative primates: Donald Mtetemela from Tanzania, Yong Ping Chung from South East Asia, and Drexel Gomez of the West Indies. Rupert Shortt quotes in full the confidential letter O'Donovan then sent on 4 July to Rowan.[4] O'Donovan is reassuring that "the predicted fire did not stream from their nostrils" and that in fact "a good deal of sympathy was expressed for you" as they "are clearly inclined to like you personally and to appreciate your contributions to the Primates' Meeting". They did, however, have a clear message "which I reproduce as much like a good CD player as I can, complete with the emphases with which it was declared to me":

> In the event of Rowan Williams' appointment, he
> must say something *as early as possible* to reassure
> the Communion; and in giving such reassurance
> *emphasising the authority of Lambeth* [I.10] *is crucial.*

O'Donovan was clear: "Should the moment arrive, you know what these primates at any rate are hoping to hear from you. It will require a twofold portion of all the sevenfold gifts to attune such a message appropriately for the whole Communion." He concluded:

> A disinterested friend would do anything to protect you
> from appointment to Canterbury; yet if that burden
> should be laid upon you, I hope you will not forget
> that even the fire-breathers can sometimes be tamed,
> and that there are one or two determined and skilful
> tamers out there in the field, on whose good will you
> can count.

With still no sign of the less dramatic Anglican equivalent of white smoke from the Vatican chimney, on 19 July Gledhill ran another story that would damage the archbishop further. Under the headline "Why the Archbishop is embracing pagan roots", she claimed he would "don a long white cloak while druids chant a prayer to the ancient god and goddess of the land", adopt a new bardic name, and so be accepted into the highest white druidic order, clothed in a druidic white head-dress and join other druids inside a sacred circle. Reassurances were given that this was a cultural ceremony at the major annual Welsh Eisteddfod, not an embrace of paganism, but this was more ammunition for his opponents. Although church criticism diminished, the tabloid press were less reasonable or forgiving. The *Sun* ridiculed him under the heading "Arch Jedi of Canterbury" and even in 2012 was referring to "Marxist Arch Druid Rowan Williams". Given the misrepresentation and mocking of this honour bestowed on him, it is understandable that Shortt reports the normally phlegmatic Rowan "remained angry about the criticism for years afterwards".

When, at last, the official announcement came, it is therefore unsurprising that Rowan Williams began his statement with the words heading this chapter. The initially "curious experience" of media exposure would become a fact of life for him over the next five months until he took office, through to his enthronement in February 2003, and then during the following ten years as archbishop. Before exploring those years and their legacy, the key characteristics of the job he was taking on and something of his stated vision on appointment need to be sketched.

Archbishop of Canterbury

The post of Archbishop of Canterbury has always been multifaceted and burdensome. It is probably now so complex and varied that it is impossible for any single individual to fit the job description. Aware of this, the church had established a review group chaired by Lord (Douglas) Hurd, the former Conservative Cabinet minister. This reported in 2001 in *To Lead and to Serve*.

For most people in England the Archbishop of Canterbury is primarily the senior bishop in the Church of England, technically, Primate of All England and Metropolitan. As Metropolitan he invariably presides at any consecration of a bishop in the province. Among his other time-consuming roles are presidency of the General Synod and chairmanship of bodies such as the Archbishops' Council and the Crown Nominations

Commission which selects diocesan bishops. Canterbury diocese's historic significance, stretching back over 1,400 years since being founded by St Augustine in 597, is the source of the office's importance although in practice most of the work of a diocesan bishop is now undertaken by the Bishop of Dover.

The established nature of the Church of England means that the archbishop has a seat by right in the House of Lords and is generally viewed as the most representative and senior Christian voice in national life. He is also a key player in deepening relationships between different faith traditions and enabling them to relate to government. As the Hurd Report commented, "The Archbishop of Canterbury may no longer be the spiritual director of the English people but he remains the nation's primary spiritual conscience." In the order of precedence he is the highest ranking non-royal in the realm, above even the prime minister and the Speaker of the Commons. This can provide interesting potential opportunities for pastoral care or Christian mission: David Blunkett noted that at the 2003 state banquet welcoming President Bush, Rowan Williams "was sitting with Condoleezza Rice and Prince Charles (which must have been an interesting experience)". He generally presides at major state religious occasions, such as the wedding of Prince William and Kate Middleton.

In relation to the wider church, the archbishop has the senior role in ecumenical relationships with other denominations within England and, increasingly, globally. During the 1990s important interfaith responsibilities were added.

All this alone would represent a considerable range and weight of responsibilities, but in the last two or three decades the archbishop has also developed a major and significant international ministry through his role within the Anglican Communion. For no holder of the office has this proved more time-consuming and often energy-draining than for Rowan

Williams. The Communion is a fellowship of self-governing churches whose historic ties mean they are in communion with the See of Canterbury. It claims 80 million worshippers in 164 countries and is thus the third largest Christian denomination after the Roman Catholic Church and the Orthodox Church.

The Anglican Communion has, since the late 1980s, understood itself as expressing its interdependence through working together by means of the four Instruments of Unity (or Communion). The Archbishop of Canterbury himself is one of these and, in the words of the Hurd Report, "his office has a spiritual and moral influence extending far beyond the limits of his jurisdiction". He also plays a crucial role in the other three Instruments. He convenes the Lambeth Conference of Anglican bishops (originating in 1867) every ten years, presides over the Anglican Consultative Council which has met roughly every three years since 1971, and chairs the Primates' Meeting, normally every two years since its first meeting in 1979. His decisive personal role in nurturing interdependence means the archbishop maintains personal contact with the Communion's rapidly growing number of autonomous provinces (rising from twenty-one in 1971 to thirty-nine by 2009). This entails a significant amount of international travel as well as correspondence. The importance of this changing role was highlighted by the Hurd Report which in Rowan's words, before becoming archbishop, "is really an attempt to free the archbishop for an international role, and we really must try to work out how that plan can be implemented".

On publicly accepting this range of responsibilities and in the months that followed, Rowan provided a sketch of some of his vision and hopes as archbishop. These provide a helpful introduction to the more detailed account and evaluation of his legacy which follows.

Setting Out a Vision and Facing Challenge

On his appointment Rowan Williams spoke of the continuity in his ministry:

> The primary job for me remains what it has long been: I have to go on being a priest and bishop, that is, to celebrate God and what God has done in Jesus, and to offer in God's name whatever I can discern of God's perspective on the world around – something which involves both challenge and comfort.[5]

His opening statement sheds light on how he would handle many issues in the years ahead as he gave substance to the "ministry of reconciliation and mission" he inherited:

> My first task is that of any ordained teacher – to point to the source without which none of our activity would make sense, the gift of God as it is set before us in the Bible and Christian belief; and within the boundaries set by that, to try and help members of the Anglican family make sense to each other and work together for the honest and faithful sharing of our belief.

He also, however, noted new areas such as speaking of God publicly in wider culture where he signalled a desire to develop "conversations... with those rather on the edges of the Church, people in the worlds of the arts, medicine, psychology, who are eager to explore what Christian faith means". He highlighted a hope which would be picked up on and regularly quoted:

> If there is one thing I long for above all else, it's that the years to come may see Christianity in this country able again to capture the imagination of our culture, to draw

the strongest energies of our thinking and feeling into
the exploration of what our creeds put before us.

Seeking to "nourish a sense of proper confidence in the Church",
he said he was "utterly convinced that the Christian creed and
the Christian vision have in them a life and a richness that can
embrace and transfigure all the complexities of human life".
However, reflecting his passion for dialogue, conversation, and
"patient willingness to learn from others", he was clear that this
had to go alongside a paying "real attention to other faiths and
other convictions".

Primed by O'Donovan's meeting the previous month, Rowan
also immediately wrote a letter to the primates. This signalled his
approach and set the parameters within which he would work. He
promised that he was "not someone elected to fulfil a programme
or manifesto of his own devising" but was committed "to serve
the whole Communion". There then followed a crucial and
succinct reading of the situation in relation to human sexuality:

> The Lambeth resolution of 1998 declares clearly what
> is the mind of the overwhelming majority in the
> Communion, and what the Communion will and will
> not approve or authorise. I accept that any individual
> diocese or even province that officially overturns or
> repudiates this resolution poses a substantial problem
> for the sacramental unity of the Communion.[6]

He distinguished "personal theories and interpretations" from
"the majority conviction of my Church" but also emphasized
the need for "continuing reflection on these matters". His hope
was "to try and maintain a mutually respectful climate for such
reflection, in the sort of shared prayerful listening to Scripture
envisaged by Lambeth" and keep a focus on "the urgent common

priority of mission and evangelism" rather than be trapped into "questions where the politics of our culture sets the agenda".

These would be consistent emphases over the next decade as would his setting of controversy within the deeper questions of life in Christ with which he concluded his letter: "I believe with all my heart that through Christ we are given a unique and immeasurable gift, and that all our work as apostles and pastors and teachers must grow from our thankfulness to God."

These words should have been a clear signal to all who hoped or feared he would be indifferent to, perhaps even support, changes in Anglican teaching or practice in relation to same-sex relationships. His approach would be different. They failed, however, to satisfy his conservative evangelical critics who continued to oppose his appointment. The following months saw a concerted campaign against him. Although focused on his views on sexuality, it broadened out into a more widespread portrayal of him as an extreme, dangerous liberal. The fullest critique came from Gary Williams whose booklet, *The Theology of Rowan Williams*, concluded by warning that "the theology of Rowan Williams puts souls at risk of perishing… To keep silence in the face of his theology is to acquiesce in the injury of souls." Committed to dialogue, Rowan tried to engage with his critics when many felt he should have ignored or rebutted them. He agreed to meet leaders of Church Society. Their report of the meeting acknowledged that "we were received graciously by Dr Williams, who had every reason to be annoyed with us and with others" but concluded "if the scripture is right Dr Williams is leading people to sin and destruction." Some of the many letters sent to the archbishop-designate were even more emphatic and unpleasant, but it was always a minority of evangelicals who were opposed to him. Those such as Alister McGrath, Tony Thiselton, and Francis Bridger who knew him and better understood his approach to theology, church, and mission made clear he was being misrepresented.

The persistence of opposition was, however, one contributory factor in the formation of a new evangelical group, Fulcrum. This sought to renew the evangelical centre, and those associated with it were sometimes viewed by more conservative evangelicals as "Rowan's evangelicals". Its origins lay in an initial private meeting in October 2002, when evangelical opponents were particularly vocal in the media, and it became public at the National Evangelical Anglican Congress (NEAC) in September 2003. After some opposition, Rowan was invited to address NEAC's opening plenary, joking to the packed hall (a small number left to attend a prayer meeting for those opposed to his invitation) that he had been tempted to speak on Psalm 71 in the Book of Common Prayer: "I am become as it were a monster unto many." Over time, opponents to varying degrees came to terms with his appointment but it revealed the range of evangelical responses to non-evangelical leadership in the Church of England and at times the different reactions to the new archbishop became a new identity marker within the different tribes of Anglican evangelicalism.

The irony was that the three main themes of NEAC – Bible, cross, and mission – were all, as his address made clear, central to Rowan's own faith and vision for the church and for Christian discipleship. In particular, his passion for a mission-shaped church would be one of his major legacies.

3

Mission-Shaped Church and Fresh Expressions

I think if there is one thing I'd like to be remembered for in the Church of England it's putting my shoulder behind Fresh Expressions. That's the thing that has most cheered me and encouraged me in recent years. (October 2009)[1]

If you enter "Order of the Black Sheep" on YouTube you will be offered a video with the intriguing title "The Archbishop and the Order of the Black Sheep". Some may at first wonder if this is a spoof or yet another "druid" story to damage the archbishop's credibility. Far from it. Watching the video reveals the archbishop sitting in his cassock in a circle of people, including young children, on a floor in a small room with a black wall decorated with skulls. They are gathered around a small table with a cross on it and are being addressed by a young clergyman, Mark Broomhead, with dreadlocks, flesh tunnels, and a lip ring. Mark hands over to Rowan who gives one of his short unscripted reflections to capture what is going on:

The one really, really unique thing about Jesus was that
he was completely not fussed about whose company
he was in. He took it for granted that if somebody was
around, that somebody was worth his company. That's
how the church started... Jesus' company is whoever
is around and whoever's prepared to spend time just
wondering, listening to what he's got to say to them. It's
as simple as that. That is the hard core around which
any church, any Christian community builds – the fact
that Jesus is there ahead of us making friends, being
in company. That's what this place is about – letting
people experience a bit of that company...[2]

In this September 2011 visit to Derby diocese and the Gates,
Chesterfield home of the Order, Rowan is doing what he regularly
sought to do on diocesan visits: experience a Fresh Expression of
church. His words capture much that is at the heart of Fresh
Expressions, why it is so important to him and why Rowan
and his vision of church and mission are so important to the
movement. This particular Fresh Expression originated with a
young trainee clergyman who had a particular passion for those
who like him were part of the alternative music culture, such
as heavy metal. It is though aimed more widely at any who
feel like "black sheep". For Mark, "what was important about
Archbishop Rowan's visit to the Order of the Black Sheep (OBS)
was not having a celebrity to open the Gates, but rather the fact
that he demonstrated to a sub-culture that has felt rejected by
the Church that they are valued and accepted and part of the
Church of England".[3]

The OBS is not just a Fresh Expression but one of the new
Bishops' Mission Orders in the Church of England and Mark is
one of the first cohort of pioneer ministers. All three categories
are significant developments in the Church of England

encouraged and led by Rowan. To understand their origins and significance and centrality to his legacy, we must go back to his time in Monmouth and early decisions he made on becoming archbishop.

Rowan became a bishop with little parish experience but he drew on what he had to great effect in relation to church growth and mission. Writing in 2005 in the launch issue of *Mixed Economy*, the journal of Fresh Expressions, he recalled an incident quarter of a century before which captures why he was so supportive of what became Fresh Expressions. He described how Renee, living on a council estate, was an occasional worshipper in the parish church who started a small Bible study group with five or six other young mums:

> I remember the awful moment at which I thought…
> under no circumstances should you go along to this
> bible study group because you will kill it stone dead.
> You will be attempting… to turn it into a parish church
> activity, and surprising as it may seem, it may just not
> have the same level of appeal if that's how it's branded…
> I left it to Renee.[4]

When he discovered similar initiatives happening on the margins or outside the normal Anglican church structures in Monmouth, he encouraged them in their distinctiveness, inviting Bob and Mary Hopkins of the Church Planting Initiative to explore what was going on outside the "mainstream" structures. His encouragement meant that, in the words of his diocesan missioner, Tudor Griffiths, "in his last year there, the numbers of people involved in 'fresh expressions' – if I can use that a little anachronistically – was roughly equivalent to the numbers who were counted more conventionally".[5] These new patterns were, however, not counted within official diocesan statistics because church growth and variety were moving ahead of bureaucratic structures!

In Wales, Rowan adopted the phrase "the mixed economy", which would become widely used within the Church of England. This phrase captured the desire to hold together different expressions of church and prevent traditionalist anxieties squashing new initiatives or those embarking on such initiatives being dismissive of well-established forms of church. Writing in the foreword to the report *Good News in Wales* (1999), he acknowledged the need for "facing up to the reality of the crisis facing our inherited structures" but discerned signs of hope: "These may be found particularly in the 'mixed economy' of Church life... in order that we might participate effectively in God's Mission, we need to consider seriously the possibilities that there are ways of being Church alongside the inherited parochial pattern."[6]

At a seminar on church planting in May 1999 he memorably articulated the theological rationale in terms of an understanding of church which would be so determinative of Fresh Expressions. Bob and Mary Hopkins recall:

> We will never forget during a Q&A and discussion section of our second presentation when an archdeacon turned to Rowan and asked "Well, Archbishop, if we are going to allow all these sorts of new things, can you help us by giving us guidance to know when something is in fact church?"... After a brief thoughtful pause, Rowan said something like "Well I suppose that anywhere where the activity of Jesus produces a response in community and worship, I would have to call it church!"... We have been living in the freedom of that pronouncement that Rowan has expanded on many times, ever since. That was

truly a Holy Spirit creative moment when all sorts of
potential was released! All these experiences convinced
us of Rowan's unique qualities as a real leader as well
as being deeply spiritual and passionately missional.
All of which made us hope and pray that one day,
when George Carey retired, he might become our next
Archbishop of Canterbury.[7]

The discovery of new forms of church in Monmouth, along with
his work on mission at Lambeth 1998, meant Rowan "felt very
strongly that I'm being called to encourage this and give it a bit
of a push; so when I first became Archbishop of Canterbury my
first thought was 'how do I use this position to further that kind
of agenda?'"

In England, a similar recognition was taking place and in
2002 the Church of England's Board of Mission set up a new
working party to review church planting and the emerging
variety of new forms of church in mission. Its chair was Graham
Cray, Bishop of Maidstone in Canterbury diocese. At his initial
half-hour meeting with his new diocesan he discovered that he
was speaking to the converted. Graham Cray filled Rowan in on
the report's main recommendations and emphases. His memory
of the conversation is vivid:

Quite literally, his eyes lit up; he was ahead of me
on every point. It immediately clearly connected to
something that was deeply important to him and he
has been the most outstanding advocate, apologist and
diplomat for the whole thing ever since.[8]

The report – *Mission-Shaped Church: Church planting and fresh
expressions of church in a changing context* – appeared in 2004
with a foreword by Rowan, which began by expressing his sense

that the Church of England was "poised for serious growth and renewal" and recognizing that "there are many ways in which the reality of 'church' can exist". Alongside the still valuable map of territorial parishes and dioceses were "more and more others" and so – a theme that crops up in various aspects of Rowan's ministry – "we are going to have to live with variety; the challenge is how to work with that variety so that everyone grows together in faith and in eagerness to learn about and spread the Good News". There followed a definition of church which polishes his impromptu 1999 answer and captures a key to understanding his time as archbishop and his legacy:

> If "church" is what happens when people encounter the Risen Jesus and commit themselves to sustaining and deepening that encounter in their encounter with each other, there is plenty of theological room for diversity of rhythm and style, so long as we have ways of identifying the same living Christ at the heart of every expression of Christian life in common.[9]

Despite being aligned with "high church" Anglo-Catholic Anglicanism often associated with strong attachment to particular traditions and liturgical forms, he here offered a definition and vision of "church" which gave space and permission for new, experimental risk-taking initiatives. The theological basis for this was clearly spelt out in 2008:

> The "strength" of the Church is never anything other than the strength of the presence of the Risen Jesus. And one thing this means is that, once we are convinced that God in Jesus Christ is indeed committed to us and present with us, there is a certain freedom to risk everything except those things that hold us to the truth of his presence – Word and sacrament and the journey

into holiness. These will survive, whatever happens to this or that style of worship, this or that bit of local Christian culture, because the presence of Jesus in the community will survive.[10]

This Christ-centred understanding of church is then intertwined with other keys in his theology – his Trinitarian understanding of God, the centrality of God's embodiment in Jesus, and his understanding of the nature and priority of God's mission in the world – to give a clear sense of the calling and mission of the church. God's will and desire is that his own Trinitarian life of loving communion should be expressed in the life of the world. It is embodied in Jesus and his relationships, supremely his relationship with his Father which he reveals and shares with those who trust him and so come to stand where Jesus stands. This pattern of divine relationship is the life which Christ calls the church to participate in, to bear witness to in its own life, and to nurture and encourage within the wider world. It does this through being drawn into relationship with the mystery of God through encounter with Christ and relationships with others in whom Christ is present and gives himself to us. The focus is not on church but on the action of God:

Church always begins with what God is doing... The Church begins with a lot of people, as it were, drawn into one room by the force of Jesus' personality and life and death and resurrection, and kind of looking at each other and thinking, "What are we all doing here together?", and working it out... A healthy church is one that constantly points to the God who takes these initiatives and invites people into that sort of fellowship of Jesus – and you take it from there, I think.[11]

When seeking to share this life with others, it is vital to go out to where those outside the church are to be found and see what God is already doing, rather than expecting them to come and conform to existing forms of worship and church life. In the simple slogan of the Fresh Expressions movement: "Going out, making friends, helping them start church where they are. That is Fresh Expressions of Church."

The Mission-Shaped Church report was well received by Synod in February 2004, strongly commended by Rowan. He had laid the groundwork in his first presidential address (July 2003), which warned things would look a "lot more chaotic than we have usually assumed" but the church had to relax and move towards a "mixed economy".

Crucially, the vision was also developed by sitting loose to a certain extent from traditional structures. Rowan looked to the financial resources and enthusiasm channelled through the Lambeth Partners who had backed George Carey's Springboard initiative. They were open to supporting something new, and Rowan was clear what he wanted. He hosted events to promote the new report and secured funding for what would become Fresh Expressions. He gave it strong backing as it launched around the dioceses and also worked to ensure that it was ecumenical from the start: a joint venture with the Methodists. That ecumenical aspect has grown over time so it now includes the United Reformed Church (URC) and the Congregational Federation. Fresh Expressions has also, in part because of his support, spread to Canada, Barbados, Germany, New Zealand, and elsewhere.

To take matters forward, Rowan sought the right team leader and identified Steven Croft, Warden of Cranmer Hall. He was appointed Archbishops' Missioner (the title being another sign of Rowan's close association) in May 2004 and Fresh Expressions launched later that year. Croft was succeeded in 2009 by Graham Cray. It is easy to forget what a visionary initiative this was.

Steven Croft, now Bishop of Sheffield, is frank:

> Fresh Expressions was not a straightforward thing to
> pitch, not the most obvious thing for an archbishop to
> do. When Rowan said to me "I want to make this the
> most important thing, one of my two priorities during
> my time as Archbishop" my honest first reaction was
> really "Do you think that is wise?" I was committed
> to this but what I think Rowan perceived and I didn't
> then was the potential enlivening impact of initiatives
> in Fresh Expressions on the rest of the Church of
> England. It's part of the renewal from the edge which is
> very much part of his wider ecclesiology, the belief that
> renewal doesn't come through central programmes but
> through what's happening on the margins, what's going
> on there. I was amazed at that commitment because it
> wasn't the most obvious horse for him to back but he
> did support it, he supported it magnificently.[12]

That bigger picture of renewal was explained by Rowan to
General Synod in February 2007:

> Essentially the Fresh Expressions programme is not
> simply about a kind of scattered set of experiments; it's
> about that gradual, but I think inexorable shift, in the
> whole culture of our Church that has been going on in
> the last few years, and which will undoubtedly continue
> to grow and develop. And that shift in culture is about
> the way in which discovering new expressions of the
> Church's life has now, rather paradoxically, become
> part of the bloodstream of the traditional, mainstream
> Church's life.[13]

Under Rowan, the report gathered momentum when under a different new archbishop it could simply have gathered dust. That momentum impacted the national church's structures. These had often made church planting beyond traditional parish or diocesan boundaries very difficult and worked with a rather narrow model of authorized, particularly ordained, ministry. The introduction of Bishops' Mission Orders in 2007 allowed bishops to facilitate cross-boundary and network patterns of church. It gave a framework for those with entrepreneurial and church-planting skills that kept them within Anglican structures and patterns of accountability. Issues surrounding church planting continued to cause some difficulties, particularly among more conservative evangelicals, but Andy Lines, mission director of Crosslinks (a mission society that questioned much of what Rowan did) acknowledges Rowan's interest in their concerns:

> In meetings each year with the heads of mission
> agencies my main recollection was his desire and ability
> to make sure that he had heard from everyone, not just
> the "key" people. He acknowledged the work Crosslinks
> had been doing to hold the ring for church planters
> who were struggling for acceptance within the Church
> of England.[14]

Similarly, the authorization and training of recognized lay and ordained pioneer ministry within the Church of England enabled it to supply risk-taking leadership. The Church of England has thus tapped the vision and enthusiasm of many, particularly younger, Christians who would have struggled to use their gifts within more traditional models of ministry and perhaps left Anglicanism as a result.

Although patterns vary across the dioceses, Rowan's time as archbishop has also seen a culture change within episcopal and other senior leadership. There is now a widespread welcoming of Fresh Expression initiatives, new forms of ministry and church planting, and a commitment as bishops to being leaders in mission. Church Army Reports in 2012 examined Fresh Expressions in the dioceses of Liverpool and Canterbury. They found that Fresh Expressions of church represented about 10 per cent of the worshipping Anglican population in these dioceses with a particular strength in attracting families. Mission and growth (and Fresh Expressions within these) have also been given prominence in the National Church Institutions. The Archbishops' Council's four objectives begin with "to enhance the Church's mission by promoting spiritual and numerical growth, enabling and supporting the worshipping Church and encouraging and promoting new ways of being Church, and engaging with issues of social justice and environmental stewardship".

The initiative has not been without its critics. John Milbank, a former student of Rowan whose wife, Alison, co-authored a major critique (*For the Parish*) was scathing of Fresh Expressions in reviewing Rowan's primacy. He claimed not only had Rowan failed to develop a strategy for the obvious "growing incompetence and theological incoherence on the ground",

> he has also – to the complete bafflement of nearly all his
> natural sympathisers – compounded the ecclesiastical
> malaise by giving financial and strategic priority to
> mostly dubious pastoral strategies (inanely dubbed
> "fresh expressions") which operate outside traditional
> parish and liturgical structures in favour of "networks"
> of the secularly likeminded.[15]

Others, however, have moved from scepticism to respect for his leadership in this area. Malcolm Brown, director of the Mission and Public Affairs Division, speaks of how impressive so much of Fresh Expressions has been on the ground and of the need to ensure it remains part of the church's core business. Rowan, he acknowledges, "was there in ten minutes, not ten years" in recognizing what was "authentic, good and true" and he has been a "doughty champion of it even when the chips were down. That is not political posturing, it's Rowan's authentic belief. I'm not sure he's had the credit he should have had for making sure that it was properly funded and really flourished."[16]

Although most dioceses have seen a significant decline in Sunday attendance between 2001 and 2010, and in that sense the vision for growth has not succeeded, almost all dioceses have seen a growth in the number of adult baptisms, the best proxy statistic for conversions. The pattern of church is definitely changing as, in Rowan's words to the Canadian Vital Church Planting Conference in September 2011, the Church of England wakes up to the fact that "for the vast majority of the population we need to rethink what a church might be like, what a congregation might just look like in a very, very different setting". Fresh Expressions and its role in creating a more mission-minded and mission-shaped church must take a significant part of the credit for the promising signs.

Its long-term impact is more difficult to ascertain, but when Rowan was asked, at a public meeting in 2008, what he hopes his legacy in this area will be, he had a clear vision:

> In about twenty years' time... I'd hope and pray for
> a church whose primary and most widespread form
> and existence in this country would be smallish
> groups meeting in living rooms with an open bible
> and a fair bit of silence. People helping each other to

become adults in Christ... And that regular, prosaic, unobtrusive, half-hidden reality of the Church would be visible from time to time in the great gatherings and celebrations that Christians want to engage in; but perhaps would see its *real* focus in terms of that growth in cultivation of humanity in God's image.[17]

4

Leader in Mission

The bishop has the opportunity of addressing large gatherings in the Church and in the wider community and of interacting with people in industry, commerce, government and education, with leaders of other religious communities and with those who form opinion in society. It is vital that these opportunities be seen in an apostolic light, as part of an intentional series of strategic actions flowing into the mission of God, not as signs of status. (Lambeth Conference 1998)[1]

Although the 1998 Lambeth Conference is most often remembered for one resolution (Lambeth I.10 on sexuality), among its most important pieces of work was the report of Section Two on mission: "Called to Live and Proclaim the Good News". Rowan co-chaired this and was a major contributor to the report; it begins with God's mission and call to mission before turning to explore the church as God's partner in mission and the world which God loves. It then expounds the missionary congregation (containing the seeds of the "mixed economy" vision), missionary diocese and "being a missionary bishop in a missionary church". Much of its account shaped Rowan's self-understanding as archbishop and his stated hopes for Lambeth 2008 were that it would "equip and empower the leadership of our church for participation in the Mission of God in the world".

In addition to enabling the church's mission through initiatives such as Fresh Expressions, as archbishop, Rowan gave a pattern of missionary leadership. Three forms of this stand out as part of his legacy as archbishop: his role and understanding of being an evangelist, his ministry as an apologist and teacher, and his extensive public conversations.

Evangelist

Rowan Williams is about as far removed as possible from the popular image of evangelists. Asked, in an interview published in *Conversations on Religion*, if it was important to him to evangelize, his initial response could appear rather tepid: "Yes, I suppose it is." John Humphrys, as part of a series of programmes in which he invited Jewish, Christian, and Muslim leaders to convert him, challenged Rowan: "You're trying to convert me... But why don't you go after the Jews, go after the Muslims and say 'come on you guys', because you don't do that do you?" Rowan's reply was telling: "No and... I don't exactly do it with you either." His reticence about seeking conversion is explained in the following recollection:

> I was asked by a group of evangelical Christians from
> Africa a couple of years ago, how many people I had
> brought into living faith in Jesus Christ? It was very
> clear to them that I was a gutless Western liberal. And I
> said, "Well, I'm not sure, because God brings people to
> living faith in Jesus Christ, not me or you. I can tell you

about a couple of people that I sat with as their minds changed, as they moved bit by bit towards faith over a longish period. And, as part of that journey they shared conversations with me. And I think of one person who was baptized on her deathbed, and one Buddhist, finding their way back into Christianity." Well, these may not be great "conversions" in a sense, but I think of them as that – they got there in the end. Though, of course, I'm not at all sure of what part I played.[2]

The primary model of evangelism Rowan has offered the church – one that fits with Fresh Expressions of church – is that of journeying in conversation. His concern with the stereotype of evangelism is clear:

I *do* want to convince people, but at the same time I need to recognize the very intuitive, unpredictable nature of how people begin to see things. The worst thing I could do is to try and manipulate people into it. But I'm happy to talk about it.[3]

Two stories capture how this works out in practice. Rupert Shortt's biography reports a theologian telling the House of Bishops how candidates for a job had been asked what answer they would give to someone who approached them in the street and said, "My bus leaves in two minutes. Tell me about the resurrection in the time remaining." After letting the bishops reflect on their response, she told them they were looking for the answer that if the man really wanted to hear about the resurrection he'd better be prepared to miss his bus. Rowan offered a better solution: "I think I'd have asked the man where he was going, then said that I'd accompany him on the journey." How he put such theory into practice in real life is illustrated by the story of how, on holiday, his wife Jane opened the door to find two Jehovah's Witnesses. She said she'd call her husband but as he approached he was recognized and the two Jehovah's Witnesses turned and fled, ignoring Rowan's protestations that he'd love to talk with them.

Despite his caution about traditional evangelism seeking converts, Rowan's public preaching and teaching was often powerfully evangelistic. Michael Green, one of the most gifted living Anglican evangelists, discovered this early in Rowan's time as archbishop:

> Rowan had not been celebrated for his evangelism.
> But I was doing a mission with a team on the south
> coast in his diocese. He had recently ordained a young
> man who wrote to him (unknown to the planners!)
> and asked if he would come for an evening in the
> mission. He was, amazingly, happy to do so. It was
> agreed that he would do the main talk and I would
> offer a challenge afterwards to link up with the follow-
> up procedure of the mission. He spoke in a cassock
> without a note and with real warmth and seriousness.
> He spoke on the cross and went to town with fine
> exegesis of Mark 10.45 ("For even the Son of Man
> did not come to be served, but to serve, and to give
> his life as a ransom for many") and showed how the
> ransom illustration was so appropriate in our day
> for people held captive by all sorts of negativities. It
> was superb and I felt that my tailpiece was otiose! He
> then interacted magnificently with local people at the
> supper which followed.[4]

The wider impact of Rowan's speaking and gentle sharing of the good news that evening is not recorded but is captured by the following testimony from Phil Groves:

My son is a Christian because of Rowan Williams. Selected with a group of young people from the Diocese of Leicester, he was living at the edge of faith, living with his school friends none of whom went to church. He was coming to a crisis: engage with his friends and throw himself in completely in their culture, or withdraw and become an isolated Christian in a non-Christian society. The young people had a tour of Lambeth Palace and then a Q&A with Rowan. My son went for it, asked Rowan questions of faith and unbelief and heard the Archbishop of Canterbury encouraging him to questioning belief. This man did not pretend to have all the answers and the effect on my son was electric. He heard the gospel of love from Rowan and it has been core to his faith ever since. He learnt in a few brief minutes that he could be true to faith and true to himself, maintain his identity and live in non-judgemental relationships with others. Any account of Rowan Williams as Archbishop of Canterbury should include these regular sessions with young people from as many dioceses as possible; vital life-giving encounters that have changed lives.[5]

His son, Jon Groves, recalls:

Rowan encouraged us to be part of the world and remain true to ourselves. What struck me was that here was someone who was not embarrassed by his faith, confident and intelligent… he gave me confidence to be a Christian with my friends.[6]

Rowan's legacy will generally be measured in relation to public initiatives but the deeper yet generally hidden and unrecorded legacy is personal encounters through which lives were changed, sometimes dramatically.

Apologist and Teacher

The first two of Anglicanism's five marks of mission are "to proclaim the Good News of the Kingdom" and "to teach, baptise and nurture new believers". Alongside his evangelism, Rowan's ministry was marked by his teaching of the faith (for example, his Holy Week Lectures in 2005, published as *Tokens of Trust: An introduction to Christian faith*) and his role as an apologist, defending the faith in response to questions and critiques from those exploring faith or those of other faiths.

Perhaps the best-known example of this, which demonstrates his ability to communicate great truths simply, is his letter to Lulu. In April 2011, journalist Alex Renton's six-year-old daughter Lulu, showing signs of an emerging faith, wrote a short letter to God – "To God how did you get invented? From Lulu xo". She left her parents the conundrum of working out how to deliver it and secure a reply, which was difficult, given they were atheists. They emailed a jpeg of the letter to various church leaders (many of whom did not reply), including to Lambeth Palace, and received this email from "Archbishop Rowan":

> Dear Lulu,
> Your dad has sent on your letter and asked if I have any answers. It's a difficult one! But I think God might reply a bit like this –
> "Dear Lulu – Nobody invented me – but lots of people discovered me and were quite surprised. They discovered me when they looked round at the world and thought it was really beautiful or really mysterious and wondered where it came from. They discovered me

when they were very very quiet on their own and felt a
sort of peace and love they hadn't expected.
Then they invented ideas about me – some of them
sensible and some of them not very sensible. From time
to time I sent them some hints – specially in the life of
Jesus – to help them get closer to what I'm really like.
But there was nothing and nobody around before me to
invent me. Rather like somebody who writes a story in
a book, I started making up the story of the world and
eventually invented human beings like you who could
ask me awkward questions!"
And then he'd send you lots of love and sign off.
I know he doesn't usually write letters, so I have to do
the best I can on his behalf. Lots of love from me too.

+Archbishop Rowan[7]

Her father, despite his scepticism and cynicism about
Anglicanism, was "touched, more than I would have imagined"
by Rowan's kindness and wisdom. Lulu, in addition to liking
Rowan's beard, "listened quietly as I read the archbishop's letter
and it went down well. What worked particularly was the idea of
'God's story'." Asked what she thought, her reply, after a pause,
was, "Well, I have very different ideas. But he has a good one",
the sort of response that one suspects Rowan would welcome
and engage with further.

What will surely become classic pieces of Christian apologetics
are two addresses Rowan gave to Muslim audiences. In 2004, on
the symbolic day of 11 September, Rowan spoke at the al-Azhar
al-Sharif Institute in Cairo, a revered centre of learning within
Sunni Islam. He followed a regular pattern of seeking to find
areas of agreement but also exploring areas of disagreement. In
this case, his concern was the doctrine of God and how beliefs

about God lead to affirmations about peace and justice. Without using the word "Trinity", he proceeded to offer an exposition of the Christian doctrine of God as triune. This sought to enable Muslims, with their fundamental conviction that God is one, to see what Christians do and do not believe, what Christianity and Islam share, and what Christians confess which means there is also divergence:

> The name "God" is not the name of a person like a human person, a limited being with a father and mother and a place that they inhabit within the world. "God" is the name of a kind of life – eternal and self-sufficient life, always active, needing nothing. And that life is lived eternally in three ways which are made known to us in the history of God's revelation to the Hebrew people and in the life of Jesus. There is a source of life, an expression of life and a sharing of life. In human language we say, "Father, Son and Holy Spirit", but we do not mean one God with two beings alongside him, or three gods of limited power. Just as we say, "Here is my hand, and these are the actions my one hand performs", but it is not different from the actions of my five fingers, so with God: this is God, the One, the Living and Self-subsistent, but what God does is not different from the life which is eternally at the same time a source and an expression and a sharing of life. Since God's life is always an intelligent and purposeful life, each of these dimensions of divine life can be thought of as a centre of mind and love; but this does not mean that God "contains" three different individuals, separate from each other as human individuals are.[8]

He sought to persuade his audience that "the disagreement between Christian and Muslim is not, I believe, a disagreement about the nature of God as One and Living and Self-subsistent". This means that when "the Christian, the Muslim or the Jew sees his neighbour of another faith following the ways of this world instead of the peaceful will of God, he must remind his neighbour of the nature of the one God we look to, whose will cannot be changed and who will himself see that justice is done".

A year later, in November 2005, he spoke to students and academics at the International Islamic University in Islamabad, Pakistan on "What Is Christianity?"[9] He sketched the annual pattern of Christian worship and responded to questions that might arise in the minds of someone observing the church's life. He thus explored central Christian doctrines and practices through reflection on prayer, Scripture, and Eucharist and set out central elements of the Christian gospel in simple, non-confrontational terms:

- "We are given the right to speak to God in exactly the same way that Jesus did, because the life, the power, the Spirit, that filled Jesus is given to us also."

- "Jesus knows the very mind and heart of God and can reveal it completely and authoritatively to those he calls to be with him."

- "When God created the world, he made all things according to his will. But the first human beings refused to obey God, although they knew what he asked of them. By rebelling against him in this way, they started a process of corruption in the world which spreads to everyone who is born into it… The law of God is there and it is plain, but we are held in prison by this history of sin and disobedience."

- "Jesus... shows us what a human life is like when it is lived as it should be. But he does more. Because of his perfect obedience and goodness, he is able to offer himself to rejection and death, so that by his death there may be a restored relationship of love between God and humanity. Christians say that Jesus, as he goes to the cross, accepts all the suffering that is the consequence for human beings of their rebellion and weakness. He 'pays the price' of human wickedness."

- "When we come in trust to Jesus and identify with him, when we stand in his place and speak with his words, the Holy Spirit gives us once again the freedom to live a life according to God's will... And because God brings him back from death to meet again with his followers, we know that his life is not a thing of the past. He is still alive, eternally alive. He calls people to be with him just as he did in his life on earth. And so day by day he creates that community of fellowship with him which gives human beings the possibility of living differently, living in obedience to God."

- "When we receive the Holy Spirit, we still have to use our freedom to choose the good. But in fellowship with Jesus, we know that we have the help of the Spirit, giving us strength to resist temptation and wisdom to see where it lies. We also know that when we fail or fall back, as sometimes we are bound to do, the forgiving love of God will give us another opportunity to serve him, to try and model our lives on the life of Jesus and to let the freedom and love which he has planted in our hearts change all that we do and say."

Although perhaps never as fully or succinctly as in this address, these basic truths of the Christian faith recur throughout Rowan's ministry as archbishop, particularly in his preaching at Christmas and Easter. These remain among the few addresses that still get a wide audience through reporting on television and in the press (although sometimes in distorted and dismissive terms – "Pious piffle" was the *Sun* editorial on Christmas 2003). In them, he spoke on pressing issues of the day or aspects of our personal lives (greed and the environment at Christmas 2007). Less often reported, he related these constantly to an explanation of the central truths of Christian faith: God's self-emptying identification with us all in Christ's vulnerable incarnation, his self-giving love leading to his suffering, reconciling and atoning death, and his resurrection power which brings good news of hope and his presence with us.

Perhaps the most difficult form of apologetics is in the face of great tragedy. Rowan responded to a number of these during his primacy. In September 2004, the world was shocked by the massacre of hundreds of people, mainly children, at the end of a siege in a school in Beslan, Russia. Rowan agreed to be interviewed on the *Today* programme by John Humphrys. Four years later, answering a sixth former's more general question about God and suffering, he admitted the difficulty he experienced and summed up the position which, drawing on an appeal to human free will, he had struggled to articulate during Humphrys' persistent interrogation:

> I think the most demanding interview I have ever had to do was with John Humphrys the morning after the Beslan massacre a couple of years ago. Essentially he got me into the studio to say, "Well how can you talk about God in the face of this level of sub-human atrocity?" And I said then and I say now that it is very strange not to let that level of suffering and human awfulness dent something about your faith. But is it morally wrong not to doubt? I don't think I could say that.[10]

On Boxing Day 2004, a tsunami in the Indian Ocean killed approaching a quarter of a million people. On 2 January, Rowan wrote a reflection for the *Sunday Telegraph* acknowledging that, faced with the question "How can you believe in a God who permits suffering on this scale?" "the traditional answers will get us only so far", and "every single random, accidental death is something that should upset a faith bound up with comfort and ready answers". He explored the importance of each person, the role of prayer, the significance of a faith which persists even in such crises, and the Christian's commitment to fellow humans, particularly those who are suffering and weak, but concluded that "what can be said with authority about these terrible matters can finally be said only by those closest to the cost. The rest of us need to listen; and then to work and – as best we can manage it – pray." Demonstrating the challenges of relying even on broadsheet media to communicate his message, the paper ran the totally misleading and inaccurate headline, "Archbishop of Canterbury: This Has Made Me Question God's Existence", and reported him as saying "the Asian tsunami disaster should make all Christians question the existence of God". As Lambeth Palace stated, any reading of the text made clear this was a misrepresentation, but the headline furthered an image of a woolly, doubting church leader.

These contributions showed how even a great theological mind struggles when asked to make sense of such tragedies. They demonstrated that any faithful attempt to speak out risks being misunderstood and distorted and must ultimately fall silent and address its pain, anger and questions to God.

Public Conversations

Rowan's practice of mission as a journeying in conversation was put to great effect in his engagement in public conversations with people on a range of issues, some very directly related to matters of Christian faith, others more focused on social and cultural concerns. Some of these were closer to more traditional interviews such as his Radio 5 Live dialogues with Simon Mayo (one of which was preceded by a lively exchange with the previous interviewee, comedian and proselytizing atheist, Ricky Gervais). Others were more clearly conversational, such as his contribution to John Humphrys' *In Search of God*. Further examples of this public conversational genre include his 2003 Channel Four series exploring issues such as childhood, rights, and bioethics and his 2004 *The Worlds We Live In* discussions on global economics and politics with people such as Philip Bobbitt, John Kay, Mary Midgley, and David Owen.

One of those involved in the Channel Four series was the children's writer Philip Pullman. Rowan re-engaged him in conversation in 2004 when his controversial trilogy, *His Dark Materials*, became a stage play. On being invited to start the conversation, Rowan illustrated how, without being contentious or confrontational, he would happily get the key questions on the table:

> I suppose one of the questions I would like to hear
> more about from Philip [Pullman] is what has
> happened to Jesus in the church in this world [of *His
> Dark Materials*], because one of the interesting things
> for me in the model of the church in the plays and the
> books, is it's a church, as it were, without redemption.[11]

That simple question led to the "conversation" continuing in a broader sense with the appearance in 2010 of Pullman's *The Good Man Jesus and The Scoundrel Christ*. Pullman traced the inspiration for this back to his conversation with Rowan: "He asked me why I hadn't dealt with Jesus in *His Dark Materials*.

And I said, 'Well you're right, I haven't, so I'd better do a book sometime.'" Rowan, in turn, reviewed the book in the *Guardian* with Pullman commenting, "I think he was generous. Much more generous than might have been expected, but he is a good and kindly man. And predictably, but correctly, in effect he said, 'This wasn't as good as the Bible.'"

Other conversation partners have been remarkably eclectic, including *Private Eye* editor Ian Hislop (September 2009), Terry Eagleton (November 2010), Foreign Secretary William Hague (June 2011), comedian Frank Skinner (in Canterbury Cathedral, September 2011), Richard Dawkins (February 2012), philosophers A.C. Grayling (May 2011) and John Gray (April 2012), and former prime minister Tony Blair and former *Spectator* and *Telegraph* editor Charles Moore (July 2012).

No previous archbishop engaged so extensively and publicly in conversation with leading names in wider society. Although not formal conversations as such, his guest-editing the *Today* programme on Radio 4 (December 2006) and, controversially, the *New Statesman* (June 2011) also enabled him to choose dialogue partners. He has become (along with the Chief Rabbi, Jonathan Sacks) one of Britain's leading public intellectuals, addressing a great range of issues in dialogue with other intellectuals but also – as with Frank Skinner – able to discuss with thoughtful popular celebrities. This pattern, behind which were doubtless private conversations with many key figures, not least through the variety of people invited to receptions at Lambeth Palace, has been a major way of fulfilling his stated ambition to "capture the imagination of our culture". It leaves an unquantifiable legacy of influence as in both academia and wider culture, sometimes explicitly as with Pullman, key thinkers find themselves subsequently interacting with a Christian perspective directly because of their conversations with the archbishop.

5

Capturing the Imagination

If there is one thing I long for above all else, it's that the years to come may see Christianity in this country able again to capture the imagination of our culture, to draw the strongest energies of our thinking and feeling into the exploration of what our creeds put before us. (July 2002)[1]

Two features of British culture which have become particularly prominent in the last ten years and are likely to remain important in shaping the church's understanding and pattern of mission are the New Atheism and the phenomenon of "spirituality" detached from traditional Christian worship and discipleship. Rowan's discussions of these, although quite theoretical, merit exploration. They reveal common misunderstandings and help explain his own vision of mission which he has bequeathed the church as it addresses these major missional challenges in the future. In addition to analysing and critiquing these alternatives to Christian faith, Rowan sought to "capture the imagination" through appealing to literature, the arts, and religious biography.

The New Atheism

Rowan has not engaged with the phenomenon of evangelistic atheism as extensively and thoroughly as other theologians (particularly Alister McGrath) but he could not avoid it given its prominence. In February 2012 he had a formal debate/conversation with Richard Dawkins whom he had previously described as having "gleefully stepped into the role of famous atheist... with tremendous panache". Although he thought Dawkins had set himself up as an "anti-pope... a great pusher in some ways of the most extreme, the most obnoxious and offensive versions of anti-religious language", he admitted that "he does it with such eloquence and even such charm that it is a great tribute to his intellectual quality". Rowan's critique of Dawkins and others was that they displayed "tremendous analytical sophistication in respect of physical processes, allied to philosophical crudity", and when asked in Winchester how he would challenge Dawkins' underlying worldview his reply began, "I think I'd probably tell him he's wrong!" Three lectures in particular set out why he thinks the New Atheists are wrong and offer a provocative analysis and response to atheism.

In March 2004, with suggestions that atheism be added to the curriculum alongside religions, Rowan explored the relationship between unbelief and belief. He pointed out that in order to understand "atheism" we need to know which gods are being rejected. The various forms of reactive atheism mean that "to speak as though 'atheism' were a belief system alongside varieties of religious belief is simply a category mistake". In addition, it is crucial to ask whether the God being rejected is the God religious people claim to worship.[2]

Later that month, he revisited some of this analysis.[3] His critique of much existing religious education was summed up in terms of it describing "positions of faith communities as finished systems for which questions have been answered". He preferred to view religions as (to borrow Alasdair MacIntyre's phrase) "continuities of conflict" where moral, spiritual, and intellectual tensions "constantly press believers towards a fuller, more comprehensive statement of their commitments". This means that most religions "require and cultivate unbelief" and "to come to the point where you disbelieve passionately in a certain kind of God may be the most important step you can take in the direction of the true God".

Three years later, his October 2007 lecture "How Religion is Misunderstood" picks up some of these themes and offers the heart of his critique of the "new atheism".[4] As in his earlier critiques, he approaches questions from a novel perspective, arguing that Dawkins has misrepresented and misunderstood what he is rejecting and that, once understood on its own terms, religion offers a challenge back to Dawkins' reductionist Darwinian worldview.

Rowan opens with a character in Dostoevsky's *The Idiot* who comments, "Atheists always seem to be talking about something else." Exploring this in more detail, he shows how religion is misunderstood by Dawkins as either a survival strategy or an explanation of the world. Religious practice is rather "learning how to occupy a certain role, a position in the universe, a position of recognized dependence". This leads to us attending to others as those who relate to God before relating to us and the development of "that contemplative skill which turns me silently and expectantly to a reality greater than myself". This requires "a sense of trust in communication and relationship". Dawkins doesn't recognize that these enable religion to be self-critical as "every religious practice involves some very deep levels of self-questioning and self-criticism". This humility feeds into the wider imaginative and intellectual world. For Christians such self-critical energy is rooted in "justification by faith": "a fundamental act of trust in the character towards which you're looking. Trust that is, in Christian terms, in the love of God." Rowan argues that such good religion, rather than atheism, is the best antidote to the bad religion which Dawkins constantly highlights. As he closes, he turns the table on the atheist secularist critic of religion, asking whether the reality of moral integrity, self-inspection, and fundamental trust is really reducible to either a personal choice or a survival strategy. Is not the explanation of the religious believer – that these are "styles of living which communicate the character of an eternal and free agency, the agency that most religions call God" – a much better one?

Spirituality

Alongside the rise of "new atheism", there has been the growth of interest in "spirituality" detached from Christian faith or "religion" generally. Drawing on similar themes Rowan often addressed this, most fully in his 2008 lecture at Westminster Cathedral entitled "The Spiritual and the Religious: Is the Territory Changing?" This not only offers a critique of "spirituality" but a vision for Christian mission.[5]

The common contrast is between "religion" (portrayed negatively due to its alleged exclusive truth claims and demand to abandon personal freedom) and "spirituality" (concerned with openness, personal depth and integrity, and the sacred). Tracing the sources of this, Rowan argues that it can be expressed in terms of a desire to be patrons in control rather than subscribers bound to the community or organization. While not belittling "spirituality", he sought to challenge the claims that we need to become post-religious. Viewing religion in terms of a power seeking us to submit our will unquestioningly to it is false. Traditional patterns of religious commitment provided an environment of a comprehensive narrative. This provided people with possible roles and projects so they could act in a way that "lets the story come through, that shows to the world what we believe is most real". The religious language of responsibility points to giving an answer to an "other" and religion, unlike spirituality, points to something like "another personal presence... an initiating agency that is independent of anything in our world". Our actions are reflections or continuations of something else, some revelation or transforming event with which we seek to be in harmony. In contrast to the "spiritual" there is interpersonal imagery and a recognition that our knowledge is incomplete as through faith and worship we explore something other than ourselves in gratitude, enjoyment, and obedience:

> The specific reality of the human self is not abolished,
> but it is dethroned or decentred. To discover who I am
> I need to discover the relation in which I stand to an
> active, prior Other, to a transcendent creator: I don't
> first sort out who I am and then seek for resources to
> sustain that identity.

Religious people generally reject the idea that they seek adherence to doctrine and policies and instead point to the need for "exposure to an action believed to be effective in altering the world we experience, human and non-human". For Christians this reality is the Kingdom revealed in Jesus. The church's response to the challenges of non-dogmatic spirituality should therefore be something which sounds not unlike the vision behind Fresh Expressions and Mission-Shaped Church:

> The believer... should be asking whether what happens
> when the Assembly meets to adore God and lay
> itself open to his action looks at all like a new and
> transforming environment, in which human beings are
> radically changed... If we who adhere to revealed faith

don't want to be simply at the mercy of this culture,
to be absorbed into its own uncritical stories about
the autonomous self and its choices, then we need to
examine the degree to which our practice *looks* like a
new world.

Or, as Rowan sometimes more memorably put it in conversation: we need churches to be living in such a way before the eyes of the world that they get the response of the fellow-diner seeing Sally's famous performance in *When Harry met Sally*: "I'll have what she's having."

Mission through Literature, the Arts, and Religious Biography

In responding to the challenge to capture the imagination of wider society, Rowan (in addition to his engagement with social and political issues discussed later) regularly turned to two approaches not often associated with offering leadership in Christian mission. First, drawing on his own love for, and remarkable knowledge of, literature, arts, and culture, he frequently gave lectures and sermons in these areas or wrote and spoke on them in the media. The range of his output is quite remarkable. He is a gifted poet and has often, in passing or in a more sustained engagement, used reflections on John Donne, John Milton, George Herbert, Henry Vaughan, W.H. Auden, T.S. Eliot, R.S. Thomas, and lesser-known poets such as Geoffrey Hill and fellow-Welshmen Waldo Williams, David Jones, and Vernon Watkins to open up questions of faith, contemplation, and human struggles and flourishing. In January 2009 at the Guy's and St Thomas' Hospital NHS Trust Annual Arts Event, he offered commentary on his favourite poems (by Wordsworth, Shakespeare, Keats, and particularly William Blake) and some of his own poetry.

Two classical writers are particularly prominent and fruitful conversation partners. To the surprise of many, he took a sabbatical at the height of the Communion conflicts (a year before Lambeth 2008) to write a major study of the Russian novelist Dostoevsky. This created opportunities to speak on the Radio 3 Literary Proms and Radio 4's *One to One* programme, at a Hay Festival discussion with A.N. Wilson, and which led to interviews, reviews, or articles in *The Times Literary Supplement* and major broadsheets. Another great passion – Shakespeare – led to a sermon in Stratford on Shakespeare Sunday (2006) and an interview on the *Today* programme. Shakespeare was the focus of yet another of his public conversations in May 2011, with actor Simon Russell Beale at the Hay Festival, and he spoke about the piece of Shakespeare that inspired him most for the 2012 BBC radio series *Shakespeare Unlocked*, choosing *Macbeth* Act 3, Scene 2 where "Macbeth and Lady Macbeth are discussing – though not discussing – the murder of Banquo".

Among more recent and contemporary writers, his interactions with Philip Pullman have already been noted. In the year of his retirement he published an expansion of his 2011 Holy Week Lectures exploring, with great profundity but also simplicity, C.S. Lewis's Narnia. He has also drawn upon and drawn attention to the theologically rich work of American writer Marilynne Robinson, most fully in his lecture on accepting the Conference on Christianity and Literature Lifetime Achievement Award. Early in his time as archbishop, in 2005, he also gave a series of four lectures (published as *Grace and Necessity: Reflections on Art and Love*) which explored Catholic philosophy and the twentieth-century artist through bringing the work of Roman Catholic philosopher and theologian Jacques Maritain into conversation with Welsh poet and painter David Jones and American novelist Mary Flannery O'Connor.

Music, too, is a great love and his *Desert Island Discs* choice of the Incredible String Band's "Hedgehog Song" provided an opportunity to raise his profile and help shake off his ivory-tower academic image. It also became an opportunity to be present as a Christian witness in unexpected places. In October 2003 he was spotted at the 12 Bar Club, a Soho jazz club, for the launch of an anthology of the band's work. One reveller remarked, "The Archbish was just mingling with the rest of us in his clerical garb. I was a bit surprised to see him at the 12 Bar – it's pretty down-at-heel." He wrote the preface for the anthology. According to the editor it was "very erudite… all about bardic and Celtic traditions, and quoted the band's songs" but, as so often in his speeches and short articles, it was the final sentences that conveyed the heart of his message and a key as to why this focus was for him a form of mission: the Incredible String Band offered

> simply a discovery of poetry; and as such – risking the embarrassment that so regularly goes with my particular vocation – I'd also have to say that it was a discovery of the holy; not the solemn, not the saintly, but the holy, which makes you silent and sometimes makes you laugh and which, above all, makes the landscape different once and for all.[6]

At other times his subject matter made it easier for more explicitly Christ-centred mission. Tom Wright recalled in his appreciation of Rowan:

> "Here to introduce Bach's *St Matthew Passion*," said the radio announcer, "is the Archbishop of Canterbury, Dr Rowan Williams." My companion and I listened eagerly to a lucid account of St Matthew's theology, and of how Bach's music involves every hearer in the events of Jesus' death. But at one moment the speaker

paused, as though searching for a word. Didn't he have a script? Next time I saw the Archbishop, I asked him. The BBC, he explained, sat him in a studio and asked him to talk about his favourite music. How many Archbishops could have done that, I wondered – at the same time as writing a book on Dostoevsky, debating with Philip Pullman, and plotting a visit to Robert Mugabe? Not to mention the thousand shocks that episcopal flesh is heir to.[7]

Alongside drawing out meaning, significance, and gospel from poetry, literature, and music, another key feature of Rowan's distinctive pattern of opening up people to the call of God is his use of religious biography. His 2004 Romanes Lecture, "Religious Lives", was an early signal of the importance of this.[8] He insists, appealing to the apostle James, that religion is not primarily about beliefs but

> a religious life is a material life… living religiously is a way of conducting a bodily life. It has to do with gesture, place, sound, habit; not first and foremost with what is supposed to be going on inside. The whole idea of an "inner life" is… what comes to light as the sense, the intelligibility, of a certain pattern of acts… religious lives are indeed recognised as habits of behaviour.

That lecture also introduced someone he often referred to: Etty Hillesum, a young Jewish woman from the Netherlands killed in Auschwitz. The insight Rowan often drew from her is captured in his words of welcome to Taizé's European Youth Meeting in Geneva at the end of 2007:

> When she was facing the possibility of deportation and death, she wrote she felt that her task was "to testify

84

that God is alive also in the midst of the horror and the folly of Nazism". These words still haunt me today since they give one of the most demanding and authentic definitions of faith of [the] modern era. To have faith is to live so as to show that God is living.[9]

The stories of those who do live in a way that shows that God is living are able to draw others into relationship with God. This was most fully explored in his 2008 address to the Hereford Diocesan Conference, "Sharing the Story". Drawing on Scripture, he argued for the power of story to invite people into a new world:

I do think that a great deal of effective sharing of the faith is done by simply pointing to certain sorts of lives and saying "human life could be like that; isn't that life inviting and challenging?" That seems to me to be one of the ways in which we can communicate our faith at a level where it's not just about inviting people to adopt a certain set of ideas, but inviting people to believe that a certain kind of way of being in the world is possible: "Life could be like that."[10]

He then illustrated this ecumenically with four of his favourite modern saints: Sergei Bulgakov, Edith Stein (whose impact Hillesum testified to), Dietrich Bonhoeffer, and Dick Sheppard. None of their lives were "sensible", but they made sense of the world by "uncovering a new world where what you think is sensible and rational doesn't necessarily work in quite the way you might have hoped or expected":

That's why sharing stories and trying to communicate the heart of the Christian vision by storytelling, is inevitably a way of trying to push people out of the comfort zone, out of comfort into joy as well as risk,

out of comfort into a homecoming so profound that it's
shocking not just consoling. That's what Jesus is after
in the New Testament, that's what redemption *is* about,
not just comfort, not just security, but the new
creation.[11]

Conclusion: Rowan Williams' Missional Legacy

Rowan's labelling as a "liberal" and his association with more
traditional "high church" Anglicanism, combined with
opposition from some evangelicals, meant that few predicted
how central missional leadership would be during his primacy
and within his legacy. These last three chapters have highlighted
various aspects of this as he helped create a mission-shaped
church through Fresh Expressions and used his position and
intellectual power to be the public face and voice of the national
church.

Some would have preferred him to offer a clearer pattern of
evangelistic mission which more confidently called for repentance
and faith and proclaimed Christian truths. However, his gentler,
more questioning advocacy of a contemplative pattern of faith
and conversational form of mission and evangelism won him a
hearing and warm appreciation in many circles. This was evident
in comedian Robert Webb's humorous *New Statesman* reflection
in which he confessed "I am troubled by how much I like Rowan
Williams". In addition to admiring his brains, Webb identified
part of the attraction being that "while I'm busy having doubts
about my doubts about my doubts, it 'helps' to have in front of
me an example of a believer I'd like to talk to":

It's an intersection of hard-won but lightly worn
scholarship and classic liberal notions of tolerance and
compassion that allows agnostics like me the space to

believe in God without feeling like a mug. In short, it makes God "attractive".[12]

Webb also shows, however, that a central part of the message had failed to get through to him: "this God seems to agree with me about everything". Even allowing for humorous exaggeration, this highlights that the challenging, unsettling, converting power of the gospel and the cost of discipleship – which Rowan could never be accused of downplaying by anyone who had really listened to him or read him – had got lost.

Although his own words and deeds are an important part of his legacy in relation to mission, his greater long-term contribution is how he challenged and enabled the church to make mission central and to change and become something different in order to reconnect with those on its margins and distant from it. Those most committed to such a vision, particularly those who are part of Fresh Expressions, almost universally share the positive assessment and appreciation of his ministry expressed by Mark Russell, chief executive of Church Army:

> Rowan has been committed to helping the church be more missional, more outward-looking. I have seen at close quarters his commitment to a mission-shaped church, his energy and passion to see the Church of England re-invent herself in new ways. Church Army has been a key partner with Fresh Expressions all the way. He has chaired countless meetings, worked to get the right people in place, and kept *Mission-Shaped Church* on the agenda of the central structures of the church, either at Archbishops' Council, or in Synod. On his watch we have seen the development of Ordained Pioneers, we have seen the Church Commissioners release more money specifically for

church planting and work with the unchurched. He has encouraged the development of new mission communities, like CMS [Church Mission Society], ourselves, Moot, and others, seeking to model the new monastic movement. Mission has been central to Rowan's vision for his ministry, and he has done so much to encourage practitioners in the field.[13]

6

The Reading Crisis and Sexuality Debates

None of us will need any persuading that the recent appointment of Canon Jeffrey John as Bishop of Reading has proved a controversial and challenging one. (June 2003)[1]

From the perspective of the media and wider society and even many Anglicans, Rowan's legacy is focused not on new, missional forms of church but on two controversial and divisive issues: battles over same-sex relationships and the move to allow women bishops. A popular picture views him simply holding the ring between two warring camps: "inclusive" or "liberal" supporters in touch with cultural change, facing "conservatives" or "traditionalists" committed to upholding the Bible and tradition. Although this has a small grain of truth, the reality is much more complex. A significant body of opinion – represented by groups such as Affirming Catholicism and Inclusive Church – does see the two issues as connected and presses for change on the basis of the gospel's inclusion of all. However, conservative opponents to women bishops are divided between Anglo-Catholics and conservative evangelicals. In addition, most evangelicals, certainly in senior leadership are, on the basis of Scripture, supportive of women bishops but not of sexual relationships outside heterosexual marriage.

Although Rowan is supportive of women bishops and has called for the church to rethink its views and practice in relation to same-sex relationships, his approach as archbishop has been shaped by the position of the wider church on both issues. In relation to women bishops, although such a development would create more problems in ecumenical relationships with Rome, it would be welcomed by other denominations. The Anglican Communion in 1988 decided that a province's decision to proceed with consecrating women bishops should be respected by other provinces. In 1998 it called on provinces "to affirm that those who dissent from, as well as those who assent to, the ordination of women to the priesthood and episcopate are both loyal Anglicans" and "to make such provision, including appropriate episcopal ministry, as will enable them to live in the highest degree of Communion possible" (Lambeth III.2). In contrast, the Communion in 1998 rejected homosexual practice as "incompatible with Scripture" and said it "cannot advise the legitimising or blessing of same sex unions nor ordaining those involved in same gender unions" (I.10). Rowan, as noted in Chapter 2, immediately made clear the significance of this resolution for his own primacy.

Underlying Rowan's approach to both issues has been the concern to respect the mind of the wider church (including on the question of at what level decisions can be made). Alongside this is his commitment to assist mutual understanding across different viewpoints and a determination to work patiently at finding solutions which will maintain the greatest unity possible, so as to enable ongoing communication and discernment together. How this played out was different with the two issues and at times Rowan's actions heightened tensions and increased conflict. This chapter explores his handling of the sexuality debates within the Church of England and the following chapter turns to debates about women in church leadership, particularly the question of consecrating women as bishops.

Sexuality: Clarifying the Issues

As soon as Rowan Williams was linked to the Canterbury post, his stance on homosexuality caused controversy, raising great hopes among those looking for the church to change and alarm among some conservatives. By the time he left office there had been a sea-change in British law and culture, but the Church of England's official stance remained basically unchanged and the church and wider Communion remained as divided as ever on the subject. Before turning to his actions as archbishop, it helps to clarify just what the debate is about and, more specifically, his understanding of the church's struggles and position in this area.

The heart of the debate was captured clearly in Rowan's June 2004 address to the Anglican Consultative Council, one of his few substantive contributions on the issue.[2] Echoing his earlier writings, he insisted Christian teaching about sex was not a list of prohibitions but "an integral part of what the Bible has to say about living in such a way that our lives communicate the character of God". Marriage's uniqueness was clear: "it speaks of an absolute faithfulness, a covenant between radically different persons, male and female; and so it echoes the absolute covenant of God with his chosen, a covenant between radically different partners". Those opposed to blessing same-sex unions view such actions as "upsetting... the balance of how we show and speak of God". However, without such blessing, "people living in such unions are at least in tension with the common language of the Church" and this "is not a good basis for taking on the responsibilities of leadership, especially episcopal leadership, whatever latitude we allow to conscience and pastoral discretion". He therefore identified two key questions: "What is the nature of a holy and Christ-like life for someone who has consistent homosexual desires? And what is the appropriate discipline to be applied to the personal life of the pastor in the Church?" He was clear that Lambeth 1998 and "the majority voice of the Communion" firmly resisted changing practice and discipline but argued that such a stance could accept the need for full theological discussion of such questions. Christians must also condemn violent and bigoted language. A key passage captured the crucial issue in a way rarely reported in the media (who reduce the debate to being for or against "gay bishops") and often not understood by many Anglicans:

> The question is… about what the Church requires in its ordained leaders and what patterns of relationship it will explicitly recognise as unquestionably revealing of God. On these matters, the Church is not persuaded that change is right. And where there is a strong scriptural presumption against change, a long consensus of teaching in Christian history, and a widespread ecumenical agreement, it may well be thought that change would need an exceptionally strong critical mass to justify it. That, I think, is where the Communion as a whole stands.

That statement holds the key as to why, although viewed as a potential reformer in this area, Rowan did so little to change things during his ten years in office. In 2003, however, it had been far from clear what respecting "where the Communion as a whole stands" meant in practice in the Church of England.

The Reading Crisis

The appointment of even a new diocesan bishop raises limited interest in the Church of England outside his diocese. The announcement of a new suffragan or area bishop registers on very few radars. It is therefore remarkable and unparalleled for the ministry of an Archbishop of Canterbury to be so seriously destabilized and constantly overshadowed by such an appointment. For Rowan Williams, however, the events of the six weeks between Tuesday 20 May and Sunday 4 July in 2003 surrounding the bishop-elect of Reading would have just such a catastrophic effect. They wounded and scarred him and his ministry throughout his primacy.

A full account of what happened, why, and its significance and implications could be a whole book. The focus here is on what the incident revealed about church tensions, Rowan's role, and why he and the church emerged from the crisis very badly damaged. His initial approval as a bishop of Jeffrey John, someone in a same-sex partnership and a leading advocate of the church blessing such partnerships, confirmed conservative critics in their suspicions. It also gave great hopes to those who thought he would provide what they saw as prophetic leadership. In the words of an unnamed leading General Synod member, reported in *The Times* in the middle of the controversy:

> Jeffrey John will be ordained bishop in October and
> everyone will have to put up with it… We are in
> the transition period between the evangelical world
> of George Carey and the gay new guard of Rowan
> Williams… This is how the Church of England works.[3]

Except it was not how the Church of England worked. As a result, supporters of same-sex partnerships felt sick after the roller-coaster ride plummeted them from the high of delight at such a bold move to the depths of shock and depression at Rowan's eventual withdrawal of support for Jeffrey John. This they could only understand as a betrayal. Colin Coward of Changing Attitude is clear about the significance of this event:

> His capitulation to the intense opposition to Jeffrey John's appointment was a defining moment. He capitulated to prejudice, to an interpretation of Christianity which allows for the set of people who claim to be "orthodox", "biblical", "traditionalist", "true Christians" to categorise other sets of people in creation as inferior, sinners, not properly Christian.[4]

The same perception took hold in North America with consequences for the wider Communion debates as expressed by Louie Crew of *Integrity*:

> Rowan abandoned his conscience regarding LGBTQ [lesbian, gay, bisexual, transgender, queer] folks. He knew full well that Jeffrey John is an outstanding cleric and fully competent to serve well as Bishop of Reading. Rowan crumbled to peer pressure when he asked Jeffrey to resign the appointment. Had Rowan allowed Jeffrey's appointment to stand, I doubt that he would have experienced opprobrium any more vicious than he experienced anyway. Nor did Rowan persuade any of the bullies that he was on their side: he had already published his "side." Instead he in effect signalled to the whole Communion that he would be led by a majority of the bishops.[5]

A similar conclusion that it proved to be a "lose–lose" outcome for Rowan is voiced by Philip Giddings, a leading conservative player in the crisis, who described the legacy of Reading for Rowan as "he lost friends but without winning over his opponents".[6]

Rowan played a crucial role at three stages: the appointment, his intervention on 23 June, and his securing Jeffrey John's withdrawal.

The Appointment

Although the public drama began with the announcement on 20 May, just over five months into Rowan's term, the seeds were sown in preceding weeks and months. The vacancy arose after a game of episcopal musical chairs going back to Rowan's appointment to Canterbury. In December 2002 the Bishop of Reading, Dominic Walker, had been elected as his successor in Monmouth. Among the unsuccessful candidates was Jeffrey John. Walker's departure left a vacancy in Oxford diocese. Although the Bishop of Oxford, Richard Harries, did not include John on his original shortlist "because of his well-known views", he reconsidered in the light of strong commendations including from the Archbishops' Appointments Secretary, Tony Sadler. Having checked that the archbishop would not object, Bishop Richard added Jeffrey John's name and concluded, following the selection process, that he was the best person for Reading. At this point, there was a phone conversation between Bishop Richard and a member of his diocesan advisory group, Philip Giddings, who later reflected,

> I was very clear about the adverse reaction that would result but I did not say to him [Bishop Richard] directly you must not make this appointment. I have agonised over whether I should have stepped over that line. I believe I made a mistake there – if I could have that conversation again I would go further, I would cross that line.[7]

There followed a second conversation between Bishop Richard and Rowan to establish he was happy to consecrate Jeffrey John. While the full details of that and the earlier conversation are not known, the Bishop of Oxford was apparently surprised the matter was finalized relatively briefly and without a face-to-face meeting. Rowan's role is best summed up in his own words in his later letter to fellow bishops:

> It is an appointment I have neither sought to promote nor to obstruct. I was informed that Canon Jeffrey John was regarded as a highly gifted candidate, was acceptable to the diocese, that he had given explicit assurances on various matters, including his personal circumstances and his willingness to work loyally within the framework of doctrine and discipline as expressed in Issues in Human Sexuality. With these assurances... and in keeping with the principle that the integrity of the process within the diocese should be respected, I raised no objection to forwarding his name.[8]

Once the announcement was made, it was a matter of waiting to see just how much trouble the appointment would cause. Given the denouement, the inevitable question is why the archbishop let it reach this stage. Even some who thought Rowan should have stood firm acknowledged afterwards that it was a proposal that was always likely to end in tears. Peter Selby, then Bishop of Worcester, said:

> I always had to confess to friends who were very angry about what happened that if I can fantasize about myself being Archbishop of Canterbury I think I might well have told Richard Harries to "pull the other one" when he came to me with that proposal.[9]

Why did Rowan Williams not respond in a similar way? A number of likely factors highlight some of the issues of substance at stake and key characteristics of Rowan's style of leadership.

- Jeffrey John's qualities and the fact that through due process he had shown himself to be the best person for the post in the minds of diocesan selectors were crucial. In such a situation, it would appear unjust discrimination not to consent.

- Jeffrey John had given assurances that his own life was in conformity with church teaching and that he would work within that teaching as bishop.

- His views on same-sex partnerships were indistinguishable from the archbishop's previously stated views. To reject him on those grounds would be to cut off the very branch the archbishop himself was sitting on.

- Rowan worked with the principle that the integrity of the process within the diocese should be respected. He thus respected the diocesan bishop's choice and the internal processes rather than use his own powers to object, intervene, or overturn these.

- As someone new to the Church of England he was advised that Canon John was the best candidate, supported by his appointments secretary, the sending bishop (Southwark), and the appointing bishop (Oxford) whom he knew well and was the longest-serving diocesan bishop.

- In his first months as archbishop Rowan had consented, on the basis of probably less strong commendations, to a number of appointments of people unknown to him. As he explained to a colleague who spoke to him during the crisis, he felt it would be wrong for him now to apply a different procedure to the first candidate for a senior appointment he knew.

- In his letter to bishops, Rowan set out the process for such appointments in terms of being "made by the Crown, on the advice of a diocesan as forwarded by the Archbishop of the province". His presentation of his own role as almost simply a postman between the diocese and the Crown led some to wonder whether he was told of his ability and authority to input more strongly into the process, even, *in extremis*, to exercise a veto by telling a bishop he would refuse to consecrate. He was probably aware of this but decided not to act on it as both temperamentally and theologically he is cautious about using his own power.

- Rowan had for some time stressed the need for theological discussion about sexuality, including listening to the experience of conscientious gay Christians. He is likely to have seen in Jeffrey John someone who would bring into the episcopate an articulate and generally irenic voice of a minority position within the church. This would enable those who held such views to feel included and able to participate constructively rather than antagonistically within church structures, thus following a well-established Anglican pattern of engaging with, some might argue "capturing", dissenting voices.

- There appears to have been a level of innocence and naivety about the extent and force of the likely response and the difficulty, perhaps impossibility, of containing its potentially destructive consequences. "Liberals" can often refuse to "face the fact that the people opposed to them believe it would be contrary to the will of God to find a compromise".[10]

Whatever Rowan's reasons, his passivity in the face of the proposed appointment would, with hindsight, seem a serious misjudgment although Philip Giddings is clear that "I have no criticism of the way Rowan handled his way through that."[11]

The Crisis

It was quickly clear the negative reaction was much greater than expected. Private letters were sent first by opponents in the diocese and then supporters as opinion polarized. Opponents focused on the substance and tone of Jeffrey John's public teaching on same-sex partnerships. He was relatively or totally unknown to most of them and many remained unaware he was gay and concerns might exist about his "personal lifestyle" until Bishop Richard's private reply of 2 June alluded to this fact. By then the tensions were spreading nationally (at the House of Bishops meeting that first week of June, some bishops expressed their unhappiness and discussed a response) and internationally. The appointment was announced as Rowan chaired his first Primates' Meeting. As it ended, conservative primates were briefed on the trouble brewing in England. Then, on 28 May, the first episcopally and synodically authorized Anglican same-sex blessing took place in New Westminster, Canada. This was soon connected with the Reading appointment, which the press reported conservative primates were seeking to reverse.

On Friday 6 June, citing an Affirming Catholicism address by John in 1998 shortly after the Lambeth conference, the *Telegraph* broke the major news about John's sexuality and partnership. This refocused attention on the archbishop: "The Archbishop of Canterbury was facing a fresh storm over homosexuality last night after it emerged that the Church of England's most recently appointed bishop had been in a gay relationship for decades." It said he was under pressure to force Jeffrey John, "a close friend and fellow liberal, to withdraw as Bishop of Reading".

The next few days added further fuel to the fire. On 7 June, Bishop Richard defended his choice on the *Today* programme and to his diocesan Synod. Revealing Jeffrey John was committed to abstinence and that his relationship had not been sexual for a very long time, he attacked the campaign against him and summed up the central argument in his defence: it would be quite wrong as a matter of principle not to appoint the best candidate especially when he was willing to make public and clear declarations of adhering to the policy of the Church of England. By Sunday morning, however, the first English bishop (Pete Broadbent) had called for Jeffrey John to step down. The Anglican Communion also gained another openly gay and partnered bishop-elect when, that same day, the diocese of New Hampshire elected Gene Robinson.

In less than three weeks and before any face-to-face meetings between the main protagonists in the diocese, the appointment of an area bishop in the Church of England had become connected to the global Anglican fault-lines over homosexuality. It had become "the Reading crisis". Barely six months into his post, attention once again focused on Rowan and his own position on the church's teaching on homosexuality. The following week saw various meetings within the diocese but with no movement on either side towards any agreed way forward.

The stakes were significantly raised on Monday 16 June with an open letter to the archbishop from nine diocesan bishops (Bradford, Carlisle, Chester, Chichester, Exeter, Liverpool, Rochester, Southwell, and Winchester) and with the support of two soon-to-be consecrated diocesans (Bristol and Durham), almost a quarter of the House of Bishops. The nine, soon labelled "the Nazgul" by their critics (after the Nine Riders who serve Sauron in Tolkien's *Lord of the Rings*), were joined by seven evangelical suffragans. Such a major break in the episcopal ranks encouraged some but shocked and angered others. *The Times*, in a prophetic editorial, warned

> If Dr John is not consecrated this autumn, as the
> conservatives plainly hope, the issue will not be
> resolved. A large group of fair-minded and tolerant

Anglicans will instead be profoundly disillusioned
and angry. And the Church's future will become more
problematic still.[12]

With the diocesan situation in deadlock – a further lengthy
meeting between opponents and the bishop was a case of
"irresistible force meets immovable object" – protestors asked
Rowan to intervene. They connected the crisis to the wider
Communion developments and made clear they were not
objecting to Canon John's sexual orientation but to his teaching
and lack of any regret about acknowledged previous sexual
activity. Bishop Richard remained confident Jeffrey John would
quickly win people's trust and gave him "unswerving" support.
Another open letter to the archbishop from a group of eight
diocesan bishops (Hereford, Leicester, Newcastle, Ripon and
Leeds, St Edmundsbury and Ipswich, Salisbury, Truro, and
Worcester) backed him. The weekend press was full of this
episcopal civil war and the role of the archbishop, with one aide
reported as saying "This is an appointment endorsed by the
archbishop, approved by Downing Street and commanded by
the Queen. The archbishop would have to resign if he did not
ordain John."

On Monday 23 June, in a dramatic development, Rowan
wrote to Church of England bishops. The letter revealed key
hallmarks of his leadership and crisis management styles, still
relatively unknown so early in his primacy. He saw his role as
to "try to clarify basic issues, in my capacity as Archbishop of
Canterbury and Chairman of the House of Bishops".[13]

Having explained his part in the appointment, Rowan
addressed key areas, offering his own interpretation of events
and proposing principles which would shape future crises. In
particular:

- He stressed the importance of proper processes of church discernment and development, denying a weakening of the bishops' commitment to "what we have declared as our common mind".

- There was a clear reassurance "to the wider Anglican Communion that we are not embarking on or colluding with any policy of unilateral local change, which I have more than once deplored elsewhere".

- He urged respect for opponents whose concerns were "theologically serious, intelligible and by no means based on narrow party allegiance or on prejudice" and "must be addressed and considered fully".

- The problem was expressed in terms of the importance of "confidence in the ability of a new bishop to minister to those in his pastoral care".

- Given that "serious questions remain in the diocese" he was emphatic the solution had to be found locally and "it is not for anyone outside the diocese to override or preempt what is obviously a painful and complex process".

- Refocusing attention on mission, he closed with what would become a constant plea during his primacy, for patience, offering a diagnosis of some of the spiritual disease evident in responses: "it does us no harm… to learn in some matters to give each other a little more time and space for thought as we try to find how we can walk in step as the Body of Christ – not falling over ourselves because of anxiety and suspicion".

Time and space were, however, running out rapidly. Within two weeks he, from outside the diocese, would act in a way that many felt did "override or preempt" its own processes. This was perhaps partly because, far from calming down, positions appeared to harden. The Bishop of Oxford demonstrated his contrasting style of leadership, giving a *Newsnight* interview, which left no doubt as to his determination to proceed, and later wrote for *The Sunday Times*. Two days after Rowan's letter, Philip Giddings chaired a gathering (including two Communion primates, conservatives from America, Oxford clergy, and others from around the UK) which, under the hastily agreed name of Anglican Mainstream, subsequently evolved into the leading conservative network based in England. Rumours began that the Queen was expressing concerns about the situation, and Damian Thompson captured the dangers as people raised the stakes "to unprecedented levels": Blocking the appointment "is not only a catastrophe for the man who chose him… it could set back the cause of homosexual equality in the Church by many years" but if the consecration goes ahead "then the evangelical lobby will face an unwelcome dilemma: should it accept the humiliation or plot revenge?"

The following week, with no meeting arranged between Bishop Richard and diocesan opponents, Jeffrey John met twenty concerned incumbents from the Reading area, and a second letter from opponents, requesting a meeting with Rowan, was signed by over 100 diocesan clergy and 110 significant lay people. Facing continued strong opposition from the wider Communion, Rowan also had the building pressure of presiding at his first General Synod, due to meet in just over a week.

The Dénouement

By Friday 4 July Rowan had decided the appointment was unsustainable. He held a phone conference with senior colleagues to tell them this and to discuss coping with the fallout. He called the Bishop of Oxford and Jeffrey John to an early morning meeting the next day. Exactly what transpired over that long day at Lambeth is not fully clear but, in the face of strong opposition from a shocked Bishop of Oxford and a reluctant Jeffrey John, Rowan secured an agreement to withdraw. An attempt the next morning to rescind that decision was rebuffed, and the letter of withdrawal was released as, for the second time in less than two weeks, Rowan made a public statement.

Why had Rowan finally concluded the appointment was unsustainable and intervened to pull the plug on it? The various reasons were summed up in the words of Jeffrey John's letter which highlighted "the damage my consecration might cause to the unity of the Church, including the Anglican Communion". As Rowan later told a very difficult meeting of the House of Bishops, there was an underlying and crucial consistency to his approach: the reasons for which he eventually came to say "No" were the same reasons for which he'd originally said "Yes" and these were about the well-being of the church. His public statement announcing the outcome set out a number of different factors which were at play in leading him to his painful and costly conclusion:[14]

- The cause of people's concern related to "accountability to biblical teaching" and "the consistency of our policy and our doctrine in the Church of England".

- Highlighting the Communion context, Rowan described the problem of "the consecration of a bishop whose ministry will not be readily received by a significant proportion of Christians in England and elsewhere", warning that "the estrangement of churches in developing countries from their cherished ties with Britain is in no-one's interests."

- There would be "a heavy price to pay" by proceeding in terms of ecumenism, mission partners and "the vulnerability of Christian minorities in some parts of the world where they are already at risk".

These comments were, however, counterbalanced by Rowan's other consistent emphases. He stressed that the withdrawal "should not be taken to mean that the Church can now stop being concerned about how it discerns the will of God in this area of ethics". Furthermore, given that "some of the opposition expressed to Canon John's appointment has been very unsavoury indeed", he was clear that Christians who collude with prejudice "are simply not living out their calling" as "our official policies and resolutions as Anglicans commit us to listening to the experience of homosexuals and recognising that they are full and welcome members of the church loved by God".

In concluding, he admitted that "this has been a time of open and painful confrontation in which some of our bonds of trust have been severely strained", but called for honest reflection in order "to find what God has been teaching us in these difficult days".

His own refocusing on God and on what the church should be were made clear in his first presidential address to General Synod. Implicitly describing the church as a community of communities, he explained how recent weeks and months had reinforced that there are "several different 'Churches of England'" and "they do not communicate with each other very effectively". Communication was needed to overcome anxiety and prevent scapegoating and help everyone "fulfil their primary task of witnessing to God's transforming power". Highlighting the mission initiatives discussed in Chapter 3, he urged Synod to:

> lift its eyes for a moment from the traumas of recent
> weeks and days – not to pretend or forget, but to
> be newly aware of what God is already doing in our
> Church. If we can see that too a bit more clearly, we
> shall not feel paralysed. We shall know gratefully that

there is indeed a Church, because of God, not because of us. And if that is so, we are free to follow where he has led, to grow and to celebrate.[15]

The Legacy

Despite these hopeful words, the Church of England was severely damaged. There was increased bitterness, confusion, anger, and mutual incomprehension threatening division. Rowan himself was the focus of much of this because of his handling of the crisis. Later in 2003, Colin Slee, Giles Fraser, and others launched Inclusive Church, while evangelicals holding traditional views on sexual ethics established Anglican Mainstream and Fulcrum. These became three key movements during the rest of Rowan's primacy, all, to varying degrees, engaging with the sexuality debate. Some, on all sides, concluded that Rowan would buckle and backtrack if put under sufficient pressure. His consistency with his fundamental principles went unnoticed by many. Rather than seeing his decision as the result of careful discernment of a changing landscape aimed at creating space for more reasoned reflection, he was portrayed as someone unwilling to follow through his commitments in the face of concerted opposition and who would do anything faced with threats to unity.

On a personal level, Rowan subsequently had a private meeting with Jeffrey John in which he reportedly asked for forgiveness and knelt for a blessing. John was appointed Dean of St Albans in April 2004 but had become a symbolic figure. The wounds, far from healing, were often reopened and later attempts to make him a bishop – most famously in relation to Southwark in 2010 – failed. This resulted in leaks to the press, recriminations from his supporters, and accusations of Rowan once more bowing to pressure and blocking his appointment. Jeffrey John being "parked" as dean thus also came to symbolize the church's official stance in relation to the substantive issue during Rowan's time in office.

Church of England Teaching and Practice

Another legacy of Reading was seeming paralysis, almost post-traumatic stress, among bishops. They had publicly disagreed and looked into the chasm of serious divisions and were aware of the difficulties the subject caused Rowan. Faced with rapid social and legal change, they struggled to find a way forward in relation to the substantive issues. Later in 2003, the House of Bishops review group issued a significant contribution to the debate entitled *Some Issues in Human Sexuality*. It was, however, never really followed through in terms of educating the wider church, and it was predicated on not reviewing the position agreed back in 1991 in *Issues in Human Sexuality* (with which Rowan had strongly disagreed). This was in line with Lambeth I:10 in that while tolerating same-sex partnerships among the laity it was not affirming of them but viewed them as falling short, and it stated that clergy should not be in any sexual relationship outside marriage. The new report thus left those pressing for new ways forward feeling further frustrated after the disappointment over Jeffrey John and Rowan's response to Gene Robinson's election.

The issues arose in a fresh way with the introduction in 2005 of civil partnerships, a new legal status for same-sex couples paralleling marriage. Again the bishops decided not to reconsider but to apply, as best they could, the long-standing *Issues* position, although in 2009 Rowan acknowledged that the attempt to do this was "one of the most difficult issues we've had to deal with in recent years". Their statement continued to prohibit blessings and while clear that the House of Bishops "does not regard entering into a civil partnership as intrinsically incompatible with holy orders" this was "provided the person concerned is willing to give assurances to his or her bishop that the relationship is consistent with the standards for the clergy set out in *Issues in Human Sexuality*". Gay clergy were expected, in other words, to be celibate. The Carey position from 1991 thus held sway, although one bishop, Peter Selby, publicly dissociated himself from the statement, while other bishops were thought to be less than rigorous in implementing it when clergy entered civil partnerships. The stance was opposed from both left and right. In February 2007 an alliance formed against the House of Bishops' statement on civil partnerships between those who disliked it because it was too restrictive and those who thought it too lax. As a result, the Synod motion simply acknowledged "the diversity of views within the Church of England" on the legislation and noted "the intention of the House to keep their Pastoral Statement under review".

The motion following another February 2007 debate on lesbian and gay Christians reflected the key principles in Rowan's own approach. It focused on unity, commending "continuing efforts to prevent the diversity of opinion about human sexuality creating further division and impaired fellowship within the Church of England and the Anglican Communion". It crucially recognized that efforts to prevent division "would not be advanced by doing anything that could be perceived as the Church of England qualifying its commitment to the entirety of the relevant Lambeth Conference Resolutions". Although it welcomed opportunities for "an open, full and Godly dialogue about human sexuality" it offered nothing to facilitate this other than to affirm that "homosexual orientation in itself is no bar to a faithful Christian life or to full participation in lay and ordained ministry in the Church", and acknowledged "the importance of lesbian and gay members of the Church of England participating in the listening process as full members of the Church".

Only in November 2010 did Rowan begin to suggest the need

for a more focused and structured engagement with the issues. Describing it as "a cardinal example of how we avoid theological debate", he spoke of the urgent need for "some thoughtful engagement that will help us understand how people who read the same Bible and share the same baptism can come to strongly diverse conclusions". He reported he was often told that "the lack of advance in nurturing this debate properly is a serious failure in the leadership of the Church and the Communion", and honestly admitted that "I am bound to accept my share of reproach."

In 2011, following the furore over Jeffrey John's non-appointment to Southwark, the bishops returned to the issue. Their statement made clear that "contrary to popular perception the House of Bishops has spent very little time over recent years discussing homosexuality". It then simply announced a review of the 2005 statement on civil partnerships (by the end of 2012) and a longer-term review. This began in early 2012 under Joseph Pilling and represents the most fundamental study and potential rethinking on the issue since the early 1990s. It should report to the House of Bishops by the end of 2013.

These two reviews began their work as the debate in society moved on from civil partnerships to same-sex marriage. The Church of England's formal response to the government consultation (June 2012) strongly reaffirmed, with the personal support of Rowan, traditional Christian teaching on marriage. It thus opposed the introduction of "equal civil marriage". This provoked strongly negative reactions from many Anglicans supportive of same-sex relationships which, combined with Jeffrey John's reissuing of his book as a defence of same-sex *marriage*, makes clear that disagreements now also exist over Christian teaching about marriage.

Conclusion

Despite the deep differences within it, the Church of England has avoided major division over homosexuality under Rowan. He has succeeded in maintaining unity and keeping official policy in line with Communion teaching, although a number of irregular ordinations by overseas bishops showed some conservative congregations in some dioceses were living on or over the edge of official structures. Many LGBT Anglicans also felt pushed to the margins or left the church. Where Rowan is open to more criticism is in relation to enabling the church to address the issues and think through the significance and implications of the recent massive cultural changes. Here he was haunted by his past statements and the controversy they had provoked on his appointment, seriously burnt by the Reading crisis, and severely constrained by his commitment to upholding the Communion's teaching, a reality creating an insuperable barrier to changes within the Church of England.

Rowan, throughout his time, clearly and consistently applied a sharp distinction between his personal views expressed as a theologian and his teaching responsibility as a bishop. Although many criticized this as hypocrisy, that is unfair. It is simply a very countercultural expression of living under authority and his commitment to the unity of the church of Christ. The more serious challenge is that put by Peter Selby:

> if he believes what he said he believed in *The Body's Grace*, he must also believe that it is in the best interests of the church that it too comes to that belief. That is part of thinking something is true.[16]

Rowan could not, however, give any hint of helping the church come to that conclusion without, as the Reading crisis showed, risking its division. He therefore maintained the status quo and interpreted different perspectives to each other, notably at Lambeth 2008. Most of his fellow bishops, perhaps out of respect for him and realizing the problems they would create if they spoke out, similarly fell silent and emphasized the need for ongoing listening and dialogue. As a result, during Rowan's primacy both supporters of traditional church teaching and those questioning it were generally left without public episcopal leadership. The debate was left to pressure groups, the most vociferous of which often dominated the media. This distorted and damaged the image of the church in the eyes of wider society even though it could be argued that the church was raising questions and struggling for answers on behalf of those outside the church.

Personally, Rowan sought to keep open conversations. He had a number of meetings with representatives of different groups and controversially presided and spoke at a Eucharist for the Clergy Consultation of LGBT clergy. In terms of initiating church action, however, he did not make this area a priority. Only towards the end of his time in office was there a serious attempt to facilitate listening and dialogue or to advance theological reflection. The outcome of that process he leaves to his successor. The best that can be said is that his critique of an emphasis on rights and simply following social change has highlighted bad reasons for the church rethinking its stance. In addition, his wider vision and practice as regards how we should live together as a complex, conflicted church may have helped prepare the ground in relation to this debate.

What is clear is that the subject must soon rise nearer the top of the church's agenda. Church practice has for many years been variable in its consistency with official teaching. That teaching is still strongly upheld by many Anglicans but is now much more counter-cultural. It is also increasingly questioned from within the church. The perceived divergence from British culture and internal tensions, not least between official policies and actual practice, make the status quo look highly unstable.

The fallout over sexuality thus remain a ticking time-bomb within the Church of England as it comes to terms with the divisions in the wider Communion. Rowan, to the amazement of many, particularly given the Reading crisis, managed to prevent it detonating in England during his time in office. His successor arrives, however, with the fuse much shorter and few processes in place to defuse it and prevent what appears to be a rapidly approaching and damaging explosion.

7

Women Bishops

It's like one of those terrible games you get in Christmas crackers sometimes where you have to get the little silver balls into holes – you always get two of them but then the other one goes off somewhere else. (June 2012)[1]

In sharp contrast to the disagreements over gay relationships, the tensions over women bishops have been a constant feature of Synod debate during Rowan's time as archbishop. Only at an extra General Synod meeting, the month before he retired, did the Church of England finally reach its decision on women bishops, dramatically rejecting the proposed legislation and causing a major crisis.

Rowan's approach was marked by two key consistent emphases traceable through the many debates and ways forward explored by the church. Firstly, along with the overwhelming majority of the church, he supported women bishops and women clergy. Secondly, he had a concern for the place of opponents within the Church of England and for the views of the wider church. He constantly stressed the importance of the handling and outcome of this debate in revealing and determining the kind of church the Church of England would become.

Supporting Women Clergy

Rowan became archbishop as a strong supporter of women priests and bishops in a church which had in 1992 voted for women priests. It had also, in the Act of Synod, created a structure of provision for those opposed to this decision in the form of provincial episcopal visitors (PEVs, or "flying bishops"). This was to enable opponents to stay within the Church of England with integrity and also to acknowledge the need for ongoing discernment and reception within Anglicanism and the wider church. Two years before Rowan became archbishop, Synod established the Rochester Commission (July 2000) to offer a theological study on the admission of women to the episcopate. As the church was waiting for this report, Rowan said relatively little on the subject although in an early interview (December 2002) he was clear he could "see no theological objection to consecrating women as bishops".

The Rochester Report appeared in November 2004. It set out the theological issues and mapped different possible ways forward given the diversity of views. In the February 2005 Synod debate, Rowan did not make a major speech on the theological issues but intervened to respond to points made by Anglo-Catholic opponents, Geoffrey Rowell and Jonathan Baker, focused on issues of gender and symbolism. In July 2005 he spoke against an amendment seeking to delay legislation to allow further consideration of the theological issues.

In the years that followed (with one exception) he supported moves to progress legislation but said little about the theological convictions which led him to support it. In contrast, he spoke and acted often in response to opponents' concerns. Some therefore felt his support could have been more vocal. One of his strongest statements came, ironically, after reports suggested his support was tentative or diminishing.

In November 2006, shortly before his first visit to meet Pope Benedict, and as the legislative drafting group was preparing to begin its work, Rowan became the centre of a media storm about his own commitment to women priests and bishops. An interview with the *Catholic Herald* led to damaging reports claiming he thought women clergy had not transformed or renewed the church and Anglicans might think again. This led to a critical press profile in which a woman, described as part of his inner circle, was quoted as saying the hardest thing for Rowan's many admirers to stomach "is that too often he seems to bend over backwards to be kinder to his enemies than he is to us". His error had been to acknowledge the theoretical possibility that he could "just about envisage" a time when Anglicans "thought again" about ordaining women. Once the reports appeared, however, he was emphatic that his careful nuanced statements about a hypothetical possibility were being totally distorted:

> From the very beginning of this issue I have been a supporter of the ordination of women and have not doubted the rightness of that decision or the blessings it has brought... I made it clear in the interview with the *Catholic Herald* – and will continue to do so – that I see no theological justification for any revisiting of this question and indicated in the interview three times that I had no wish to reopen it, whatever technical possibilities might theoretically exist. The presentation of this to mean anything else is wilful misinterpretation. My convictions mean that I feel nothing less than full support for the decision the Church of England made in 1992 and appreciation of the priesthood exercised.[2]

Despite this, the high-profile reports of the interview, combined with the long-drawn-out legislative process and his determination to achieve strong provision for opponents, left some women clergy feeling that, despite his personal support for individual women clergy, their archbishop was not listening and could have done more practically to show his support.

These concerns peaked with the archbishops' attempted amendments to the draft legislation in 2010. As a result, Rowan established a mechanism for information and communication between various women's groups and Lambeth Palace. Out of this arose one of the most significant but unsung signs of his commitment: his sponsorship and support of the "Transformations – Theology and Experience of Women's Ministry" initiative. The initial expression of this was his invitation of over sixty (mainly women) members of the Church of England to a consultation at Lambeth Palace in September 2011 where an American woman bishop gave the keynote address and presided at the Eucharist. The consultation sought to review experiences of women's ordained ministry but also "to consider what women's experience could tell us about the inherited models of ordained ministry in both theology and practice and how these might be changed for the better".[3] Rowan spoke at the consultation, arguing that two common models surrounding women's ministry – "co-option" into male patterns and "messianism" – were inadequate and that fully accepting women's ministry should lead to rethinking models of ministry for men and women. His concluding remarks acknowledged that the group wanted bishops to hear that "the House of Bishops and the College of Bishops need to prepare for a change of culture" including rethinking the nature of the episcopacy. He ended on a celebratory note, promising to carry on listening and emphasizing that

in arguing for and working for the full inclusion of
women in the ordained ministry of the church, what
we're after is not simply justice... but... the humanising
of the ordained ministry and all that that might mean
in terms of mission and the health of Christ's body.[4]

The consultation produced a full report and recommendations including the need to change the dominant male pattern and culture of ordained ministry, increase flexibility in patterns of ministry and awareness of the needs of clergy couples, and address theological incoherence that feeds discriminatory culture and practices.

The Steering Group, comprising ordained women from across different theological traditions, continued its work with Rowan's support, and a year later, in September 2012, he invited them to share their research findings with the whole college of bishops at their annual meeting. The research celebrated major changes during Rowan's primacy: 31 per cent of clergy were women in 2011, compared to 16 per cent in 2000, more women than men are now being ordained, and there are increasing numbers of women deans and archdeacons. However, it also highlighted several problems and challenges including that only 18 per cent of incumbents are women, very few of them in larger churches, and the number of women under forty being accepted for ordination is declining. Rowan's hope is that having initiated and sponsored the original consultation and brought the group's findings to the bishops, this work will be continued by his successor. The concerns of women clergy will then be heard in a way that shapes the Church of England's ministry at every level.

Seeking Adequate Provision for Opponents: What Kind of Church?

Given the widespread support for women bishops, many are confused about why the process has been so drawn out and complicated. Rowan humorously captured the situation in the July 2006 Synod debate:

> It's usually the apparently simple questions that are
> hardest to answer. My faint recollections of A-level
> history include echoes of the dispute in the 1860s
> over the Duchies of Schleswig and Holstein, whether
> they should belong to Denmark or to the German
> Confederation. A "yes or no" question, you'd think,
> but Lord Palmerston observed in 1864 that only three
> people had ever really understood the issues involved; of
> whom one was dead, the second was mad and the third
> had forgotten. "Women bishops or not?" sounds like
> a simple "yes or no" question to the world around as
> well as to many of us but it shows every sign of turning
> into a Schleswig-Holstein case, as discussion spirals
> as to what might be necessary and the technicalities
> proliferate... How soon before we reach the situation
> Palmerston described, you may ask?[5]

In the first "Take Note" debate on the Rochester Report (February 2005) Rowan had presciently noted that "God's way forward might be less clear to us than the various ways forward that we might at this stage map out for ourselves." The central question with which the church was grappling was named as "the idea that we should be modelling working with difference".[6] He also introduced what would become a golden thread through the next seven years: given Anglican differences, there needs to be "sensitivity to genuinely felt conscientious scruple" and proceeding to women bishops requires "mutual prayer and patience and mutual understanding". Central in this is the question of "what kind of church we think we want to be" and the need "to model for the world around ways of doing our business responsibly, lovingly, and at the same time creatively and courageously".

In July 2005 the Synod voted by a clear majority to proceed with legislation (Bishops: 41 to 6; Clergy: 167 to 46; Laity: 159 to 75) but in February 2006 Rowan was already preparing the church for the long haul. He argued that "the 'how' of proceeding is as much a theological question as the 'whether' or the 'when'", and warned that "because the journey is unavoidably long and uncertain… we need to move with sure steps at each stage".

He had long been clear that in proceeding to agree women bishops there were large questions about what happened to the minority and in 2002 had even signalled sympathy for the idea of creating a Third Province (alongside Canterbury and York) for opponents as "the least evangelistically and spiritually damaging form of separation". He wouldn't fly that kite again but this tension in his own position – wanting change but with perhaps significant changes to church structures to meet the concerns of the minority in order to maintain the greatest unity – would be key in his oversight and it slowed developments.

In 2006 the focus of attention was on the Guildford Report, the first of a number of groups working to find an agreed way forward. It proposed Transferred Episcopal Arrangements (TEA) under which parishes opposed to women priests and bishops could opt for their diocesan bishop to request the archbishop to arrange episcopal ministry by a provincial regional bishop. He would exercise jurisdiction in certain matters transferred from the diocesan bishop. Rowan was an (unsuccessful) advocate for TEA or something very similar to it. It was, he pointed out, agreed by the group unanimously and the bishops by a majority that "simply providing for dissent by means of a code of practice would leave too much to discretion, create too great a variety of practice and fail to preserve that highest possible degree of communion in the Church of England". This meant contentious issues about jurisdiction should be addressed in the primary legislation. Although language of "safeguards" sounded unpleasant and it would be better if there was sufficient mutual trust, he urged people to "go the extra mile" asking what might, in love, be done "to carry us forward together, rather than apart. Even if that togetherness is more fractured and more untidy than many might like." He urged "sustained and prayerful reflection" as the church was now in "uncharted territory" and "there is no option for not changing". Recognizing the church was already living in schism he sought to "minimise the damage and the risks of mutual isolation" by recognizing integrity and negotiating a process of "managing diversity and conflict".

The process was, he again insisted, a learning one, as the hope was that the church might be discovering

> something about ourselves as a church and about each
> other that we didn't know before and thereby perhaps
> beginning to model something for the Church Catholic
> and the world at large. Integrity need not mean
> absolute division; it can mean a process of admittedly
> painful, often untidy, but finally deeply evangelical self-
> discovery, the discovery of what God purposes for us.[7]

He stressed that opposition to the development came from those for whom this was a matter of "obedience to scripture, or obedience to the consensus of the Church Catholic" and appealed for "common conversation, common culture" where "we try to find ways of talking which are absolutely fully conscious of the 'there-ness' of others that it's easier to forget".

His own commitment to such "common conversation" extended beyond the Church of England. In June 2006 he invited Cardinal Kasper to offer a perspective from the Vatican to the House of Bishops. Kasper pointedly challenged Anglicans on the coherence, given their ecumenical agreements and understanding of the church's unity, of creating a college of bishops in which some (traditionalist opponents) would not recognize others (women) as bishops. The following month part of Rowan's reply – spelt out more fully in Rome in November 2009 – acknowledged the ecumenical costs would be "heavy and serious" but raised questions about why, given the level of ecumenical agreement now reached about ministry, suddenly the issue of the ministers' gender was such a serious roadblock.[8]

That July 2006 Synod created a group to draft legislation and Rowan's contributions again highlighted his constant concerns and challenges to the church. He characteristically set out the issues from different perspectives, seeking to interpret people to each other and addressing questions to different groupings. The "theologically convinced majority" had to ask whether "they still want to see particular styles of catholic and evangelical theology, witness and mission, as a routine and recognisable part of Anglican life". The "theologically unconvinced minority" needed to consider "how Anglican" they wanted to be, "accepting the unavoidable anomalies and possible contradictions of a Church that makes decisions in the way we do".

Once again he emphasized the underlying issue was "very searching questions about what kind of Church we are. Indeed, what we believe about the Church of God itself, not only about the Church of England". His concern was at least as much about how to nurture virtues and establish good practices of discussion as about procedural technicalities and issues of substance. A key principle was that "if decisions take a little longer but are more genuinely owned at the end of the process, the time is not wasted". This taking of time held out hope if the church could "see this process of exploring discovery and testing our mutual loyalty and our sense of obligation... as the seed bed for the creative ministry of the future".

The legislative drafting group's report was debated in July 2008, just before the Lambeth Conference. Synod made the crucial decisions that special arrangements should be "within the existing structures of the Church of England, for those who as a matter of theological conviction will not be able to receive the ministry of women as bishops or priests", and that "these should be contained in a statutory national code of practice to which all concerned would be required to have regard".

Rowan found himself "in the very difficult and unsatisfactory situation of abstaining in a Synod vote". In his speech explaining why he hoped for more he distinguished between "tolerating an uncomfortable and unrepresentative minority in the Church" ("I suppose I can live with people who hold those sorts of view"), and "recognizing that certain minorities in the Church are part of the defining agenda of the national Church" ("People with those sorts of view are actually a rather important element in how I am an Anglican and how we are Anglicans"). He clearly saw evangelical and Anglo-Catholic opponents of women bishops in the latter category and set out his wrestling with two principles and the importance of this tension for Anglican identity:

> I want to say very strongly that I am deeply unhappy
> with any scheme or any solution to this that ends up
> as it were structurally humiliating women who may
> be nominated to the episcopate... At the same time
> I am as unhappy about solutions that systematically
> marginalize, if not finally exclude... those whose
> presence is part of the necessary abrasion that we need

to keep our theology vigorous and independent and not simply at the mercy of whatever fashions or currents in society to which we are vulnerable.[9]

His answer, pressed repeatedly, controversially, and often unsuccessfully on Synod over future years was clear:

So I come not very comfortably to the conclusion that originally I had not thought I would reach, namely that if we want to preserve that kind of Anglican identity which embodies those sorts of conversation, those sorts of accountability, I would want to see a more rather than a less robust form of structural provision and accommodation.[10]

His final words again highlighted the significance of the changes taking place:

Whatever happens this afternoon and subsequently, we are going to find ourselves in a deeply changed Church of England. My question is: what sort of change will it be – the change of the fundamental complexion of the sort of Anglicanism that we have inherited with all its almost unbearable tensions, or the kind of change… that organisms have to undergo in order to stay the same?[11]

His February 2009 presidential address brought to the forefront another key theme of his leadership: those who cannot in conscience accept women bishops "will not got away". He therefore warned about unrealizable "dreams of purity and clarity" (which "liberals" are susceptible to as well as "conservatives") and hoped the good news of women bishops could "carry with it some good news also for these others who are still going to be our brothers and sisters and companions in mission". Rather than a fantasy pure church, people should seek a church honest about its sometimes embarrassing and unwelcome diversity.[12]

Before the end of 2009, the possibility of going to another Communion opened up for Anglo-Catholic opponents, with the Vatican's creation of the Ordinariate (discussed in Chapter 11). This did not lessen Rowan's commitment to find a solution within the Church of England. In February 2010 he recognized the "tragic" element in the women bishops' debate as people felt they were not being listened to as they defined their position. But he also drew attention to the promising realities which helped destroy the fantasies each group can sometimes have of the other:

> The priest from Forward in Faith finds himself going
> to a woman priest for spiritual counsel because he has
> recognised an authenticity in her ministry from which
> he can be enriched. The Christian feminist recognises
> that the Resolution C parish down the road has a better
> programme for community regeneration than any other
> in the deanery.[13]

This locating of the political disagreements in the complex lived reality of the church's life and the spiritual growth of its members is another classic feature of Rowan's approach.

The Revision Committee working on the legislation issued a draft Measure in May 2010, but on 20 June the two archbishops issued a joint statement explaining an initiative to amend the Committee's proposal.[14] They identified the most difficult issue as that of "jurisdiction" and "provision for someone other than the diocesan bishop to provide episcopal oversight for those who are unable to accept the new situation". The debate had divided between oversight *either* coming from the diocesan by way of delegation (a problem for those who had difficulty with the diocesan's oversight) *or* providing alternative oversight by "removing some part of the diocesan's jurisdiction" (a problem for those supporting women bishops as it makes them "second-class"). The archbishops sought to square this circle by proposing "co-ordinate" jurisdiction. Under this the diocesan (male or female) would keep their jurisdiction intact but would refrain from exercising various functions in parishes which requested such restraint. As a result, "women ordained to the episcopate will enjoy exactly the same legal rights as men within the structures of the Church of England and… there will be no derogation of the rights of any diocesan bishop, male or female". In parishes requesting episcopal ministry from another bishop this would be provided by a bishop who received authority not by delegation from the diocesan but from the legislation itself. This "solution" was summed up in these terms:

> Since the amendments would not divest the diocesan
> bishop of any jurisdiction, they would involve no
> change in the Church of England's understanding of
> the episcopate. But for those seeking ministry under
> this provision from a nominated male bishop, there
> would no longer be the difficulty that this authority
> was derived in law from an act of delegation by an
> individual diocesan.[15]

Although proposed to facilitate mutual trust, this action set the proverbial cat among the pigeons. Opponents were encouraged, but those wanting women bishops were very unhappy with both the substance (which they felt *did* undermine women bishops) and the archbishops' attempt, less than a month before the key debate, to trump the Committee's proposals.

The defeat of these amendments was perhaps the most

significant setback for Rowan's leadership since the Reading crisis. Criticism was often personal, directed at how, once the amendments were proposed, the archbishops inadequately sought support. There was no concerted attempt to encourage Synod members to speak and vote for the proposal. Although Rowan probably would consider such action crude, political lobbying, the closeness of the final vote suggests that personal conversations with a few key individuals, encouraging them – particularly women clergy – to speak and vote for the amendments could have secured approval.

In defending the amendments, Rowan explained to Synod why stronger provision was needed and expressed concern that key theological issues were not being recognized. In doing justice to the majority, more was required "to do justice also to the fact that opponents do not necessarily belong in a totally different, radically unacceptable theological world which we can no longer recognize as part of our conversation".

Despite his commitment to the amendments, Rowan's (and the Archbishop of York's) presentation of them to Synod left their supporters disappointed, many blaming their performance for the defeat. Many felt Rowan was too detached (even speaking of "the archbishops" in the third person) and failed to express the amendments' significance or how much he wished them to succeed. Crucially, he explicitly stated that the archbishops "should both be very disappointed if this were seen as some kind of covert loyalty test". Some Synod members considering supporting the archbishops probably thereby felt released from any obligation to follow their lead. When the vote came, more Synod members voted for the amendments (216) than against (191) but they fell in the House of Clergy (Bishops 25 to 15; Clergy 85 to 90 with 5 abstentions; Laity 106 to 86 with 4 abstentions) and so were lost. This was a major setback for the archbishops' authority and their attempt to find a way forward.

Reflecting on the defeat later in Synod, Rowan again made clear the process of legislation and discernment was not finished and urged everyone to be "working for the interests of those who will be taking different decisions from our own... so that all may grow up into Christ as best they can". He reiterated the need to hold together the two principles which guided him throughout – women bishops, but with adequate provision for opponents – and acknowledged that "we all know that we have not yet cracked how to do that".

Following the defeat of the archbishops' amendment the proposed legislation had to be considered by diocesan synods. Their debates suggested many thought the problem had already been "cracked". There was overwhelming support for the Measure (only two dioceses voting against) but with signs that some, like Rowan, would welcome stronger provision. His commitment to opponents was signalled when two of the three "flying bishops" resigned in November 2010 to join the Ordinariate. One of them, Andrew Burnham, writes positively of his experience working as a PEV under Rowan:

> Rowan inherited me as a suffragan bishop rather than chose me... I found him to be a warm, sympathetic, and generous pastor... One was given absolute trust and, in practice, autonomy, almost as if one were a diocesan. He was ready to offer sympathetic advice but, inevitably, the problems we presented him with periodically were along the fault-lines of the Act of Synod and, though he sometimes offered to intervene, there was little sign that these interventions were successful, such is the real autonomy of the diocesan bishops with whom we were dealing. He once wrote to me to congratulate me on some initiatives in the area of evangelisation that we were undertaking in

Ebbsfleet parishes and that summed up his warm and encouraging approach... He was – and is – searching for ways for traditionalists to remain in the Church of England without being simply herded into a township where sexual discrimination is somewhat patronisingly permitted as a concession to human weakness. In short, he wants to permit some sort of ecclesiological rationale even though he himself is unlikely to agree with its detail.[16]

Some clearly hoped the PEVs' departure would mark the end of this pattern of ministry established by the Act of Synod following the 1992 vote. Rowan, however, made clear in his response to the resignations that he would be filling the vacancies, and new appointments were made in May 2011.

His determination to find a different way forward was signalled at the February 2012 Synod when he again sought more work on provision for the minority that respected their theological integrity and gave "some sort of ecclesial and sacramental integrity". Recognizing the impatience and suspicions of many, he remarked, "I would quite like Synod – no, I'd very much like Synod – to consider whether leaving a door open for the bishops to revisit some of those questions in the light of where we have got to might not be a good idea at this juncture." He again expressed a desire the Synod "find something we can all more-or-less *gratefully* live with" and so celebrate the fact that, despite divisions, they were reaching a point where the Church of England could say "this is the kind of church we could, with celebration, with affirmation, live in".

Gratitude, celebration, and affirmation were not, however, the response of Synod or the wider church to what happened next. The bishops decided in May 2012 to bring back to Synod a few amendments they hoped would ensure sufficient support for the final Measure which needed a two-thirds majority in all three Houses of Synod. In reality, one proposed amendment destabilized the whole legislation, which looked like it could be lost at the final hurdle by, paradoxically, supporters of women bishops voting against the legislation which would secure their goal. The issue focused on what the legislation would require the code of practice to give guidance on in relation to the selection of male bishops or male priests for those opposed to women bishops and priests. The amendment proposed that the code require the selection of men "the exercise of ministry by whom is consistent with the theological convictions" stated as behind the opposition to the consecration or ordination of women. This reference to "the theological convictions" of opponents within the legislation itself and the need to provide bishops whose ministry was "consistent with" such convictions created a firestorm of criticism from supporters of women bishops. They had already reached the very limits of compromise (many had wanted a "single clause" Measure) and were horrified at such a significant change at a late stage, giving theological status within the legislation to unacceptable views.

In the midst of that controversy, speaking to young people at Lambeth Palace, Rowan captured the situation he and the Church of England seemed to be constantly caught in with the vivid image quoted at the start of this chapter:

> I'm speaking as somebody who really very much wants to see women bishops as soon as possible... I share the frustration of a lot of people that we're tangled-up in trying to get the maximum support for it in the Church of England and every move in one direction makes other people move away. It's like one of those terrible games you get in Christmas crackers sometimes where you have to get the little silver balls into holes – you

always get two of them but then the other one goes off somewhere else.[17]

Once it was clear that approving women bishops was now in danger of being lost, the July Synod, which should have been Rowan's last as archbishop, sent the legislation back again to the bishops for more work. Rowan admitted the proposal had created "a reaction of real hurt and offence in the Church at large", which could not be ignored, and that bishops had "under-rated the depth of that sense of hurt and offence". This meant that "if other bishops feel as I do, they will need to examine themselves and feel appropriate penitence that they did not recognize just how difficult that was going to be". Given the many clear signals the amendment would produce such a reaction, this underestimation is surprising. It represents yet another crucial misjudgment on Rowan's part as to the effects of his actions, ranking alongside those in relation to the Reading appointment and the Church of England's response to the covenant. The goals and principles remained the same: securing women bishops (see Chapter 9) but in a way that "will feel like something that the Church of England can celebrate together... good news for all, a true witness to Jesus Christ in the world". He made clear he thought a major issue still needed addressing before the final vote and was not persuaded by the criticisms: "I don't, myself, feel convinced that we were *wrong* in the wording we selected, but that is clearly a conviction that has now to be tested and discussed." The final stage was now set to try and sort things out at an extra Synod meeting in November, a month before Rowan retired.

In September, the House of Bishops, with greater consensus among themselves and to the initial satisfaction of many, offered an alternative wording. Rather than speaking of providing clergy whose ministry was "consistent with the theological convictions" of the requesting parishes, the amendment spoke of selection "in a manner which respects the grounds" for the request. In commending it to the church and Synod members, Rowan appealed for the church to pass the legislation: "I am convinced that the time has come for the Church of England to be blessed by the ministry of women as bishops and it is my deep hope that the legislation will pass in November."

It soon became clear, however, that opponents were not convinced by the revised wording and felt that it did not meet that desired goal of being "something that the Church of England can celebrate together". Showing signs of having learned from previous political failures, Lambeth Palace, in the weeks prior to the Synod debate, mounted a strong campaign. Leading Anglicans urged Synod members that the time had now come to move on and permit women to become bishops.

In the day-long debate on 20 November, just over twenty years after the Synod voted to allow women priests, both Rowan and the archbishop-designate, Justin Welby, spoke powerfully in favour of the Measure. Rowan, describing the step as a "potentially liberating moment for us all", stressed the anomaly of not testing the vocation of a whole group of priests to the episcopacy and urged opponents to abstain or vote in favour if they could possibly do so in good conscience. His final question to Synod, which he described as "deeply troubling", was stark: "How much energy [do] we want to spend on this in the next decade? And how much [do] we want to bind the energies and skills of a new Archbishop into a new agenda?"

Despite this clear lead and challenge, as well as the overwhelming support of both the Bishops (44 for, only 3 against) and Clergy (148 for, 45 against) the Measure failed. Although the Laity were also strongly in favour (132 for, 74 against), the majority fell six votes short of the necessary two-thirds required to pass in that House and so it failed to pass overall.

It is hard to imagine a more disastrous and depressing final synod for a retiring archbishop, leading to a last month in office where he foresaw "a great deal of very uncomfortable and very unpleasant accusation and recrimination... and there is no easy way of getting through that except to endure it". Speaking of his "deep personal sadness" and "a great grief and great burden", he acknowledged that many would feel "rejection and unhappiness and deep disillusion with the institution of the Church".

The church overwhelmingly wants women bishops. Even opponents accepted that they cannot prevent this from happening in the future. Despite this, the Synod rejected the Measure that it had agonised over for years. The widespread perception is therefore that it has rejected women and resisted their equality with men. As Rowan said,

> We have, to put it very bluntly, a lot of explaining to
> do... a great deal of this discussion is not intelligible
> to our wider society. Worse than that, it seems as if we
> are wilfully blind to some of the trends and priorities of
> that wider society... We have, as the result of yesterday,
> undoubtedly lost a measure of credibility in our
> society.[18]

As the national, established church, that explaining also has to be given to politicians, some of whom were quickly signalling sympathy with calls to remove church exemptions from equality legislation or even consider disestablishment. Certainly, the church can expect many to take a much more sceptical and dismissive attitude to its contributions in the public square.

As this chapter has shown, the real problem has always been deciding what structures to provide for opponents of women bishops and Rowan spent much of his primacy seeking to secure a strong form of provision for those opponents that would enable the church to proceed with legislation to consecrate women bishops. In the end, what was on offer was less than he had sought, and although he urged opponents to accept it and work with it, they, and some who personally supported women bishops but wanted better provision for those who did not, refused and had the necessary blocking power among lay members.

As in other areas – notably the Anglican Communion discussed in the following chapters – Rowan therefore bequeaths his successor a situation where the deep divisions among Anglicans which have marked his primacy remain as serious as ever. His constant attempts to find an agreed way forward together have been rejected by concerted opposition from both extremes, leading to a situation of apparent deadlock.

The challenge as he leaves is whether the church continues to seek what Rowan sought: a solution that offers provision that both supporters and opponents of women bishops can embrace. But, despite opponents claiming this solution will become clearer given more time, in Rowan's words in the final debate, few "blindingly fresh ideas" are likely to arise. The hope would therefore be that greater trust can develop and either supporters will become more positive towards something like the Archbishops' amendments or else opponents will become more accepting of the proposal they have rejected. Given the reactions to the final vote, and the fact that the sexuality debate will become increasingly divisive, both options appear to require a miracle. The main alternative would be to stop trying to satisfy opponents and seek, in 2015, to elect enough members to support a Measure that offers them little or no legal framework. Such a campaign would, however, be deeply divisive and, even if successful in elections, would likely fracture the House of Bishops who have taken their responsibilities as a focus of unity so seriously.

A narrow final vote in favour would have created its own challenges, but the need to start all over again has created many more. Just as it looked as if the crucial last ball would fall into its hole, the whole game has been jolted and all the balls are now rolling around with little sign of the calmness and patience needed to restart it. That legacy threatens to cast a dark shadow not just over Justin Welby's opening years in office, but also back over all of Rowan's primacy. The light in that darkness is that with the church in such a mess, it may focus afresh on God and heed Rowan's closing, characteristically hopeful, words in his very last presidential address to Synod the day after the vote:

> God remains God, our call remains our call, our Church remains our Church and it is in that confidence that, with a good deal of deep breathing and as they say heart-swearing, we prepare ourselves to do our business today in the hope that the grace and strength of the Holy Spirit is what it always is, and always was and always will be.[19]

8

Canterbury and the Anglican Communion

The Anglican Communion is on the way to being a Communion, but still learning. (July 2003)[1]

As Rowan Williams' appointment to Canterbury was announced, the fracture lines which had long been evident within the Anglican Communion began to widen and deepen. As a result, Anglicans were trying throughout his tenure to crack what it means to be a global fellowship or communion of churches while watching the Anglican Communion crack under various pressures.[2] Rowan's constant efforts to address the problems and enable the Communion to develop structures to sustain relationships long-term have repeatedly floundered. For most of his time in office he found himself, in the words of the then Primate of Scotland, Idris Jones to *Time* in June 2007, "occupying the Christ-like position. He is crucified between two extremes and they're pulling him apart." It would, however, be wrong to imply he was simply passive – his approach was also proactive and generally consistent.

This chapter and the two chapters which follow seek to understand Rowan's legacy and assess his intentions and actions in relation to the Communion. They explore key elements in his response as he sought to prevent the Communion finally breaking under the strain and instead help it learn to become a communion.

This chapter focuses on his personal ministry as Archbishop of Canterbury. After sketching the nature of that role in the Communion and the situation he inherited on taking office, it explores how he sought to nurture the Communion's wider mission and shared life in part through his visits to provinces and how he also worked through Primates' Meetings. Seeking to respect and serve the Communion as a whole, his central commitment was to maintain the highest degree of communion by following the vision set out in Lambeth I.10: upholding Anglican teaching and enabling ongoing listening. The next chapter describes the more specific shape of these commitments which was provided by the 2004 Windsor Report. This gave him four further approaches: moratoria on blessings and consecrations of same-sex partnered people, a moratorium on interventions so as to find an internal solution to American divisions, a formal listening process, and – a longer-term solution – the development of an Anglican covenant. Alongside these he offered his own reflections and guidance through public letters and statements on the Communion's life. Finally, as discussed in Chapter 10, his reshaping and presiding over the 2008 Lambeth Conference was particularly significant, as was his subsequent sponsorship of the Continuing Indaba Project. His first presidential address at the Conference captured some of his fundamental vision across these different elements of his ministry within the Communion:

> It's my conviction that the option to which we are being led is one whose keywords are of council and covenant.

It is the vision of an Anglicanism whose diversity is limited not by centralised control but by consent – consent based on a serious *common* assessment of the implications of local change. How do we genuinely think *together* about diverse local challenges? If we can find ways of answering this, we shall have discovered an Anglicanism in which prayerful consultation is routine and accepted and understood as part of what is entailed in belonging to a fellowship that is more than local.[3]

The Archbishop of Canterbury and the Communion

Before assessing Rowan's own oversight it helps to recall the archbishop's role in the Communion and particularly its limits. The Archbishop of Canterbury is the focus of unity for the Communion and for its other three Instruments of Communion (the Lambeth Conference, the Anglican Consultative Council, and the Primates' Meeting) that co-ordinate relationships between churches. He has, however, very little power. He gathers and presides over Primates' Meetings and the Lambeth Conference at his own discretion but lacks formal executive function within the Communion. The executive functions are carried out by the Anglican Communion Office under the secretary general (John Peterson until 2004, Kenneth Kearon from January 2005) with whom he usually meets once a month. He and the secretary general have carefully delineated roles and responsibilities. The archbishop also lacks (with very minor exceptions) legal authority in any Communion church. Each province is autonomous, governing itself according to its own constitutions and canons. Despite such limited powers, Communion work took up about 20 per cent of Rowan Williams' time as archbishop.

Anglican provincial self-government was traditionally exercised within the context of "bonds of affection" expressed in part by mutual commitments to common counsel and respect for the Instruments' considered decisions. These decisions had significant moral authority even though they lacked legal authority within each church's life. Historically this pattern of relationship enabled the Communion to navigate difficult decisions and from the 1970s to accept some churches proceeding with women's ordination as priests and then bishops without major fracture. By the time Rowan became archbishop, it was clear that developing the teaching or practice of Anglican churches in relation to same-sex partnerships would be much more tempestuous and divisive.

Rowan's Inheritance

Many date the crisis in the Communion to Gene Robinson's 2003 election as Bishop of New Hampshire. This distorts the immediate context and fails to set that development in the context of the preceding three decades. Since the 1970s, the American church (ECUSA/TEC) had been debating same-sex partnerships and openly ordaining people in them. Through the 1980s and 1990s it increasingly interpreted sexual identity and questions about same-sex unions through the same lens as earlier conflicts over issues of race and gender. In relation to women priests there had been pre-emptive irregular ordinations prior to the American church agreeing. In relation to women bishops, although the Instruments were consulted, many felt they had little choice but to consent. During the 1980s, many American Anglicans reached the conclusion Rowan himself had reached: faithful, committed, loving same-sex partnerships were not incompatible with genuine Christian discipleship but could be a means of grace and bear witness to Christ. As this happened, with limited awareness in the wider church, the battle lines were being established among American Anglicans for the conflict Rowan would face.

Other churches were also addressing homosexuality, which received some attention in Lambeth 1978 and 1988 resolutions and at the 1991 Primates' Meeting. Matters came to a head in America with the Righter trial of 1995–96 when traditionalist bishops unsuccessfully brought charges in a church court against Bishop Righter for knowingly ordaining a partnered gay man. From then on the conflict went global. Stronger links began to develop between American "traditionalists" (the American Anglican Council (AAC) and Ekklesia, both formed in 1995) and African and other provinces. These were based on a shared theological vision (including concern about wider liberal theology, viewed as underlying developments in America) and a commitment to mission and evangelism. This linkage was intertwined with growing frustration among newer, growing Anglican provinces. They were seeking to be heard within the Communion structures and to move towards a postcolonial global Anglicanism.

Against this background, the crucially important Resolution I.10 of the 1998 Lambeth Conference was passed. This restated earlier resolutions but, driven particularly by African bishops, took a more definitive stance than the report by the sub-section discussing sexuality. The resolution upheld traditional Christian teaching, crucially stating that the Conference rejected homosexual practice as "incompatible with Scripture". It also set out the limits it saw resulting in terms of church practice by opposing the blessing of same-sex unions and the ordination of those in such unions. In addition, it recommitted the Communion to listen to the experience of homosexual persons.

Despite overwhelming support, it was clear ECUSA/TEC would not receive and implement this teaching. This produced a backlash: in 2000, with the American church disregarding the Lambeth resolution, the Anglican primates of South East Asia and Rwanda consecrated two American priests as missionary bishops (four more were consecrated in 2002). This created the first formal split in the American church over this issue as the Anglican Mission in America (AMiA) formed. Alongside this, since 1998 the diocesan synod of New Westminster in Canada had been asking its bishop to authorize clergy to bless covenanted same-sex unions. Just five days before the leak that Rowan was headed to Canterbury, it did so again. It was clear that on taking office Rowan was facing a situation in which there was more than one powder keg of explosives and a number of Anglicans playing with fire.

Rowan's Arrival

Rowan's letter to the primates on his appointment immediately set Lambeth I.10 as a key boundary outside which the Communion risked fragmentation. The first Primates' Meeting he chaired (May 2003) discussed "True Union in the Body?", a booklet on same-sex relationships and the Communion. Its communiqué stated, "The Archbishop of Canterbury spoke for us all when he said that it is through liturgy that we express what we believe, and that there is no theological consensus about same sex unions. Therefore, we as a body cannot support the authorisation of such rites." Immediately, however, the cracks appeared with the first blessing in New Westminster, the Reading crisis, and Gene Robinson's election on 7 June as Bishop of New Hampshire.

Robinson's election needed the confirmation of ECUSA/TEC's General Convention in August. In advance of this Rowan wrote to the primates describing how the Communion was "on the way to being a Communion, but still learning" and that "a number of the choices faced by various provinces are choices that will clearly take us either nearer real communion or further from it". Around the same time he signalled he knew what was coming:

I suspect that those who speak of new alignments and new patterns, of the weakening of territorial jurisdiction and the like, are seeing the situation pretty accurately. But what then becomes the danger to avoid is an entirely modern or post-modern map of church identity in which non-communicating and competing entities simply eradicate the very idea of a "communion" of churches... I don't expect the next few years to be anything other than messy as far as all this is concerned. The question is not whether we can avoid mess, but whether we can hang on to common convictions about divine grace and initiative. There is a real issue there, not often enough named and faced.[4]

Rowan's concern was that in changing teaching and practice there needed to be a clear sense of accountability and a focus on "the conviction that what makes a church a church, even through the struggles of major disruption and disagreement, is a shared divine calling".

General Convention approved Robinson's election and also recognized "that local faith communities are operating within the bounds of our common life as they explore and experience liturgies celebrating and blessing same-sex unions". Now the trouble really began, both within the American church and in the Communion as provinces distanced themselves from ECUSA/TEC. "Major disruption and disagreement" would continue until Rowan's retirement and shape his legacy.

Before focusing on that disruption and disagreement, this chapter looks at Rowan's wider and more personal ministry within the Communion.

Building Up Common Mission and Shared Life

We must hope that, in spite of the difficulties, this may yet be the beginning of a new era of mission and spiritual growth for all who value the Anglican name and heritage. (July 2009)[5]

The Communion continued under Rowan to develop many areas of common mission and shared life, through partnerships between dioceses and between provinces as well as through the various Anglican Communion Networks. Rowan's Easter 2005 message to the Communion, following the difficult Dromantine Primates' Meeting, drew attention to one major element, the Millennium Development Goals. He noted that the communiqué's paragraph on this had "barely been mentioned by any commentator, inside the Church or outside" and concluded pointedly:

> This is not an additional extra – the boring bit of
> a message in which all the excitement is generated
> by church politics. It should really shock us that a
> document like the Primates' communiqué has been
> read as if it were only intended to be about our internal
> struggles. It means that we have not been heard to speak
> about the Resurrection.[6]

Other Communion initiatives during his primacy included continued support for ministry among those with HIV/AIDS and developing the work of TEAC (Theological Education for the Anglican Communion). This, along with support for Anglican women theological educators, was a major concern given his commitment to theological education. The Communion Office also continued to provide training and orientation for new bishops from across the Communion. Important new initiatives included the work on biblical interpretation through the Bible in the Life of the Church project and – a major part of his Communion legacy – the launch of the Global Anglican Relief and Development Alliance working at the grassroots to co-ordinate various relief agencies. In an interview on announcing his retirement, he identified the Anglican Alliance as one of the things "I look back on with greatest satisfaction". Primates' Meetings, though at times swamped by crisis management, also made important contributions in responding to violence against women and the situation in Zimbabwe.

All these examples demonstrate that, under Rowan, many areas of Communion life flourished. Sharing together across the Communion in these and other forms of common mission, service, education, and development helped limit the damage done by the conflict and demonstrated the importance of nurturing the Communion's life.

Another key element was Rowan's regular visits to Communion provinces. This often unreported aspect of his ministry helped confirm the significance of the office of Archbishop of Canterbury and established Rowan as a global Christian leader.

Visiting Provinces

An enormous gift and privilege (Advent 2011)[7]

Every year Rowan visited different Communion provinces. Often very intensive, these visits were a highlight of his ministry and provided some of the glue holding the Communion together. Reflecting on his ten years and the "big positives" he included his travels around the Communion: "It's enormously stretching and inspiring, because you see people really work in the middle of appalling circumstances – heartbreaking in some ways, but a great enrichment." His words to the primates in 2011 about recent visits to parts of Africa could be applied more widely: "I can truthfully say that each of those visits has in its own way been an enormous gift and privilege."

The visits enabled him to listen to and learn from Anglicans worldwide. He encouraged them in their discipleship and mission and then spoke for them (not simply for the Instruments) as a focus of unity within the Communion. He supported churches in difficult social, economic, and political contexts (most notably in the Middle East, Sudan, Congo, and Zimbabwe) and acknowledged and strengthened the various expressions of "bonds of affection" by sharing his experiences with the wider Communion. As he told Simon Mayo in 2005,

> I have to spend a fair amount [of] time travelling
> around bits of the Communion… Burundi this
> summer, visit to the Sudan coming up next year some
> time; and on the ground what matters most often is the
> kind of support that's given informally by Christians in
> one bit of the world to Christians in another bit, the
> links that exist through the Mothers' Union, through
> informal networks of friendships and partnership.[8]

He often met political leaders, most famously his historic meeting with Mugabe. Rowan used these opportunities and the status of his office to empower the local church and to speak for the vulnerable and oppressed, particularly persecuted Christians. He illustrated the effect of such visits in a 2007 interview:

> When I visit Angola or further afield, as in Pakistan,
> sometimes it's possible because the Archbishop of
> Canterbury is a high profile visitor… for me to take a
> local church leader in to meet a president, or a cabinet
> minister, in a way that they wouldn't necessarily have
> the clout to do on their own… In Pakistan I can

remember one particularly lively exchange where I went in with a local bishop to meet a provincial governor and it was really an occasion for me simply to say to the local bishop "OK now you tell the provincial governor what you've been telling me about the problems of Christians in this area!" So that kind of opening doors is part of the international ministry of the Archbishop of Canterbury.[9]

This global ministry enabled him to speak on the media and to governments about the needs of some of the most troubled parts of the world. He particularly sought to do this in relation to the Middle East and Zimbabwe, and Archbishop Deng in 2010 described him as a "colossally effective advocate for Sudan". Such visits also equipped him to be an authoritative witness to England and other parts of the Communion of the work of God through the global church as it impacted on wider society, an important counter to secular critics of religious influences. As he said in his important 2007 address to the international TEAM (Towards Effective Anglican Mission) conference in South Africa:

Not only in this continent, but certainly very visibly in this continent, the Church is probably the only organization in civil society that can deliver goals concretely at grass-roots level, in modest but real ways: whether it's the work of the Mothers' Union… whether it's micro credit initiatives in a village somewhere; whether it's a small school in the back of beyond like the little school that we visited meeting under a tree in southern Sudan at this time last year. All of those are examples of the real difference that no-one else can make.[10]

Experiences such as that "meeting under a tree" were particularly important to Rowan. They capture in their simplicity a central element in his ministry, as the Communion's secretary general, Kenneth Kearon commented:

> He admires honest faithfulness – in Congo and in Sudan. Extraordinary faithfulness to the church and actually working out your faith in the context. That's what he admires. Big events can just irritate him. You don't impress him easily. He'd much rather have lunch with a few people from a parish or meet the Mothers' Union for a while. I think that's really quite important for him and not everyone does that as well as he does. He really does squeeze round into the kitchen and likes to be there. It's part of his listening to the Communion, which he does very, very well.[11]

Rowan's experiences on these visits revealed some of the hurt and damage caused by unilateral actions and the greater harm if further fractures followed. They thus strengthened him to persevere so determinedly in keeping the Communion together in a way many in the Church of England failed to understand. The received way of doing such work of maintaining unity was through the Instruments and during his primacy this role was particularly taken by the Primates' Meeting.

Working with the Primates' Meetings

Can we continue to be friends? (June 2005)[12]

Following confirmation of Robinson's election, Rowan called an Emergency Primates' Meeting in the context of concerns that not only the American church but the whole Communion could divide in coming months. It ended with a stark and strongly worded communiqué. The view of the Communion's primates was that the actions of New Westminster and ECUSA/TEC

> threaten the unity of our own Communion as well
> as our relationships with other parts of Christ's
> Church, our mission and witness, and our relations
> with other faiths, in a world already confused in
> areas of sexuality, morality and theology, and polarise
> Christian opinion.[13]

Using categories which would be important in years to come, and objected to by some, they clarified the American actions did not alter "the teaching of the Anglican Communion" or express the "mind of our Communion as a whole". They did "jeopardise our sacramental fellowship with each other". The key and subsequently much quoted paragraph in relation to Gene Robinson's election stated:

> If his consecration proceeds, we recognise that we have
> reached a crucial and critical point in the life of the
> Anglican Communion and we have had to conclude
> that the future of the Communion itself will be put in
> jeopardy. In this case, the ministry of this one bishop
> will not be recognised by most of the Anglican world,
> and many provinces are likely to consider themselves
> to be out of Communion with the Episcopal Church
> (USA). This will tear the fabric of our Communion at
> its deepest level, and may lead to further division on
> this and further issues as provinces have to decide in
> consequence whether they can remain in communion
> with provinces that choose not to break communion
> with the Episcopal Church (USA).[14]

Rowan described the meeting as "anything but easy" but it had been "honest and open and I hope that we have grown in some real shared understanding as a result". In reaching unanimity it appeared to have experienced something close to a miracle. That sense was quickly shattered when ECUSA/TEC's presiding bishop almost immediately made clear that, despite having signed the statement agreeing that there would be dire consequences, he intended to proceed with the consecration. This apparent instant rejection of the primates' grave concerns further diminished, in some cases totally destroyed, the already low levels of good faith which had traditionally been the oxygen of the Communion's common life.

The meeting's substantive outcome was a well-worn response to difficulties: a Commission chaired by Archbishop Robin Eames. Its vision of life together and specific recommendations – published in October 2004 as the Windsor Report – established many of the key building blocks of Rowan's approach to the crisis and these are discussed in the next chapter. It was received at the February 2005 Primates' Meeting in Dromantine, which again miraculously found a way forward. The *Church Times* reported "universal admiration for the Archbishop of Canterbury's leadership", and Greg Venables from the Southern Cone described how, in contrast to previous meetings where many from the Global South had felt unable to speak freely:

> Now under Archbishop Rowan's leadership, either because he's got a Celtic background, or perhaps because of his personality or perhaps because of his emphasis on spirituality and the need for prayer, we've been able to get to a stage where we can talk very openly, very strongly even but somehow keep the thing open and keep going.[15]

This success was, however, overshadowed by the conscientious decision of over a dozen primates not to share in Holy Communion alongside the presiding bishop. This fracture of eucharistic fellowship demonstrated the seriousness of the situation and caused Rowan great distress: for him, gathering together around the Lord's Table is central to the identity and unity of the church. Mark Russell, a member of the Archbishops' Council, recalls, "I have spoken with him after successive Primates' Meetings and seen the pain in his eyes when he talks about how Primates cannot even share Eucharist together."[16] Some argued that Rowan should have refused to allow those withdrawing from table fellowship to participate in the meeting's discussions. Others argued that Presiding Bishop Griswold's consecration of Robinson and refusal to express regret should have led to him being asked to withdraw or just observe. Rowan, however, continued throughout his primacy to invite and welcome all the Primates of the Communion to the meeting table, mirroring Christ's invitation and welcome at his table, even though some primates (a diminishing number) refused to take communion or, in 2011, even to attend. His pained appeal a few months later at ACC (Anglican Consultative Council) was, "If it is difficult for us to stand together at the Lord's Table as we might wish, can we continue to be friends?"

After Dromantine, Rowan described the situation as "more in marriage counselling than in the divorce courts" but further counselling was needed. The 2007 Primates' Meeting at Dar es Salaam in Tanzania (where the Archbishop of York represented the Church of England for the first time and there were fourteen new primates) was in many ways the hardest of Rowan's primacy. Although it again reached agreement, the failure to follow that agreement through (Rowan went on sabbatical shortly afterwards) when its proposals were rejected, was a major failure. It led to further unhappiness on the part of many Global South Primates some of whose provinces then stayed away from Lambeth 2008.

The Alexandria meeting of 2009 succeeded in gathering primates from across the Communion, but Rowan's final Primates' Meeting in 2011 left a mixed legacy for his successor to pick up. The professionally facilitated meeting was viewed very positively by those present and set out a vision for the meeting's future role. However, a significant number of primates stayed away in protest at the lack of action taken against the presiding bishop of ECUSA/TEC following her consecration in May 2010 of another same-sex partnered bishop, despite the clear appeals of Rowan and the other Instruments for a moratorium.

The Primates' Meeting during Rowan's time in office met less often than towards the end of George Carey's time but took a lead role in responding to the conflict (even, at Dromantine, controversially requesting provinces to withdraw from the ACC). It could appeal to the enhanced responsibility recommended by Lambeth Conferences to justify this development, but its actions upset some provinces. The inability of Rowan or anyone else to follow through the primates' actions alienated others. The cracks which opened up with the breaking of eucharistic fellowship in 2005 therefore continued and widened so that for his final Primates' Meeting Rowan was unable to persuade a significant minority of primates to attend the meeting. This Instrument of Communion, which had for most of his primacy worked to repair the cracks and seek unity in the Communion, had itself fractured, leaving his successor the major challenge of finding a way to bring the Communion's leaders back round the table for common counsel.

9

Cracking Communion?
1. The Windsor Path

We stand in the middle of one of the most severe challenges to have faced the Anglican family in its history. (Lambeth Conference 2008)[1]

Supporting the Windsor Report

It's been said that the Windsor Report is the only game in town. I think that's probably right. (February 2005)[2]

The Lambeth Commission on Communion, established by the primates in 2003 to address the crisis in the Communion, reported on 18 October 2004. Its report was determinative for much that followed in Rowan's leadership and the legacy he leaves. Its opening section set out the purposes and benefits of communion, offered a diagnosis of the Communion's recent ills, and identified key categories for addressing them. There followed an articulation of fundamental principles. Drawing on Scripture, earlier Anglican statements, and a shared ecumenical theology of life in communion, these two sections set out an Anglican vision combining provincial autonomy with recognition of interdependence and mutual accountability between provinces. The third section addressed how this vision could be made a reality, making a number of proposals for the Communion. It stressed the archbishop's role "as the central focus of both unity and mission within the Communion" (para. 109) and his "very significant teaching role... The Communion looks to the office of the Archbishop to articulate the mind of the Communion especially in areas of controversy" (*Ibid.*). It proposed he be supported by a Council of Advice, one proposal Rowan made clear he did not want to be taken forward although he agreed the report was "the only game in town".

With the support of the primates and ACC, and in the face of some strong opposition, particularly from supporters of ECUSA/TEC, Rowan made Windsor's other main proposals central:

- moratoria on blessing gay partnerships and consecration of bishops in such partnerships;

- a moratorium on interventions in North American churches by other provinces;

- a listening process on sexuality; and

- an Anglican Communion Covenant.

The implementation of each of these and the legacy they leave are the concerns of this chapter. They need to be explored in the context of the report's final paragraph, the inclusion of which caused some controversy within the Commission as it offered a stark assessment of the paths facing the Communion:

> There remains a very real danger that we will not
> choose to walk together. Should the call to halt and

find ways of continuing in our present communion not be heeded, then we shall have to begin to learn to walk apart... Our aim throughout has been to work not for division but for healing and restoration. The real challenge of the gospel is whether we live deeply enough in the love of Christ, and care sufficiently for our joint work to bring that love to the world, that we will "make every effort to maintain the unity of the Spirit in the bond of peace" (Eph. 4.3). As the primates stated in 2000, "to turn from one another would be to turn away from the Cross", and indeed from serving the world which God loves and for which Jesus Christ died.[3]

Seeking Moratoria on Same-Sex Blessings and Consecrations

A period of gracious restraint in respect of actions which are contrary to the mind of the Communion is necessary if our bonds of mutual affection are to hold. (December 2009)[4]

The Windsor Report called for statements of regret for certain controversial past actions and a commitment not to repeat them. In particular, it sought "a moratorium on the election and consent to the consecration of any candidate to the episcopate who is living in a same gender union until some new consensus in the Anglican Communion emerges" (para. 134) and for "all bishops of the Anglican Communion to honour the Primates' Pastoral Letter of May 2003, by not proceeding to authorise public Rites of Blessing for same sex unions" (para. 143). These appeals would be repeated constantly by Archbishop Rowan and the other Instruments, but ultimately both would clearly fail.

The initial response of ECUSA/TEC bishops in 2005 was to "offer our sincerest apology and repentance for having breached our bonds of affection by any failure to consult adequately with our Anglican partners". They effected a moratorium on all consents for new bishops until General Convention 2006 and pledged "not to authorize any public rites for the blessing of same sex unions" although they recognized some offered services as a form of pastoral care.

Some bishops had personally presided at such blessings. Demonstrating that Rowan did much more behind the scenes (most still largely unknown), Bishop John Chane of Washington received from him an email which he read as an instruction to "cease and desist". The bishop then reciprocated by entering into a "very challenging" correspondence about his pastoral care and responsibility to the clergy in his diocese and said that if he "believed one bishop in the American Church could destroy the structure of the Communion, then the Communion was in far worse shape than I thought it was".[5]

The constitution of ECUSA/TEC meant the full response had to await General Convention in 2006. This struggled to find a way forward. It failed to address the question of rites and passed a last-minute resolution on consecrations calling on Standing Committees and bishops with jurisdiction "to exercise restraint by not consenting to the consecration of any candidate to the episcopate whose manner of life presents a challenge to the wider church and will lead to further strains on communion". Those most unhappy with ECUSA/TEC were not satisfied.

The Primates' Meeting in February 2007 accepted the apology offered but spoke of a "lack of clarity" in the American church's response. They asked that, by the end of September 2007, the American House of Bishops clarify the church's stance on blessings and consent to candidates for bishop in same-sex unions warning that

if the reassurances requested… cannot in good
conscience be given, the relationship between The
Episcopal Church and the Anglican Communion
as a whole remains damaged at best, and this has
consequences for the full participation of the Church in
the life of the Communion.[6]

Rowan attended the American House of Bishops in September. It pledged "not to authorize for use in our dioceses any public rites of blessing of same-sex unions until a broader consensus emerges in the Communion, or until General Convention takes further action". It also acknowledged that "non-celibate gay and lesbian persons" were included in the group General Convention called bishops and others not to consent to being consecrated. The Communion's Standing Committee was broadly positive about this reply, but consultations showed many remained sceptical. Rowan's Advent 2007 letter therefore concluded that "we have no consensus" about the adequacy of the response and then drew a line under the matter:

It is practically impossible to imagine any further
elucidation or elaboration coming from TEC…
A good deal of time and effort has gone into the
responses they have already produced, and it is
extremely unlikely that further meetings will produce
any more substantial consensus…[7]

Over the next five years, actions spoke louder than words. Many American dioceses continued to permit or authorize rites, a trend also seen in some Canadian dioceses. The number of such dioceses in ECUSA/TEC rose after the 2009 General Convention passed a resolution encouraging experimentation and authorizing further work in this area. That work led, in 2012, to General Convention authorizing for provisional use, with the consent of the bishop, a rite for "The Witnessing and Blessing of a Lifelong Covenant". For the first time, Rowan made no public statement about this clear abandonment of the moratorium. This was perhaps because in 2010 the other requested moratorium had been broken despite the bishops' promise in 2007 of which Rowan had written, "I do not see how the commitment not to confirm any election to the episcopate of a partnered gay or lesbian person can mean anything other than what it says." Mary Glasspool, a priest in a lesbian partnership, was elected a bishop in Los Angeles in December 2009, confirmed by the bishops and dioceses, and consecrated in May 2010.

Writing to the Fourth Global South Encounter in April 2010, Rowan stated that the Glasspool decision "deepened the divide" and that he was in discussion about "consequences" but reissued his constant call for patient and penitent waiting on God:

> I hope also in your thinking about this and in your
> reacting to it, you'll bear in mind that there are no
> quick solutions for the wounds of the Body of Christ. It
> is the work of the Spirit that heals the Body of Christ,
> not the plans or the statements of any group, or any
> person, or any instrument of communion. Naturally
> we seek to minimize the damage, to heal the hurts,
> to strengthen our mission, to make sure that it goes
> forward with integrity and conviction. Naturally, there
> are decisions that have to be taken. But at the same
> time… we must *all* share in a sense of repentance and
> willingness to be renewed by the Spirit.[8]

His May 2010 Pentecost letter set out the consequences. Representatives of churches which had rejected agreed moratoria were removed from Anglican ecumenical dialogues and IASCUFO (the Inter-Anglican Standing Commission on Unity, Faith and Order). This was "to confirm what the Communion as a whole has come to regard as acceptable limits of diversity in its practice", although the IASCUFO decision was rescinded in March 2012. Rowan's letter noted other bodies where such consequences may be implemented but he then took no further action, leading to many primates refusing to attend the 2011 Primates' Meeting.

The American church (along with some Canadian dioceses) is clearly unwilling to show "gracious restraint" in the form sought by Rowan on behalf of the Communion throughout his primacy. Although consequences have been enacted, they are minimal and have not satisfied many. Rowan thus leaves a major unresolved problem for the new archbishop, Justin Welby. He will need to decide how he, the Church of England, and the rest of the Communion should relate to those who are convinced the Spirit is calling them to act in ways that reject the teaching and the appeals of the rest of the Anglican Communion.

Working for a Moratorium on Interventions and Seeking Provision for Conservative Anglicans

It's an experiment; pray for it. (February 2007)[9]

The Windsor Report also called for a moratorium by "those bishops who believe it is their conscientious duty to intervene in provinces, dioceses and parishes other than their own" (para. 155). This need arose because of the actions of ECUSA/TEC conservatives and the response by some other provinces.

Rowan, as a Communion primate, had been wrestling with American divisions since 2000. From his appointment he had exchanges with American conservatives about their future, reflecting his pastoral concern, particularly for minorities and those presenting as marginalized and suffering. This would create problems with both sides of the American divide. He was also creative in his thinking about adapting church structures to enable what in wider society he often spoke of as "interactive pluralism" (see Chapter 13).

In September 2003 he met with conservatives, one of whom, Martyn Minns, subsequently wrote that Rowan suggested the need for a Network of Confessing Dioceses and Parishes. Seeking a possible navigation through the new alignments he could foresee, Rowan had turned to the "network" language of the 2002 Primates' Meeting. Plans for this were announced on 8 October and soon claimed Rowan's backing (he met its leaders the day after the Emergency Primates' Meeting). Such claims were never denied by Lambeth Palace who stated (in September 2004) that no proposals for the Network's "potential form, structure or outworking were advanced". The form, structure, and outworking were, however, quickly developed by the American Anglican Council (AAC), which launched the Network of Anglican Communion Dioceses and Parishes in January 2004.

Two major problems Rowan faced were the lack of a structure of oversight within ECUSA/TEC acceptable to conservatives and the differences among conservatives about how to respond to this difficulty. Many American Anglicans committed to Communion teaching remained outside the Network, which included a spectrum of opinions about the way forward. Some (represented by the Anglican Communion Institute (ACI)) were seeking, like Rowan (in his words to General Synod), "arrangements which will secure a continuing place for all Episcopalians in the life of the Episcopal Church in the United States". Their hope was an agreed form of differentiation and alternative structures. This would maintain the province's unity while connecting those committed to Communion teaching to the wider Communion if the province continued to go its own way. Others were either open to or actively seeking a more separatist outcome as shown by the leaked unofficial December 2003 "Chapman memo":

> Our ultimate goal is a realignment of Anglicanism on North American soil committed to biblical faith and values, and driven by Gospel mission. We believe in the end this should be a "replacement" jurisdiction with confessional standards, maintaining the historic faith of our Communion, closely aligned with the majority of world Anglicanism.[10]

Achieving this goal involved offering parishes oversight by bishops elsewhere in the Communion and building the "Common Cause Partnership". This partnership included earlier breakaways and sought to demonstrate what a June 2004 letter to Rowan described as "our commitment to make common cause for the gospel of Jesus Christ and common cause for a united, missionary and orthodox Anglicanism in North America".

Rowan could not personally provide episcopal oversight and clearly wanted an internal solution. However, his comments in private pastoral conversations and the public spin put on them embroiled him in the internal American conflict. Conservatives portrayed him as backing their plans but he had no control over their actions. They were increasingly divided among themselves and there was increasing breakdown of trust between them and ECUSA/TEC's leadership. This made it impossible to broker an internal solution. Over time most became disillusioned with Rowan's inability – often seen as unwillingness – to secure the form of Anglican church life in America which they believed he had encouraged and blessed.

The unhappiness with Rowan from Gene Robinson supporters was quicker and deeper. They saw his actions as an abandonment of beliefs they thought he shared with them and an undermining of their church's life. The September 2004 words of Mark Harris are an early statement of an attitude which became increasingly common:

> The Archbishop must be understood to have taken
> an active and initiating part in the internal ecclesial
> struggles of this Province, seeking with others to
> negate the effects of decisions made by the General
> Convention, and barring that to set a new course
> for an "orthodox" Anglican Church in the US. This
> sort of action by an Archbishop of Canterbury is
> not anticipated, agreed to, condoned or contracted
> for in the Constitution or Canons of the Episcopal
> Church...[11]

At Dromantine in early 2004 the primates established a Panel of Reference to seek resolution of specific cases of conflict. They committed themselves "neither to encourage nor to initiate cross-boundary interventions" but the Panel's work was widely acknowledged a failure and interventions continued.

Decisions at General Convention 2006 heightened the conflict. Its response to Communion requests was inadequate for conservatives and, to everyone's surprise, the bishops elected Katharine Jefferts Schori as presiding bishop, the first woman to hold primatial office in the Communion and someone supportive of pursuing "full inclusion" of gay and lesbian people. The murkiness of church politics at the time was such that at least four conservative bishops voted for her.

Almost immediately, several conservative dioceses appealed to Rowan for alternate primatial oversight (APO) claiming "there are effectively two churches under one roof... Separation of the two churches became all but inevitable and irreversible at the

General Convention of 2006". Network moderator, Bishop Bob Duncan, made clear the challenge: "This is a kairos moment in the life of the Anglican Communion, especially as regards the evolving role of its leadership by the Archbishop of Canterbury."

Another key development in June 2006 was Nigeria's election of Martyn Minns to be a missionary bishop in America. This followed their 2005 decision to revise the constitution by deleting all references to "communion with the see of Canterbury", memorably summed up in Archbishop Akinola's sound bite that people "did not have to go through Canterbury to get to Jesus". When David Frost asked Rowan, "presumably not straight to your face, that wasn't, was it?" he honestly replied, with a laugh, "No, but I think if he had said it to my face I would have agreed entirely."[12] The cracks in the American church were now spreading into the Communion and reaching to Canterbury.

Divisions were also appearing in the Network. The Camp Allen "Windsor Bishops", resourced by the ACI and connected with the Bishops of Durham and Winchester, offered an alternative to Common Cause. They sought Canterbury's support for a grouping within ECUSA/TEC (including some who had voted for Robinson) committed to Windsor's proposals.

A September attempt in New York at finding an agreed internal solution came close but ultimately failed. The conservative grouping withdrew from the planned second meeting and rejected the presiding bishop's subsequent proposal. The Global South Primates meeting in Kigali declared the time had come "to take initial steps towards the formation of what will be recognized as a separate ecclesiastical structure of the Anglican Communion in the USA". Rowan was honest about what could lie ahead and what he was working to avoid:

> If Canterbury doesn't help, there will be other provinces that are very ready to help... I don't want to see in

the cities of America the American Anglican Church,
the Nigerian Anglican Church, the Egyptian Anglican
Church and the English Anglican Church in the same
street… My nightmare is that action is now going
forward that will tie us all up in law courts in ten years,
in disputes about property. That would take so much
energy from what we're meant to be doing.[13]

The difficult 2007 Dar es Salaam Primates' Meeting took place against this backdrop, surrounded by campaigners seeking to influence it. Rowan, always committed to conversation, invited three American bishops to meet with the primates. After hard negotiation, the primates offered a way forward: a Pastoral Council to act on their behalf in addressing the problems in a way that would end interventions and create some structure to provide "sufficient space for those who are unable to accept the direct ministry of their bishop or the Presiding Bishop to have a secure place within The Episcopal Church and the Anglican Communion". Rowan's final words at the closing press conference captured the precariousness of the situation: "It's an experiment; pray for it."

The experiment was – even in the turbulent life of the Communion – one of the most short-lived and also something of a tipping point. Widely seen as a victory for conservatives, it was quickly and robustly rejected by American bishops. Stephen Bates, under the headline "Bishops to Primate: Drop Dead", described the American response as "a kick in the balls for Dr Williams" while Damian Thompson opined, "Rowan Williams is finished as Archbishop of Canterbury. His authority has been utterly destroyed by the decision of the American bishops to reject his scheme to hold together the Anglican Communion." Interventions escalated into inter-provincial consecrations, as more American priests were quickly elected missionary bishops by Nigeria and Rwanda but also by Uganda and Kenya. As a result, the cracks between American conservatives also widened and Rowan's task became even harder.

Network moderator, Bishop Bob Duncan, attacked Rowan whose support he had originally claimed, making the claim that "never, ever has he spoken publicly in defense of the orthodox in the United States". He concluded that "The cost is his office. To lose that historic office is a cost of such magnitude that God must be doing a new thing." His criticism was simple: "The Archbishop of Canterbury has not led in a way that might have saved his office and might have saved Lambeth... In this crisis, we've had no leader to lead." Duncan's energy now focused on the Common Cause Partnership, which in September 2007 "pledged to take the first steps toward a 'new ecclesiastical structure' in North America".

Other Network bishops took a different path and Rowan set out his underlying theology and approach when responding to a letter from one of them – Bishop Howe, who was struggling to hold together his diocese. Rowan wrote, "the organ of union with the wider Church is the Bishop and the Diocese rather than the Provincial structure as such". Rowan's 2007 Advent letter contained some of his strongest words against those intervening and separating off but some were determined to pursue that path. Four dioceses left ECUSA/TEC and, through 2008, worked to create a new province. This was formally launched as the Anglican Church in North America (ACNA) in June 2009 supported by a number of Communion provinces. It presents a challenge for the new archbishop as some English Anglicans are eager for the Church of England to recognize it formally.

Attempts continued to be made to enable the Communion to support and give structure to marginalized conservatives remaining within ECUSA/TEC, gathered around Communion Partners. However, neither the work of the Windsor Continuation

Group (2007–09) nor the Pastoral Visitors succeeded, and a Pastoral Council was never constituted. As a result, Rowan's legacy in this area is summed up in the words of Philip Turner, who remains within ECUSA/TEC and had high hopes that Rowan shared his vision of a way forward: "From where I sit, he left those within TEC who supported him dangling in the wind. It is hard not to feel in some ways betrayed."[14]

Launching the Listening Process

The last Lambeth Conference asked for listening to go on and the Communion has taken that seriously. (January 2008)[15]

The 1998 Lambeth resolution on sexuality committed the Communion to "listen to the experience of homosexual persons", and the Windsor Report, though not addressing disputes over sexuality, called on the Instruments to "find practical ways" (para. 135) to take this forward. The primates requested ACC "to take positive steps to initiate the listening and study process", and later in 2005 the ACC passed a resolution which, at the initiative of Rowan and Kenneth Kearon, extended the listening beyond LGBT Christians to a wider "mutual listening". ACC members also heard presentations from the North American provinces giving the reasoning behind their actions, one of the few structured attempts to listen to views on sexuality in the Instruments during Rowan's time because a plan to focus the 2011 Primates' Meeting on this was subsequently reconsidered.

The Listening Process, in itself and through shaping the Indaba Project described in the next chapter, became a major constructive legacy of Rowan's work in the Communion. Led by Canon Phil Groves from January 2006, it monitored work on sexuality in the Communion and encouraged and enabled mutual listening, including to homosexual people. On arriving in post Canon Groves discovered "I had a mandate, but no other guidance; frankly no one had a clue – especially not me."[16] He set about building relationships and establishing networks that would enable listening instead of persuasion, debate, or securing a compromise. Listening concentrated on questions such as "'What would I feel in that situation?' 'What would I have done?' 'How does that person think, what is her worldview?' rather than, 'How can I counter that argument?'"

The Listening Process requested and published reports from provinces about their own listening processes and engagement with issues of sexuality. One major fruit of this process was the publication at Lambeth 2008 of a volume of essays, *The Anglican Communion and Homosexuality*, which had the potential to be a major resource although it is unclear how widely it was used. It also provided online resources including a website with material from people of opposing viewpoints about sexuality but sharing a commitment to the view that, in the important words of the Dromantine primates' communiqué, "the victimisation or diminishment of human beings whose affections happen to be ordered towards people of the same sex is anathema to us". This was also a strong emphasis from Rowan who frequently spoke out on this issue, calling on the church to become a safe place for gay and lesbian people and challenging societies to recognize that "in many places – including Western countries with supposedly 'liberal' attitudes – hate crimes against homosexual people have increased in recent years and have taken horrifying and disturbing forms". In 2011, for example, he issued a clear statement that proposed anti-homosexuality legislation in Uganda was "of shocking severity and I can't see how it could be supported by any Anglican who is committed to what the Communion has said in recent decades".

Perhaps Rowan's most striking personal contribution in

relation to listening to each other on sexuality was his second presidential address at the Lambeth Conference. There he used his gifts to role-play mutual listening:

> I want to imagine what the main messages would be, within an atmosphere of patience and charity, from those in our Communion who hold to a clear and traditional doctrinal and moral conviction, and also from those who, starting from the same centre, find fewer problems or none with some recent innovations.[17]

In fewer than 1,000 words, he gave clear voice to two different viewpoints, capturing the key points in the Anglican discussion and the feelings and perceptions found within and between provinces. His challenge summed up the Listening Process's vision: "If both were able to hear and to respond generously, perhaps we could have something more like a conversation of equals – even something more like a Church."

Creating the Anglican Communion Covenant

The idea of a 'covenant' between local Churches... seems to me the best way forward... There is no way in which the Anglican Communion can remain unchanged by what is happening at the moment. (June 2006)[18]

In addressing the Communion's longer-term health, the Windsor Report urged "the adoption by the churches of the Communion of a common Anglican Covenant which would make explicit and forceful the loyalty and bonds of affection which govern the relationships between the churches of the Communion" (para. 118). Rowan quickly signalled his support for this in his 2004 Advent letter. He would consistently and strongly commend it only to see it, like the moratoria, face concerted opposition and, most damaging of all, rejection by the Church of England.

A large part of the covenant's difficulties throughout was that it constantly got caught in the mutual suspicions, competing "solutions", and crossfire of the current conflicts. As Philip Giddings commented, "when you are having your first big row is not the time to make the rules you don't have but now need".[19] Responses to the covenant also made clear a deeper problem: very different and incompatible visions existed of "being a communion", as Rowan would acknowledge in his first presidential address at Lambeth.

A March 2006 report to the Joint Standing Committee set out what would remain the main areas of contention.[20] Opponents worried that any covenant would redefine the Communion into a "narrowly confessional family" and become "a test of authentic membership" threatening Anglican comprehensiveness. They feared it would create "a bureaucratic and legalistic foundation at the very heart of the Communion" with "a centralised jurisdiction" which would constrain "inspired and prophetic initiatives in God's mission". Supporters argued it would "clarify the identity and mission" of Communion churches by "articulating our ecclesiological identity" and help to re-establish "a fundamental basis of trust, co-operation and action" by making explicit the "house rules" to which people were accountable. It could help "develop a disciplined and fulfilling life in communion" and assist Anglican self-understanding and ecumenical relationships. In supporting the covenant's development, the report said it should be relational (assisting reconciliation), educational (offering a vision of being Anglican), and institutional ("providing what is currently lacking – an agreed framework for common discernment, and the prevention and resolution of conflict").

Rowan appointed a Covenant Design Group (CDG) during 2006 and it began work in January 2007. He had already set out more fully his vision for the covenant but his way of doing so fuelled divisions. Describing it as an "opt-in" commitment, his 2006 "Challenge and Hope" letter acknowledged that

> We could arrive at a situation where there were "constituent" Churches in covenant in the Anglican Communion and other "churches in association", which were still bound by historic and perhaps personal links, fed from many of the same sources, but not bound in a single and unrestricted sacramental communion, and not sharing the same constitutional structures.[21]

As the crisis reached its height in 2007 the covenant thus became seen – by supporters and opponents – as a possible way of structuring, perhaps even effecting, a measure of "walking apart". In his last-minute attempt to save the covenant in England, Rowan said:

> one of the greatest misunderstandings around concerning the Covenant is that it's some sort of centralising proposal creating an absolute authority which has the right to punish people for stepping out of line. I have to say I think this is completely misleading and false.[22]

That was, however, how it had come to be seen by many, rather than as a model of "consensual Catholicism".

Throughout the next two years the CDG produced three drafts in continuous consultation with the Communion. The covenant's basic structure remained constant: a set of affirmations and commitments in three sections relating to faith, mission, and common life. These appeared to gain widespread support but the recurring challenge was how to address actions thought incompatible with these affirmations and commitments. The final 2009 draft included a Section Four. This set out a process of requesting a halt to controversial actions and determining "relational consequences" if these requests were ignored, or action undertaken which was judged "incompatible with the covenant". Although not as strong as earlier drafts (losing the covenant support from more conservative Anglicans), this was controversial and, in a confused debate not helped by Rowan's intervention, ACC in 2009 sought more consultation. With minor amendments, the covenant was issued for provinces to consider adopting in December 2009. Rowan spoke once again in support, concluding:

> We hope… that many provinces will feel able to adopt this… that in the long run this will actually help us to become more of a communion – more responsible for each other, presenting to the world a face of mutual understanding, patience, charity and gratitude for one another. In other words, we hope and pray that the Covenant for the Anglican Communion will be a truly effective tool for witness and mission in our world.[23]

An international campaign was mounted against the covenant and its first major success was the Church of England, with the final killer blow being struck just after Rowan announced his retirement. It was clear some still thought only in terms of being a national church, not understanding what it meant to be part of a communion of churches. At the February 2009 General Synod, Rowan responded to a speaker who complained about the covenant "handing over to the communion rights of decision". He set out clearly his fundamentally different vision which explains so much of his action as archbishop and lay at the heart of the covenant:

I don't believe that a process of shared discernment is a handing over of something that belongs to me to someone to whom it doesn't belong, because I have a rather more, excuse the word, robust doctrine of our participation in the body of Christ than that. I don't believe that when I invite someone else to share my own process of prayer and decision making I'm resigning something which I ought to be clinging on to. I believe rather that I'm trying to discover more fully who I am in Christ by inviting others who share my life in Christ into the process of making a decision.[24]

For Rowan, a key to the covenant was accountability, another crucial concept in his understanding of the church. This was not accountability to a confessional document but rather "accountability to Jesus Christ in his body but also Jesus Christ beyond and calling his body". This means holding together the task of "trying to discover Jesus Christ in our fellowship with one another" with "learning together how to listen to the Jesus Christ who is not imprisoned in, or exhausted by, his body".

General Synod sent the covenant for consideration by diocesan synods during 2011–12. Suggestions were made to prepare the ground, educate those voting, or present the case for what was a major part of Rowan's legacy, but little of substance was done. Even when opponents won key votes, Rowan took some time before acting by producing a video explaining the covenant and urging backing for it. Despite this intervention, and the acknowledgment of the covenant's importance to Rowan, most dioceses rejected it (although more people voted for it than against it and the Church of England was effectively split down the middle).

As his primacy drew to a close this was a crisis and defeat for Rowan paralleling that of Reading as he began. In retrospect, it too could have been foreseen and probably prevented by earlier action. Its consequences for the Communion and the Church of England's role within it are potentially very serious. The place of the covenant in Rowan's legacy remains uncertain. It may gather support from most provinces and even be adopted by the Church of England in future, or it may prove another failed route out of the crisis. For Rowan, the covenant offered a rich vision of what it would mean to be a communion. If, following rejection by his own province the covenant is not widely accepted, then without having in place his main proposed means of preventing fragmentation, the cracks in the Communion are likely to widen and deepen.

Writing "Challenge and Hope" and Other Letters

The Archbishop of Canterbury presides and convenes in the Communion, and may do what this document attempts to do, which is to outline the theological framework in which a problem should be addressed. (June 2006)[25]

One of the features of Rowan's ministry in the Communion was his regular writing of public letters and reflections to fulfil his responsibility as focus of unity speaking for and to the Communion as a whole. Previous archbishops wrote letters to the primates, but Rowan, through their frequency, length, and depth, made this a much more significant part of Canterbury's service in and for the whole Communion. The most significant of these is undoubtedly his "The Challenge and Hope of Being an Anglican Today". Its subtitle "A Reflection for the Bishops, Clergy and Faithful of the Anglican Communion" shows it to be similar in form, though not authority, to a papal encyclical. Written after the response of ECUSA/TEC's General Convention to Windsor in 2006, it stands out as a major statement which interprets and responds to the crisis by articulating his vision of both being Anglican (discussed in the final chapter) and being a communion.

Rowan addressed the regularly raised question of the relationship between unity and truth and acknowledged that "witness to what is passionately believed to be the truth sometimes appears a higher value than unity". However, he highlighted the risks of this, arguing that "unity is generally a way of coming closer to revealed truth ('only the whole Church knows the whole Truth' as someone put it)". He rejected the idea of dissolving international relationships – the fractures are not just between provinces and we are bound deeply in various ways – and pointed out that "an isolated local Church is less than a complete Church" and "our unity is something given to us prior to our choices". The Anglican expression of this – "neither tightly centralised nor just a loose federation of essentially independent bodies" – is one Rowan consistently sought to preserve and nurture:

> The reason Anglicanism is worth bothering with is because it has tried to find a way of being a Church that is… seeking to be a coherent family of communities meeting to hear the Bible read, to break bread and share wine as guests of Jesus Christ, and to celebrate a unity in worldwide mission and ministry. That is what the word "Communion" means for Anglicans, and it is a vision that has taken clearer shape in many of our ecumenical dialogues… We have tried to be a family of Churches willing to learn from each other across cultural divides… a community trying to respond to the action and the invitation of God that is made real for us in ministry and Bible and sacraments… There is an identity here, however fragile and however provisional.[26]

A similar weighty reflection appeared three years later entitled "Communion, Covenant and our Anglican Future" and there were letters to the Primates of the Communion particularly at Advent but also at other points in the church year, notably his Pentecost 2010 letter.

These communications were very personal letters and reflections, written by the archbishop based on his listening to God and to the Communion; the secretary general would see them once written and before publication. In them Rowan offered leadership to the Communion through his teaching and interpretation of what he saw God doing and calling Anglicans to do in the Communion's common life, not least its conflicts and disagreements. They show his patient wrestling with the difficulties, his perseverance in advocacy for moratoria, listening, and the covenant, and his passionate and unswerving commitment to a vision of life together as a communion of churches within the body of Christ. Like his addresses to General Synod within the Church of England they combine biblical, historical, and theological depth with pastoral encouragement (and occasionally gentle rebuke), and a call to spiritual growth and maturity. Both in content and in form they represent a significant part of his legacy to the Communion.

10

Cracking Communion?
2. Lambeth, Indaba, and the Future

There are no quick solutions for the wounds of the Body of Christ. (April 2010)[1]

Lambeth Conferences, where the Archbishop of Canterbury gathers the bishops of the Communion together, traditionally occur every ten years and are a major part of any archbishop's legacy. The Conference's status was summed up by Rowan in his Advent letter to primates prior to the 2008 Conference:

> It is not a canonical tribunal, but neither is it merely
> a general consultation. It is a meeting of the chief
> pastors and teachers of the Communion, seeking
> an authoritative common voice. It is also a meeting
> designed to strengthen and deepen the sense of what the
> episcopal vocation is… I would insist that only in such
> a context can we usefully address divisive issues.[2]

This chapter describes Rowan's significant role at the 2008 Conference and how he then developed one of its key features – Indaba – into a major new initiative within the Communion. It then offers a concluding assessment of Rowan's legacy in the Anglican Communion.

Presiding at the Lambeth Conference 2008

The chief need of our Communion at the moment was the rebuilding of relationships – the rebuilding of trust in one another – and of confidence in our Anglican identity... I believe that the Conference succeeded in doing this to a very remarkable degree – more than most people expected. (August 2008)[3]

The Lambeth Conference over which Rowan presided in 2008 was, on a number of counts, significantly different from its predecessors. It was, however, not as different as originally expected when he took office. The early plans were to locate it in South Africa rather than England and combine the Conference with the less well-known and less frequent tradition of Anglican Congresses which would include clergy and laity. The international planning group, with hardly any "Northern" representation, began work in 2004 planning for such an event but it soon became clear it was not feasible. Rowan nevertheless insisted the same group continue the work and develop its mission-focused vision. As he wrote in his Advent 2005 letter, "The main focus I long to see at this Conference is the better equipping of bishops to fulfil their task as agents and enablers of mission, as co-workers with God's mission in Jesus Christ." Each year the group met three times for a whole week including a day with Rowan.

In March 2006, Rowan made clear that "I do not hear much enthusiasm for revisiting" the 1998 sexuality resolution and focused attention on "equipping the people of God". At this stage the most significant change had yet to occur as he assured the primates that although the conference would be different, "there will still of course be plenary sessions and resolutions". It was the St Augustine seminar in autumn 2006 that, in part through interaction with the Listening Process, changed this. Phil Groves recalls:

> I was asked to talk to them on homosexuality and
> how it could be handled at the Lambeth Conference.
> I spoke of listening and mutuality. I remember John
> Holder of Barbados and Terry Brown of Melanesia
> getting excited and the calm coolness of Bishop Thabo
> chairing the meeting. Kenyan delegates and those from
> India began to warm to the idea and suddenly I was
> aware they were talking about listening and the whole
> of the conference.[4]

At some point Bishop Thabo Makgoba from South Africa said the plans taking shape sounded like "indaba" (a Zulu word for what he described as "a gathering for purposeful discussion"). Thus was born the most distinctive feature of Lambeth 2008.

Unsurprisingly, given his own gifts and passion for listening, this shift was encouraged by Rowan. In the words of Colin Fletcher, a member of the Design Group:

> Whilst the idea for the "Indaba" framework came from
> the Group, it was Rowan who enabled it all to happen.
> Conversation, and reflection, is very much a part of
> where he is coming from, with all the possibilities and
> problems that brings in its wake.[5]

So, in issuing invitations in May 2007, Rowan spoke of being "hugely excited by the possibilities the programme offers for a new and more effective style of meeting and learning, and for greater participation, which will help us grow together locally and internationally".

The issuing of invitations was, however, politically contentious. Provinces routinely supply names of serving stipendery bishops in their province to the Anglican Communion Office, and that list provided the basis for invitations to the Lambeth Conference. Rowan reserved the right "to withhold or withdraw invitations from bishops whose appointment, actions or manner of life have caused exceptionally serious division or scandal within the Communion". He exercised this right in relation to a few bishops (including the Mugabe-supporting Bishop Kunonga in Harare). Among them, on the basis of the Windsor Report's strong advice, was Gene Robinson. It appears the names of "missionary bishops" were never submitted by their provinces, but if they had been they are unlikely to have been invited. Other controversial bishops received invitations, both those intervening and – upsetting conservatives – those who consecrated Gene Robinson or authorized same-sex blessings. Rowan did, however, make clear in his Advent 2007 letter that "acceptance of the invitation *must be taken as implying willingness to work with those aspects of the Conference's agenda that relate to implementing the recommendations of Windsor, including the development of a Covenant*" (italics original). He signalled his intention "to be in direct contact with those who have expressed unease about this, so as to try and clarify how deep their difficulties go with accepting or adopting the Conference's agenda". This apparently led to private exchanges with some American bishops and, in April 2008, Tom Wright referred to the Advent letter and publicly stated, on the highest authority, that "those letters, I understand, are in the post as we speak, written with apostolic pain and heart-searching but also with apostolic necessity". It appears, however, that they were never sent and there were no dis-invitations or withdrawals on this basis.

There were, however, withdrawals from several conservative provinces. Frustrated by the failure to implement Dar es Salaam, the weak response to the inadequate "clarifications" from ECUSA/TEC on moratoria, Rowan's rejection of a request to postpone the Conference, and the generous invitation list to Lambeth, their leaders announced at the end of 2007 they would organize a gathering in Jerusalem, known as GAFCON (Global Anglican Future Conference). This included lay and clergy members as well as bishops, most of whom did not then attend Lambeth. It, and its Jerusalem Declaration, rallied those most unhappy with ECUSA/TEC and Rowan's handling of the Communion crisis. Its launch meant that for a time the divisions among American conservatives were replicated among the Communion's conservative provinces represented by the Global South.

As a result of the divisions within the Communion and the launch of GAFCON, over 150 invited bishops (mainly from Africa) did not attend Lambeth 2008. The nearly 700 bishops who did attend experienced something quite different from previous Conferences. The heartbeat of the Conference was the small Bible study groups of eight bishops. These then merged to create the Indaba groups of up to forty bishops. They discussed ten topics over the two weeks, with a developing focus on mission but also engaging the divisive issues in the Communion's life. In contrast to previous conferences, there were few plenary addresses although Rowan gave five opening retreat addresses, three presidential addresses, and opening and closing sermons. Their magisterial quality and the lack of alternative voices led some to comment that it was the most papal of all Lambeth Conferences and it was only someone as clearly un-papal as

Rowan who could get away with it. Though having a grain of truth, Mark Langham recalls "Catholic delegates during difficult debates at the 2008 Lambeth Conference [were] amazed that Archbishop Rowan did not simply tell people what to do". Rowan's high profile was also not one he had sought or insisted upon. The vision was that of the Design Group and, as Ian Douglas recalls, Rowan was far from politically engineering this or pushing himself forward:

> Rowan believed we needed to begin with deep prayer.
> We in the Design Group interpreted that as retreat
> and we said "We really need a global Christian who
> is a leader of incredible integrity who can expound
> Scripture from the deep well of knowing and being in
> Christ. Who would that be?" It was obvious to us but
> it was so funny – and this is classic for Rowan – we all
> knew who it needed to be; we walked into the room at
> Lambeth and said "We have the perfect person". We
> set out the description and he looked at us and said
> "Right, yes, that's exactly who we need to get" and he
> was really on the edge of his seat as to who we came up
> with. Completely self-effacing and clueless. And we said,
> "Actually, it should be… the Archbishop of Canterbury".
> He was rather taken aback and I so remember his
> response. He said "I'll have to pray about that."[6]

Rowan's significance was further highlighted by the decision to abandon reports and resolutions expressing the mind of the bishops. In large part this was because the process of creating these was thought to disempower the majority of bishops and privilege those with English as a first language and used to parliamentary procedures. As Rowan made clear in his first presidential address, these Western and tightly procedural ways were not necessarily effective:

> this sort of method guaranteed that the voices most
> often heard would be the voices of people who were
> comfortable with this way of doing things; but what
> would it take to guarantee that everyone's voice has a
> chance of being heard?[7]

Instead of resolutions, a "Reflections" document was produced which sought to summarize the conversations in Indabas and other forums. Few claimed this was as valuable a document as past reports and resolutions. Many wished for something more concrete.

The primary fruit of the Conference was its effect on those attending. Rowan had said in his opening address that "The Conference seeks to build up a trustful community" and in his final address he emphasized the importance of what they took away from it:

> It is *your* work, your patient, lively, impatient, hopeful
> engagement with each other that has, by God's grace,
> brought us where we are... As you return, be bearers of
> good news to all your communities – above all, of the
> Good News of Our Lord's promise that where he is,
> there his servants will be. There is our unity, there is our
> hope, there is the gift we have celebrated and, I trust,
> rediscovered in our time together.[8]

Rowan's presidency won near-universal acclaim from those attending. Despite the absences and the desire of some for more definite outcomes, the Conference was a major success for which the archbishop rightly gained much of the credit, although some were disappointed he did not then build on that as well as he might in the period which followed. It did, however, highlight how precarious things remained and the difficult legacy left for his successor, as Tom Wright observed:

> The 2008 Lambeth Conference showed that three of the "instruments" that are supposed to unite the Communion (the Anglican Consultative Council, the Primates' Meeting, and the Lambeth Conference itself) aren't working well. Only the fourth one, the Archbishop himself, held things together, giving powerful addresses and inspiring personal loyalty. It may not be possible, and it certainly isn't desirable, for a successor to rely on doing the same.[9]

In the longer term, whether and how the next Lambeth Conference will return to articulating a common mind, and whether or how it can address divisive issues of sexuality, remains a major question for his successor. Part of what will shape the answer is the final key element in Rowan's oversight of the Communion – the Continuing Indaba Project.

Supporting the Continuing Indaba Project

We can point to the methods currently being developed in the "Continuing Indaba" project, with its success in creating many such spaces for face-to- face discussion across cultures. This project, which is considering a wide range of actually and potentially divisive matters, has been pursued with heroic energy and imagination by many people of profoundly diverse convictions in the Communion and needs prayer and support. (November 2010)[10]

In 2007, with the cracks becoming wider and the Lambeth Conference approaching, Rowan took the bold step of commissioning research on how best to take an initiative to move matters forward in the Communion and address the problems. A proposal was developed in April 2008 building on the methodology of the National Consensus Process (NCP) on Sexuality and Sexual Health in the US. This was then revised in the light of the Indaba experience at Lambeth. It was announced at ACC in May 2009 that funding had been secured from the Morehouse School of Medicine for the Continuing Indaba Project (CIP) with Phil Groves as Project Director.

CIP became an unprecedented international experiment in mutual listening and dialogue across cultural and theological difference with the aim of intensifying relationships across the Communion so genuine conversation can take place across difference in order to foster energy for mission that is both global and local. Its structure and method were shaped predominantly by what had been learnt from the Listening Process, the Lambeth Indaba, and Groves' doctoral work (on partnership in Paul's letter to the Philippians and the Communion's recent history, particularly the vision of Mutual Responsibility and Interdependence). Another key element in the design was the experience of Cecelia Clegg who had been involved in the Northern Ireland peace process.

Between 2009 and 2012 a pilot project was developed in which four groups were established (the most politically difficult grouping including dioceses from the Southern Cone and ECUSA/TEC did not progress). Each involved three dioceses whose teams of eight participants formed a group of twenty-four people committed to journey together over a year by hosting each other in their dioceses for a week and then participating over three days in a final, externally facilitated Indaba conversation. The groups included an all-Africa trio (from South Africa, Ghana, and Kenya), a partnership established after Lambeth 2008 involving Gloucester, El Camino Real, and

Western Tanganyika, another also comprising dioceses from the UK (Derby), US (New York), and the Global South (Mumbai), and one bringing together three postcolonial contexts (Canada, Hong Kong, and Jamaica). Rather than focus on areas of contention, the framing issue was mission and the bishops of the three partnered dioceses identified areas of common concern in the light of this. Alongside this a number of resource centres ("hubs") were established across the Communion to produce theological and practical material for Indaba, drawing on different cultural contexts and perspectives. These were published online and as *Creating Space*.

The visits and final conversations were a great success for those involved and offered a marked contrast to the image of contention and fracture associated with meetings of the Instruments during Rowan's time. They built relationships between Anglicans across the Communion within which listening and conversation deepened and developed, with all final conversations discussing (though not seeking any consensus on) difficult subjects including sexuality. The Indaba approach has also spread into different dioceses and provinces as a better way of working and deliberating together.

It remains to be seen what long-term impact CIP and its vision and approach of conflict transformation could have on the Communion. The Indaba style was introduced into the 2011 Primates' Meeting facilitated by Cecelia Clegg and was appreciated but, as at Lambeth, those Communion leaders most unhappy with Rowan's handling of the conflict stayed away. Although its future remains unclear now the initial funding has ended, the initiative could prove to be a major part of Rowan's legacy to the Communion. It has some similarities with Fresh Expressions, his main legacy in England: an initiative begun outside the main structures, with the support of Rowan but working "bottom-up" rather than "top-down" or, to change the topography, drawing on the edges to change the centre; it focused on mission and relationships and drawing in committed people on the ground rather than relying on established structures and their leaders.

What remains to be seen is how CIP will relate to the work of the established Instruments (widely agreed to be in need of urgent reform) and whether it can develop so as to go beyond encounter, listening, and conversation to enable the formation of a common mind and the reaching of decisions on contentious issues which, even if they cannot heal existing divisions, might prevent the Communion from breaking apart further.

Rowan's Communion Legacy

There can be no dispute that, as Rowan predicted, the Communion is more obviously "messy" as he leaves office than when he was appointed. One of his clear strengths is his ability to live with such mess but what is less clear is the extent to which he is responsible. The problems clearly were not generated by him but presented to him by others. One senior Church of England bishop comments:

> In assessing Rowan's ministry I think we have to be realistic about the extraordinary adverse situation in which he found himself. To use a slightly farfetched metaphor, in the Roman Empire a General of whatever brilliance in the first decade of the 5th century AD would at best go down as a glorious failure, whereas a much less talented leader could have conquered nations towards the beginning of the 2nd century AD.

Rowan's major weakness was, the bishop ironically continues, "an incapacity to work the miracle of changing the attitudes of so many people who were determined to wreck whatever good initiatives were put forward".[11] His major strengths were his refusal to impose his own views and his perseverance with such initiatives and graciousness under pressure in the face of these difficulties. He has acted in the Communion much like the abbot is called to do in the Rule of St Benedict, which he himself summed up in these words:

> Obedience for the monk is the practice of constantly being ready to suspend a purely individual will or perception for the sake of discovering God's will in the common life of the community... The abbot has to discern the needs and the common calling of the community... has to listen and attend with intense concentration to the specific requirements and gifts of the individual members of the community (chapter 2.31–2). The one to whom obedience is due is one who is called to exemplary obedience to the Rule itself (65) but also to a sort of "obedience" to every brother. If obedience is the silencing of the purely individual will, the abbot must above all be a model of this silencing, someone who will not pursue an individual agenda but seek the immense, elusive goal of a common life in which each can recognise their good and their flourishing in the life they share and their mutual dependence.[12]

Two interviews in March 2006 capture what drove his leadership. Talking to David Frost in Sudan, he reflected:

> I can try, I think, to find ways, as long as possible, of getting these two sides to make sense of themselves

to each other. The biggest problem is people don't listen very much. That's... human nature, and the Church is no exception... Now the point may come where people say "well we no longer have enough in common" and we may reach that point – I don't know. Meanwhile, my first priority is to try and keep the conversation going, to say "do you understand why this matters?"... I suppose my anxiety about it is that if the Communion is broken we may be left with even less than a federation... And there will have to be an awful lot of bridge-building; it would take absolutely decades to restore some sort of relationship there.[13]

Asked later that month, "Can you hold all this together, realistically? And is there a point where it is better to admit you can't?" he replied,

I can only say that I think I've got to try... I'd rather try and see what can be done to recreate or reinforce trust. And I think it's worth doing, because the Anglican Communion as a multicultural, an international body, is, I dare to say, more important, more significant than an Anglican Communion fracturing along... cultural lines... Coming back from Sudan, that's clearly much underlined for me, it matters a lot to a Church in vulnerable situations, to have partners elsewhere... There might come a moment where you say we can't continue, we can't continue with this? I don't know when or if.[14]

To allow innovations on sexuality to continue unchallenged was not a realistic option for Rowan. It would have fractured the Communion and probably the Church of England. The more serious question is whether, despite the rhetoric, Rowan has, in practice, effectively left the innovations unchallenged. Once it became clear the requests for moratoria were not being heeded, rather than use his moral authority as archbishop to develop the logic of his approach and the Windsor vision, he allowed business to continue much as usual, despite the decisions reached and commitments made in the Instruments. The main alternative would have been at some point to undertake what Michael Scott-Joynt, Bishop of Winchester, called for in 2008 in terms of "a negotiated 'orderly separation' as the best and most fruitful way forward for the Anglican Communion".

That would, of course, have been to admit defeat and embrace a "second best" solution, and Rowan never reached that point. The question is whether, and for how long, his successor can avoid doing so, given the reality he faces. He inherits a situation where Rowan has sown many seeds for the Communion's medium- to long-term flourishing by developing new positive approaches to communion, notably the Anglican Communion Covenant, a relationship-building Lambeth, and the CIP. However, the failures of the moratoria and existing Instruments remain largely unaddressed, the Covenant has divided Anglicans as much as united them and been defeated in the Church of England, and Continuing Indaba is still in its early stages of development and implementation. New ways therefore need to be found to address the wounds of the body of Christ for which there are no quick solutions and the words Rowan used shortly after taking office remain as true as ever: "the question is not whether we can avoid mess, but whether we can hang on to common convictions about divine grace and initiative".

11

Anglicanism and Other Churches

If the Good News of Jesus Christ is to be fully proclaimed to a needy world, then the reconciliation of all Christians in the truth and love of God is a vital element for our witness. I say this, conscious that the path to unity is not an easy one. (November 2006)[1]

Having traced and assessed Rowan's ministry within Anglicanism, this chapter widens out and turns to his work with other Christian churches, those with whom Anglicans are one in Christ through faith and baptism but from whom they are divided institutionally. The following chapter widens the vision even further to look at his engagement with those of other faith communities who share the image of the one God. Each chapter summarizes the teaching Rowan has given to guide the church as it faces new challenges and explores key features of his practice and lasting legacy.

Many of the characteristics already identified are hallmarks of his primacy and his legacy in these two arenas: a teaching ministry focused on the centrality of Christ and the priority of mission; the catholicity of the church in and through which Christ is present to us; and the importance of generous listening and honest conversation which seeks to acknowledge common ground, be open to challenge, and engage respectfully across differences.

A Vision for Ecumenism

Rowan brought to his ministry with other churches a respect for and deep knowledge of the breadth of Christian tradition. This is evident throughout his writing from his earliest book, *The Wound of Knowledge*. Prior to Canterbury, his writing specifically on ecclesiology and ecumenism was not a significant part of his academic output, but he had engaged in depth with key thinkers from across the breadth of the church both in the modern period and through the centuries. This meant that as an Anglican he could understand and engage sympathetically with Roman Catholics, the Orthodox, and the other churches of the Reformation.

Two key elements within his understanding of the church also helped shape his approach. First, as discussed in relation to Fresh Expressions, there is his Christocentric focus which emphasizes the priority of the action of God rather than human decisions and collaborations. Second, and flowing from this, the primary truth – despite the obvious divisions – is the unity of the church, a unity which is the gift of God through our union with Christ. The combination of these two truths means that the ecumenical task is not to be understood in terms of us creating unity or securing agreements through our activity. It is rather walking the path of discernment together, learning to recognize Christ in one another across the divisions that wound his body. As a result, Rowan's emphasis is on what Mary Tanner calls "the qualitative life before the institutional and structural". His approach to building relationships across historic divides was also helped by his ability to live with mess within the life of the church and by his commitment to enable different traditions within a community to maintain connection and conversation with each other.

Such emphases could result in downplaying the goal of full, visible unity, but Rowan was clear that he had not abandoned this. When asked by Vatican Radio in November 2010 whether "many in the Protestant world have settled for a mutual recognition of each others' differences, a unity in diversity kind of solution which smacks of relativism", his reply was clear:

> I think it's perfectly proper to think of our goal as unity in diversity but not a diversity as endless multiplication of institutions. I still think we have to pray for visible sacramental communion, the recognition of ministries, the ability to function intelligibly as one body across the globe.[2]

Rowan's fullest account of his vision of unity among Christian churches is found in an address that same month at a conference to commemorate the fiftieth anniversary of the Pontifical Council for Promoting Christian Unity (PCPCU).[3] He began by offering three New Testament dimensions of the unity God desires. These apply beyond the church to God's intended destiny for humanity as a whole, reflecting how the church in his theology shows all humanity what it is called to be. The three dimensions are:

- unity in Jesus Christ with God the Father and so unity with Jesus' prayer and action;

- unity with one another in the body of Christ, which is a

dynamic upbuilding in holiness through communion; and

• unity with the witness of the apostles.

These mean that the visible concrete life of the church must express and realize who we are in Christ (leading to the centrality of the Eucharist and prayer more widely), mutual and outward-looking service, and continuity with the apostolic witness to cross and resurrection. This last requires a ministry "recognisable throughout all communities of belief" and "held to account for its transmission of the apostolic truth by the agreed doctrinal discernment of the whole body".

In relation to ecumenical dialogue, his threefold understanding points to areas where there has been progress in conversations between churches: the importance of baptism as sacramental entry into Christ's life and the shared search for holiness and mutual service. But it also highlights the continued differences over ministry and securing faithful transmission of the apostles' witness. Rowan is clear that these cannot be ignored but require "some self-searching or self-questioning theological work". He concluded by proposing two focal points for future ecumenical theology – "a shared discussion of eucharistic theology across a number of confessional groups" and, with reference to the claims of papal primacy, "the need to clarify what is the service that can and should be given to an apostolic church by the petrine ministry".

Rowan's practical commitment to building relationships between Anglicans and other Christian denominations has already been signalled. One of the hallmarks of his Fresh Expressions initiative has been its ecumenical nature. In relation to Church of England debates on women bishops, he not only invited Cardinal Kasper to address the English bishops but has reminded the church of the ecumenical cost that will have to be borne. One of his motivations in keeping the Communion together and supporting the covenant has undoubtedly been the ecumenical dimension. Cardinal Kasper's response to the Windsor Report was significant in its recognition that "this approach is fundamentally in line with the communion ecclesiology of the Second Vatican Council" and

> the core recommendations of the Report would have
> a positive ecumenical impact… it would provide for
> a greater coherence within Anglicanism, allowing an
> enhancement of our understanding of the Anglican
> Communion precisely as a communion. For the
> continuation of our ecumenical dialogue, it is
> important for us to have a clear understanding of who
> our partner is.[4]

The Church of England and British Churches

Within England, Rowan continued to work alongside other Christian leaders in various forums, particularly as one of the presidents of Churches Together in England. Among his first ecumenical actions after his enthronement was signing a personal covenant between the presidents, while his sermon in 2009 (during the Week of Prayer for Christian Unity) at Cardinal Murphy O'Connor's last service as a co-president opened with words revealing the core of his ecumenical vision:

> The heart of our search for unity is very simply the
> search for that silence where we are able together to hear
> the voice of Jesus. As we come together as Christians,
> we open our hearts and our minds so that we may
> listen for Jesus. We try to listen for Jesus in one another,
> to hear what Jesus Christ is saying to us through the
> mouth of a stranger, somebody with another loyalty,

another theology. We seek together, in silence, to hear
the word of God, in Scripture, in the voice of God's
people throughout the ages. And we pray that when we
are at last silent enough, free enough, patient enough,
loving enough, we shall hear his voice. Then, and only
then, there will be one flock and one shepherd.[5]

In addition to shared silence, Rowan also participated in shared
speech, issuing joint statements with other Christian leaders
on a number of important issues including the Iraq war, the
environment, and global poverty.

For the Church of England's relationship with other English
churches, two events are of particular note during Rowan's primacy
and relate to past divisions within Anglicanism. One of these
historic splits led to the birth of the Methodist Church. A great
tragedy for Michael Ramsey (Rowan's joint favourite archbishop
alongside Anselm) was the failure of a proposed union with the
Methodists. For Rowan, this was a relationship where a proposed
covenant did succeed. On 1 November 2003, he was one of the
signatories of the Anglican–Methodist covenant comprising
joint affirmations and commitments which continued to shape
relationships between the two churches in England throughout
his time in office. His sermon at the ceremony reflected on
"how the providence of God works in and through even our
divisions" and noted how, in the midst of Anglican divisions, the
celebration of closer relationships was timely:

It is a reminder that when we can no longer see
how to hold together, God will still teach us in our
separateness; and one day we shall be led, in both
thankfulness and repentance, to share with one another
what we have learned apart; to bring to one another a
history not without its shadows and stresses, but still

one in which something quite distinctive has been learned. And if all God's gifts are given to be shared, we have no option finally but to offer them to each other in reconciliation.[6]

At the other end of his primacy, in 2011, another significant event was when the General Synod and the URC agreed a joint report entitled "Healing the Past, Building the Future". The following year marked the 40th anniversary of the founding of the United Reformed Church and the 350th anniversary of the Great Ejection, which had seen 2,000 non-conforming ministers leave the Church of England following the 1662 Act of Uniformity. A powerful joint service of reconciliation and commitment was held at which Rowan preached. Stressing the need for Christian faith to grow and mature he celebrated the questioning and challenging offered by the Dissenting tradition within England. He then drew attention to a neglected feature of the church's divisions within much ecumenical thought and activity:

We have to take a deep breath and expect to be challenged by one another. We have to assume that our discoveries will sometimes be painful and that they will not be without rupture and misunderstanding. But we have to trust the irresistible pressure – and I use the word "irresistible" in deliberate genuflection toward John Calvin here – within us of Christ seeking to be mature in us. That is what we celebrate in and through any number of conflicts, ruptures and tensions.[7]

Alongside participating in these important acts of reconciliation, recognition of Rowan's stature in other churches led to him being invited to address a wide range of gatherings from leaders of charismatic house churches (who were particularly excited by his commitment to Fresh Expressions) to the Methodist Conference (in 2004 and 2010) and the Church of Scotland's General Assembly (2012). Through his contributions on such occasions the influence of his theological vision of the church and in particular its call to mission has spread much wider than the Church of England.

Finally, within England, a further significant part of Rowan's ecumenical legacy is in relation to the many vibrant Pentecostal and black majority and ethnic churches. Leading up to the 200th anniversary commemorations in 2007 of the abolition of slavery, Rowan made building relations with black majority churches one of the priorities for his ecumenical ministry in England. He gathered black church leaders together at Lambeth Palace in 2008 and 2010. As a result of this initiative, the presidents of Churches Together in England now aim to meet annually with the leaders of Pentecostal and black majority and ethnic churches as they did in autumn 2011 at Jesus House, Brent Cross, one of the largest congregations of the Redeemed Christian Church of God. In a speech at General Synod in July 2012, Rowan spoke of "ongoing liaison with the black-led and black-majority churches in this country" as "already a serious priority for the CCU [Council for Christian Unity] and for Lambeth Palace", and his ministry in this area has contributed to the steady increase in recognition of the importance of these churches by the Church of England and other historic churches.

Anglicans and International Ecumenism

Although Rowan's ecumenical relationships within Britain have been important, it is within the global church that he has been particularly prominent, firmly establishing the office of Archbishop of Canterbury as one of international leadership within the church. Bishop Geoffrey Rowell emphasizes that "there are only three people in the Christian world who by virtue of office have a global ministry – the Pope, the Ecumenical Patriarch and the Archbishop of Canterbury",[8] and Kenneth Kearon, acknowledging the international ministry of earlier archbishops, suggests that Rowan

> reinvented the role in a way that made it comparable to the papacy or the Ecumenical Patriarch but completely different and decidedly Anglican. It's noticeable the extent to which many of the Reformed churches now look to the Archbishop of Canterbury for the sort of global religious leadership that they don't have. The notion that one person could embody, represent and speak for Anglicanism is something that I think the other Reformed churches feel in a sense also speaks for them because Rowan has spoken a very authentic Christian voice… That sort of figurehead outlines the way the Archbishopric of Canterbury could develop in the future.[9]

In addition to his part in proceedings of the World Council of Churches (WCC), including an important plenary address on Christian Identity in 2006 at the ninth meeting of the WCC Assembly in Brazil, three relationships particularly stand out in assessing Rowan's work with other churches on the world stage with the attention here focusing on Rome.

First, he has built good relationships with, and been warmly received by, Lutherans. The Church of England has a strong relationship with them through both Meissen (with the EKD, the German Protestant Church) and Porvoo (with Scandinavian and Baltic Lutherans), and Rowan's important 2004 lecture on Michael Ramsey as a "Lutheran Catholic" captures much of importance in his own thinking, including his debt to Luther who "witnesses to a Church that is truly an organic unity, created by the act of God in Christ; even more significantly, he is absolutely clear about the centrality of the cross in the Church". An even stronger Lutheran influence on Rowan is Dietrich Bonhoeffer at whose centenary celebrations in Germany in 2006 he was invited to play a major role. Four years later, he gave the keynote address at the Eleventh Assembly of the Lutheran World Federation, its highest decision-making body, offering reflections on "Give us this day our daily bread". Although in some ways his own theological emphases are closer to the East and to Rome, his ministry has strengthened and deepened Anglican bonds with Lutherans and other churches of the Reformation.

Second, and of particular significance for Rowan, has been the deepening during his primacy of Anglican relationships with the Orthodox churches. Their tradition so decisively shaped his own theology and spirituality that he has even said that "pretty well every useful thought I have ever had on Christian unity has derived from my studies of Orthodox theology – Orthodox theology rooted in the Fathers. Orthodox theology breaks the terms of western debate and brings it to a different theological level". The personal relationships, nurtured by visits to the Ecumenical Patriarch of Constantinople (in 2003 and 2009) and hosting him at Lambeth in 2007, were clearly strong, but the most significant lasting legacy of this particular ecumenical relationship is the Cyprus Agreed Statement, "The Church of the Triune God". This was issued in 2007 by the International Commission for the Anglican–Orthodox Theological Dialogue (ICAOTD), a Commission on which Rowan himself served from 1989 until 2003 as it worked on the subject of the report. It is the most significant agreed ecumenical statement during Rowan's primacy and one in which he personally had a major role.

As Rowan explained to Synod, at the heart of the landmark

report is the conviction that the doctrine of the Trinity as existing in relation "dictates and shapes everything we say about the Church and indeed about everything else".[10] The church is "to be a manifestation of God's life, a life in communion" as acting in interdependence is fundamental. Salvation is about restored relationship as God's life in communion is translated into human life and we experience "a diversity brought together in reconciliation". The report relates this theological and relational vision to areas of contention between the churches such as the ordained ministry in the light of a "sense of convergence on a vision of the Church which is fundamentally about God being the way that God is, (and) salvation being what it is because of the way God is, and all the structures and practices of the Church, likewise, being what they are because of God".

Third, there is Canterbury's relationship with Rome. In contrast to the warmly received fruit of the Anglican–Orthodox Dialogue, the formal Anglican–Roman Catholic dialogue (ARCIC) struggled through most of Rowan's primacy. Following its first phase of work (1970–81), its second phase had begun in 1983 and ran until 2005. Its 1999 report *The Gift of Authority* addressed issues relating to authority in the church including the papacy as a universal Petrine ministry for the whole church. It was not debated in General Synod until 2004 when, as archbishop, Rowan welcomed it but also raised questions. He appreciated its model of authority as gift and emphasis on communal discernment but pointed to further work needing to be done about the language of "infallibility" with its legal frame and focus on facts. He would rather ask "how does a trustworthy structure steer and co-ordinate discernment in the church overall". He also called for further work on the relationship between the universal and local church as Anglicans emphasize the local generating the universal through common action rather than the universal preceding the local.

Rowan's concerns were captured in an interview before he visited Pope Benedict in which he was asked why he was an Anglican not a Roman Catholic and replied:

I don't believe the essential theological structure of the Church is pyramidal: that it has one absolute touchstone embodied in a single office. I'm certainly prepared to believe that there's a role for the Petrine ministry of conciliation, interpretation, and mediation in the Church. I don't see that as an executive centre; so I'd start from what would historically be called a conciliarist position. And the thing that always held me back from becoming a Roman Catholic at the points when I thought about it is that I can't quite swallow papal infallibility. I have visions of saying to Pope Benedict: "I don't believe you're infallible" – I hope it doesn't come to that. [Laughs][11]

Unsurprisingly, the more Protestant elements within the Church of England were even more cautious about this particular ARCIC report. The same was true of the next report – *Mary: Grace and Hope in Christ* – issued in 2005. Many felt this failed to do justice to concerns among Anglicans about Rome's teaching and practice in relation to Mary. By the time of its release ARCIC was also a victim of the Communion's divisions over sexuality. The Anglican co-chair was the presiding bishop of ECUSA/TEC, but he resigned in 2003 following his consecration of Gene Robinson. When the second phase came to an end, Rome took considerable time to agree a further phase for ARCIC, which did not start until May 2011.

Securing agreement on a new phase – to consider issues of the relationship between the local and the universal church especially in relation to discernment on ethical issues – was a major success for Rowan after seeing ARCIC in abeyance for most of his primacy, although the International Anglican–Roman Catholic Commission for Unity and Mission (IARCCUM) continued its work and produced the important "Growing Together in Unity and Mission", which gathered together the conclusions of four decades of conversations.

A further complicating factor in relations with Rome appeared on the scene in October 2009. The Congregation for the Doctrine of the Faith (CDF) within the Vatican issued an apostolic constitution (entitled *Anglicanorum Coetibus*) which established a new structure – the Ordinariate – to welcome Anglicans into full communion with Rome. This was interpreted by many as an aggressive move against the ecumenical spirit. Its origins were twofold. For some time, there had been requests for some new structure for Anglicans wishing to join the Roman Catholic Church from a body called the Traditional Anglican Communion (which is unconnected to the Anglican Communion and not in communion with the Archbishop of Canterbury). Traditionalist Anglo-Catholics in England were also concerned that the move towards women bishops would also make it impossible for them to remain Anglicans and so began talks with the Vatican. As one of their leaders, Bishop Andrew Burnham, comments "clearly an ecclesiological crisis was brewing for Anglo-Catholics, a crisis which Archbishop Rowan well understood".[12]

In March 2008, with Rowan's knowledge, Andrew Burnham and another "flying bishop" visited Rome and had high-level talks with both the CDF and the Pontifical Council for Promoting Christian Unity (PCPCU). The latter only dealt with whole denominations but the former, whose remit includes dealing with anyone seeking to embrace the Roman Catholic faith, said it was sympathetic to the notion of *groups* of Anglicans being reconciled with the Roman Catholic Church and promised to work further on this. Others – including Cardinal Kasper at the

PCPCU and the Archbishop of Westminster, Cardinal Murphy O'Connor – were more cautious about new structures and were kept in the dark as the CDF pressed ahead. Through 2008 and 2009 other conversations were taking place. These included highly confidential meetings involving a number of serving diocesan bishops within England, some of whose concerns were more about Anglican disarray over homosexuality than the imminence of women bishops.

As Vatican plans came to a head, Rowan knew a few weeks in advance that something was likely to be announced. He was not, however, made fully aware of its significance until he met with Cardinal Levada, the head of the CDF, who was on his way to inform the Catholic Bishops of England and Wales (equally in the dark) about the Pope's new initiative to be announced the following day. This was one very rare occasion when Rowan expressed his anger to colleagues about what was being done. Although he "agreed to make" (as he wrote to the primates) a public joint statement with the Archbishop of Westminster it was clearly a very uncomfortable situation. When George Pitcher asked him about it two months later, he declined to comment on whether the Pope had apologized when they met shortly after the announcement ("private conversation, I think"), although it is understood that Cardinal Kasper did phone Rowan to apologize, and Pitcher reported,

> he does concede that the hastily convened press conference, at which he sat uncomfortably alongside the Roman Catholic Archbishop of Westminster, Vincent Nichols, was a big mistake. "I think everyone on the platform was a bit uncomfortable... I know the Congregation for the Doctrine of the Faith on the whole doesn't go in for much consultation – we were just on the receiving end of that."[13]

Rowan's typically gracious response continued to be evident when two "flying bishops" left to join the Ordinariate. One of them, Andrew Burnham, comments:

> I have no idea whether Rowan regards us as blackguards and villains or dreamy fools. He might even think well of us for doing something radical and well outside the normal comfort zones rather than joining the comfy armchair chorus of conventional ecumenical aspiration.[14]

The initial signs are that although providing a way forward for some Anglicans, the Ordinariate is unlikely to have a major impact in England or the wider Communion and that Rowan was wise not to react but to stress continuing to build cordial ecumenical relationships.

Despite these struggles and setbacks, in many ways Anglican–Roman Catholic relationships have continued to flourish. This owes a lot to the fact that Rowan's successor inherits a very strong relationship between the Archbishop of Canterbury and the Pope.

For Rowan's enthronement, Pope John Paul II sent him a pectoral cross signalling that (despite the formal legal position) he did not consider him a lay person. Such symbolic acts have been important throughout recent decades of relationships and they grew during Rowan's primacy, aided by his own more catholic spirituality. On his first visit to the Vatican in October 2003, his first ever visit to Rome, he knelt before Pope John Paul II and kissed his ring only for the Pope to in turn kiss the archbishop's ring (originally given to Michael Ramsey by Pope Paul VI). His Greeting included the statement that "here at the Chair of Peter, from which Augustine was sent to be the first Archbishop of Canterbury, I am glad to reaffirm my commitment to the full, visible unity of the Church of Christ".

Rowan was accompanied by Geoffrey Rowell, Bishop in Europe, who had insisted he must visit the Scavi – the excavations below the Vatican Basilica – and recalls:

> We went straight from the audience with John Paul and went right down for a private tour of the Scavi… We were taken round the other side of the red wall and there was a perspex screen which they opened up and there were the relics of Peter. If I'd had a camera… Rowan kneeling at the bones of Peter. Very, very moving. And then we were all allowed in. There *is* a special relationship.[15]

His first major visit to Pope Benedict in November 2006 was the occasion for one of his most significant lectures – on St Benedict and the future of Europe. Christopher Wells, who was present, highlights its importance:

> That he chose Benedict's Rule as a common, old text to lift up publicly for his first meeting with *Pope* Benedict evinced a graciousness not lost on his hosts. And the talk itself went over wonderfully to a packed house of Roman Catholic dignitaries and religious, not least as Rowan's extraordinary erudition came to the fore in the wide-ranging q&a following. Cardinal Kasper was sitting in the front row grinning from ear to ear for the duration.[16]

An ecumenical celebration of vespers with the Community of Sant'Egidio the following day memorialized the Anglican martyrs of Melanesia, seven religious murdered as they worked for peace in the midst of civil war in the Solomon Islands. Wells recalls that "finding Christian unity now in a common martyrology was one of the most profound experiences of my life, and I know meant a great deal to Rowan".[17]

Marking forty years since Michael Ramsey's historic first visit to Rome, a Common Declaration was issued. This highlighted "a process of fruitful dialogue, which has been marked by the discovery of significant elements of shared faith and a desire to give expression, through joint prayer, witness and service, to that which we hold in common". It had, though, to acknowledge "the challenge represented by new developments which, besides being divisive for Anglicans, present serious obstacles to our ecumenical progress" while "renewing our commitment to pursue the path towards full visible communion in the truth and love of Christ". In addressing what the declaration called "the emerging ecclesiological and ethical factors making that journey more difficult and arduous" Rowan used his good relationship to raise challenging questions of Rome, notably in his November 2009 lecture at the Gregorian University. With explicit reference to the Vatican's strong opposition to women's ordination he asked, "when so very much agreement has been firmly established in first-order matters about the identity and mission of the Church, is it really justifiable to treat other issues as equally vital for its health and integrity?"

The following year saw the Pope's visit to England, further strengthening the relationship and including worship together during the first papal visit to Westminster Abbey. Mark Langham of the PCPCU points to the importance of this and other events during that visit:

> I was at Lambeth Palace in 2010 as Anglican and Catholic Bishops together recited the Lord's Prayer in the presence of the Pope and the Archbishop. Reaching the Doxology, everyone stopped: it was Pope Benedict who continued, "*For thine is the Kingdom, the Power and*

the Glory..." A gesture of courtesy and thoughtfulness that did more than several pages of speeches to move the ecumenical agenda forward. That memorable visit also yielded images of the Pope and archbishop kneeling together in prayer, blessing together, easy in each other's company. These are not insubstantial moments; they provide a broader context for difficult questions. They lift the spirits of those whose ecumenical task is otherwise daunting. As Pope Benedict said during the recent visit, his presence together with the archbishop at the Basilica of San Gregorio is a reminder *and a stimulus* to Catholics and Anglicans to renew their commitment to unity.[18]

A further sign of the advances made by Rowan as archbishop was the honour of being the first Archbishop of Canterbury to be invited to address the Synod of Bishops when it met in Rome in October 2012 and marked the fiftieth anniversary of the Second Vatican Council. He spoke on contemplation and evangelization, stressing that Christians "have a distinctive human destiny to show and share with the world".

Rowan's legacy here is therefore much stronger than would appear from focusing on ARCIC or the Ordinariate but, even more than in other areas, it is also highly personal. He clearly built a good relationship with Pope Benedict who, going to Naples for a conference where Rowan was involved, remarked, "I am going to see my friend, Rowan." Rowan has described how in their meetings

what we tend to talk about... is really just the question of the Mission of the Church in Europe, the common challenges we face in Europe, how to present the Gospel of Jesus Christ more effectively, and we also like to talk a bit about theology as we're both former professors and we like to go back to that from time to time.[19]

Part of the personal chemistry is rooted in that shared academic background and interests. Rowan explained, before his first visit, how he hoped to talk theology given they shared much common ground:

> We both have a fairly solid formation in Patristics, and he did his research on Augustine; so at least we have Augustine to talk about. We both have a critical but none the less quite enthusiastic acquaintance with Hans Urs von Balthasar's theology… I think there's what you might call a broadly classical and sacramental theological perspective, shaped very much by mid-century, just-pre-Vatican II French and German thinking.[20]

In addition to lacking such theological common ground, his successor may be less comfortable with some of the precedents of shared practice introduced by Rowan. His pilgrimage to, and sermon at, an international Mass at the shrine of Our Lady at Lourdes was the first visit there by an Archbishop of Canterbury. It clearly reflected the place of Mary in his own spirituality and that of the bishops who went with him, but this is a spirituality which many Anglicans would not share. Mark Langham also describes how "the request of the Archbishop of Canterbury to pray with the Pope before the Blessed Sacrament at San Gregorio earlier this month caused astonishment to some who had naturally assumed that this sort of thing did not go on in the Anglican Communion". Comedian, and Roman Catholic, Frank Skinner, in conversation with Rowan was also astonished, hearing him describing taking Anglicans on pilgrimage to Jerusalem and seeing them crossing themselves and kissing things:

> Frank Skinner: Were you OK with that?
>
> Archbishop: Yes, one hundred percent.
>
> FS: I thought you'd have been rapping knuckles. You people are OK with idolatry now are you? Maybe it's time we got back together Your Grace, what do you say?
>
> ABC: Will you write to the Pope or shall I?
>
> FS: I'll text him.
>
> ABC: There isn't a live Twitter feed this evening is there?[21]

Conclusion

"Getting back together" with Rome is still a long way off but here, as in his other ecumenical relationships, Rowan's personal qualities, his respect for the diversity of expressions of the Christian faith and his catholic breadth of understanding have enhanced the standing of his office and strengthened Anglican bonds with a wide range of other churches.

12

Anglicanism and Other Faiths

In a good dialogue between people of different faiths, part of what happens is learning to see what the other person's face looks like when it's turned to God. Because something will be given or realized for me in that encounter and I mustn't shut out that possibility. (March 2010)[1]

The move from relationships with other churches to those with other faiths is one whose significance is not always grasped either by some Christians or by the wider media. There is a fundamental difference between Anglican relations with others who confess Christ and those who do not. Rowan Williams has been quite clear about the difference as he explained to a group of sixth formers in 2008:

> I believe that Christian faith is true, that it gives the
> most comprehensive and exciting and life-giving version
> of reality that is available to human beings. That's what

I want to grow up in, that's what I want to live and die in. And that means that when I look at other faiths I can't relate to them in the same way.[2]

However, he immediately went on to say that he can "find all kinds of echoes, points of contact, points where I want to discuss and engage", to speak of his role in interfaith dialogue, and to stress that "I don't try and make God's decisions for him".

This chapter sets out some of the key elements in Rowan's theological thinking behind these short answers before sketching some of the most significant and long-lasting elements of his practical work in relation to interfaith dialogue and co-operation.

A Theological Vision for Interfaith Relationships

Early in his time as archbishop, Rowan set out some of the central elements of his own approach to how Christians should relate to those of other faiths and how secular society should understand religious traditions. As so often, he begins by challenging standard ways of thinking and categorizing. He argues that many people are confused about what we are talking and thinking about when we talk of "religions". We assume different religions each represent

a distinct system of ideas, beliefs that connect the world as we see it with a whole lot of non-visible powers or realities, which have to be paid attention to, worshipped or at least negotiated with, in order to have the maximum security in life.[3]

Particularly in the secular West, we then assume that this whole world of religion is one that is inevitably pluralistic (because it deals with invisible powers) and is best left to private preferences, unrelated to the ordinary "unreligious" world or discussions of public policy. Such an account is, he points out, simply not true to the reality of the phenomenon. Religions are holistic and relate everything to "the holy": "it is about what lives should look like when they find their meaning as a whole in relation to holy reality".

From this perspective the question of religious difference also takes on a new and different hue. Disagreements are about "the kind of universe we inhabit, what that universe makes possible for human beings; and what is the most truthful or adequate or even sane way of behaving in the universe". This explains why they are so serious but it also challenges the common view that "all religious claims are answers to the same questions".

On this basis, Rowan resists two common views. First, he rejects the view that religions simply divide into one with the right answers and those which are wrong. Second, he rejects the view that religions are all basically the same and need to somehow pool their answers to find the truth, as in the Indian story of blind people offering accounts of an elephant on the basis of feeling only the trunk or the feet. He therefore does not approach other faiths either with "conversion" primary or with "convergence" and "consensus" as what he is seeking to achieve:

> I don't think that religious relativism or pluralism will do, as this seems always to presuppose the detached observer (the one who sees the whole elephant); but neither can we expect to find a tribunal to assess right and wrong answers.[4]

Conversion is, therefore, not seeing the right answer and abandoning the wrong one but a new experience of the world which "exposes a whole frame of reference as somehow inadequate". Although painful for former fellow-believers, it should lead to deeper self-critical understanding. This is also what can happen through building relationships and sharing each others' worlds across different faiths.

A properly secular society should thus not privatize religious difference but enable "real contention about religious truth" by "giving space for different experiences and constructions of the universe to engage with each other, to be themselves". In doing this, each religious tradition reveals in practice its own particular claim that it can "tell a truth which will comprehend any human situation it may encounter". In contrast to theocratic societies, religiously pluralist societies allow time and space to explore these different claims including through education systems which allow faith schools. In relation to Christians and other faiths, Rowan is therefore clear that rather than arguing about different answers to religious questions or seeking to reach agreement on shared answers, "significant interfaith encounter arises from our being able to see each other doing whatever it is we do as well as possible – teaching, worshipping, reflecting, serving".

This early lecture concludes by setting out some of the key claims that come from Christian faith and shape Christian practice, what he calls "the Christian universe in (very) small space". Without using technical theological terms he effectively speaks of God and creation, human sin and God's work of redemption:

- "The world exists because of the utterly free decision of a holy power that is more like personal life than anything else; that we can truthfully speak of as if it had mind and will" and "the purpose of this creation is that what is brought into being from nothing should come to share as fully as possible in the abundant and joyful life of the maker". This means that "the world is for joy and contemplation before it is for use".

211

- "For intelligent beings, this involves exercising freedom – so that the possibility is there of frustrating one's own nature by wrong and destructive choices" and so "our account of our own human nature and its needs is dangerously fallible and we are more limited than we can know in our self-understanding".

- "The purpose of God to share the divine life is so strong, however, that God acts to limit the effects of this destructiveness and to introduce into creation the possibility of an intensified relation with the divine through the events of the life of Jesus of Nazareth, above all in his sacrificial death". As a result, "it is God's gift in a particular and unique set of events in the world that it becomes possible for us to be released from some of the most lethal effects of this fallibility".

- "This new relation, realised by the Spirit of God released in Jesus's rising from the grave, is available in the life of the community that gathers to open itself to God's gift by recalling Jesus and listening to the God-directed texts which witness to this history". This means that "the new possibility is bound in with life in community centred on praise and listening and mutual nurture".

In light of this, Rowan shows how this Christian view of the world and our place and calling within it differs from that of other faith traditions:

- In contrast to Buddhists, Christians hold that "the world comes from and as deliberate gift".

- In contrast to Jews and Muslims, Christians hold that "our self-deception is so radical and deep-seated that we cannot be healed by the revelation of divine wisdom and law alone".

- In contrast to Muslims and Hindus, Christians believe that "our healing is a 'remaking' effected through a once and for all set of events".

This acknowledgment of incompatible truth claims is important in dialogue and not to be ignored or downplayed. Indeed, in a 2004 contribution, reflecting on atheism and faith traditions, Rowan suggested that "we spend more time looking at what is *disbelieved* in other religious discourses". In dialogue, rather than asserting itself as true against the other's falsehood or sidestepping the differences, each faith needs to "be prompted to ask whether the God of the other's disbelief is or is not the God they themselves believe in". Rowan's lecture to Muslims on God as Trinity, discussed in Chapter 4, is perhaps the best example of his own implementation of this model of dialogue.

Rowan acknowledges criticisms raised against his claims, and the challenge presented by non-Christian lives which "look as though they are in harmony with the Christian universe", but he is clear that:

> The Christian must argue that because this picture of the universe makes the fullest allowance possible for human failure and self-deceit and gives the most drastic account possible of divine presence in addressing this failure (God coming to inhabit creation in Jesus), it has a good claim to comprehensiveness as a view of how things are.[5]

Within this view, the person of Christ is absolutely central and Rowan is willing to talk about the "exclusive claim" being made and the "finality of Christ" as he made clear in his 2010 lecture exploring the moral, political and philosophical challenges to such claims:

What we encounter in Jesus Christ is simply the truth. It is the truth about God and the truth about humanity. *Not* living into that truth and accepting it, has consequences because this is the last word about God and God's creation. So we speak of the *finality* of Christ. There's nothing more to know. Or we speak of the uniqueness of Christ. No one apart from Jesus of Nazareth expresses the truth like this.[6]

This is not, however, the "exclusivism of a system of ideas and conclusions that someone claims to be final and absolute". As he explained to the WCC:

The place of Jesus is open to all who want to see what Christians see and to become what Christians are becoming. And no Christian believer has in his or her possession some kind of map of where exactly the boundaries of that place are to be fixed, or a key to lock others out or in.[7]

In addition, the Christian must recognize there are other perspectives and not dismiss these:

If I say that only in this place are hurts fully healed, sins forgiven, adoption into God's intimate presence promised, that assumes that adoption and forgiveness are to be desired above all other things. Not every perspective has that at the centre. What I want to say about those other views is not that they are in error but that they leave out what matters most in human struggle; yet I know that this will never be obvious to those others, and we can only come together, we can only introduce others into our perspective, in the light of the kind of shared labour and shared hope that brings

214

into central focus what I believe to be most significant
for humanity. And meanwhile that sharing will also tell
me that there may be things – perhaps of less ultimate
importance, yet enormously significant – that my
perspective has not taught me to see or to value.[8]

Thus the Christian emphasis is to be on "witness to the place and
the identity that we have been invited to live in" as we "reproduce
the life of God as it has been delivered to us by the anointed". In
relating to other faiths we need to be open to what reflects our
perspective as Christians and, when the difference is stark, not
set about correcting error but persevere patiently in seeking to
see what they see of the truth. This means that

in true dialogue with people of different faiths or
convictions we expect to learn something: we expect to
be different as a result of the encounter… We expect
to receive something from their humanity as a gift to
ours… I may emerge from my dialogue as confident as
I have ever been about the Trinitarian nature of God
and the finality of Jesus, and yet say that I've learned
something I never dreamed of, and that my discipleship
is enriched in gratitude and respect.[9]

Starting from fundamental Christian convictions there can,
therefore, be dialogue which acknowledges the differences. The
church is offered, through engagement with other faiths, neither
a means solely for conversion nor a denial of difference through
seeking convergence on some common core faith. What Rowan
has set out as a vision for future implementation is an approach
of genuine and respectful conversation across difference. In
this approach, Christians witness to God in Christ out of what
his foreword to the important 2008 Anglican Communion

215

resource, *Generous Love*, called "that double conviction that we must regard dialogue as an imperative from Our Lord, yet must also witness consistently to the unique gift we have been given in Christ".

Relationships with Other Faiths: The Practical Legacy

This theological vision has shaped Rowan's own extensive engagement with other faith traditions. Indeed, he is on record as having said that one of the unexpected features of his time in office has been the amount of time spent on interfaith relationships, an element of Christian ministry in which he had comparatively little experience before the move to Canterbury. One feature has been the great diversity of faith traditions with which he has built relationships including, for example, making the first ever official visit by the Archbishop of Canterbury to a Zoroastrian place of worship. Of particular importance have been the dialogue and partnerships with Judaism and Islam discussed in more detail below.

Despite Rowan's strong commitment to working together and deepening understanding and relationships, he has not been an advocate for interfaith worship. He explained some of the practical parameters within which he worked in a lengthy interview with *The Hindu* newspaper in India:

> We can't pray publicly together, for many reasons.
> Prayer follows conviction. But we can sometimes keep
> silence together. We can certainly look together at the
> sacred texts of one or another tradition. We can watch
> how other people handle their sacred texts and their
> rituals and learn from that. And in that process we
> become able to recognise some kind of integrity and
> some kind of depth in one another. It doesn't mean I

say, "Oh well, you must be right." But I can at least
say, "I know you're serious." And that's dialogue for
me – the recognition of the serious. And therefore if
we find we can do things together after all in servicing,
witnessing, peace-making, then it will come out of
depths, not shallows.[10]

Out of the wide range of his involvements, five areas in particular
stand out as of particular and long-term significance. First,
following a practice of the Vatican's Pontifical Council for
Interreligious Dialogue, Rowan has firmly established a tradition
of the Archbishop of Canterbury sending greetings to members
of other faith traditions at the time of their major festivals: Jews
at Rosh Hashanah (the Jewish New Year), Muslims at Eid ul-Fitr
(the end of Ramadan), and Hindus at Diwali.

Second, Rowan encouraged a range of different initiatives
which brought Christians together with people of other faiths
in partnership for the benefit of wider society. Two examples
in particular stand out here as of lasting value. The Muslim–
Christian Forum, announced in 2004, was launched in January
2006 with Rowan as Founding Patron. It built on a listening
initiative stretching back to 1997 and taking shape from 2001
under George Carey. This had begun developing a new vision for
greater mutual understanding and partnership. The forum brings
together Christians and Muslims (across different traditions
within the two faiths) who are involved in community life,
together with specialists including academic scholars. It is very
rooted in local communities but also organizes national events
such as major consultations. It seeks to build open, honest, and
committed personal relationships between leading Christians
and Muslims to enable shared reflection on how their traditions
can resource citizenship in British society and working together
for the common good.

Rowan has also given major support to the "Faith in Leadership" initiative, an independent leadership programme for young people in their twenties and thirties from different faith communities. This selects individuals and helps them develop leadership skills alongside one another. Steven Croft, Bishop of Sheffield, who attended a dinner to celebrate its work at Lambeth Palace highlights Rowan's crucial role in helping to develop this:

> Five years ago the Archbishop made a visit to Sheffield and went into some of the Further Education colleges. He saw the work that Krish Raval was doing on educating young people in deprived areas in leadership using a course he had developed called Learn to Lead. Krish asked Rowan to be a Patron of the charity and he agreed. It has now grown into a programme offered in Cambridge University under the auspices of David Ford... It's people from different faith backgrounds coming together not to do inter-faith work in the narrow sense but to learn about leadership in an inter-faith context. It's a fantastic piece of work, way below the radar. You can see [as with Fresh Expressions] that Rowan simply spotted something going on which was really interesting, has picked up this person and encouraged them. He has taken it forward through using his office and has connected that person with people like David Ford. Something has grown which will go on. Rowan spoke at the event and the warmth and affection with which he was regarded by the whole room was immense – this was Jews, Muslims, Sikhs, Hindus, all there.[11]

Third, connected with these initiatives, Rowan as archbishop has sought to address issues in wider society alongside leaders of other faith traditions. Among the areas in which he and other faith leaders united were: to speak at the start of the Iraq war in 2003; to advocate on behalf of the world's poor before the G8 summit in 2005; to respond together to the 7/7 terrorist attacks in London; to write a letter to *The Times* in 2006 on assisted dying; and to sign the 2008 Faith in Human Rights statement. There have also been interfaith consultations on various issues such as the 2010 discussions with government ministers on religious communities and "the big society". Of even more lasting significance is his argument, explored more fully in the next chapter, that religious voices need to be heard in public debates. From his first major lecture as archbishop – the Dimbleby Lecture in December 2002 – he has repeatedly challenged the view that in a secular society religious voices need to be silent or express themselves in non-religious terms. Instead he has argued that religious leaders need to ask "fundamental and challenging human questions" and that "the requirement that religious believers leave their most strongly held and distinctive principles at the door when they engage in public argument" is "not a good recipe for lasting social unity".

Fourth, in relation to Judaism, Rowan has always been clear about the unique relationship between Christians and Jews. In a 2004 lecture he rejected the idea of two covenants (one for Jews, another for Christians) and instead explored how Jews and Christians challenge each other to be faithful to the covenantal God and can take a stand together against certain beliefs. He acknowledged Christians had to be open to critique here:

> The Jew may want to charge the Christian with undermining the whole point of the covenantal story by acting and speaking as though the covenant celebrated by Christians had been substituted for that with the Jewish people, thus suggesting that God does not keep faith and that we cannot hope for him to make one story of our diverse human histories.[12]

He calls on Jews and Christians to be faithful to each other in a sort of mutual human covenant, "to be amazed at each other and in that amazement to find something of God; and from that will flow a strange but real shared testimony to the world, about God's nature and our own". The theme of covenant was also taken up by the Chief Rabbi in his important address to the Lambeth Conference of 2008.

Rowan has also highlighted the importance of the Holocaust, issuing an annual statement on Holocaust Memorial Day and making a powerful 2008 pilgrimage with the Chief Rabbi and others to Auschwitz saying that "our hope is that in making this journey together we also travel towards the God who binds us together in protest and grief at this profanation".

Some of the most difficult situations have arisen in relation to contemporary Middle Eastern politics, where Rowan has often been involved through public and private visits and through public statements. A particularly difficult situation arose in early 2006 when Rowan wrote to the Chief Rabbi expressing his "deep regret" at how a General Synod decision in relation to ethical investment and Israel had been perceived. Later that year, however, it was clear that no lasting damage had been done as he was able to sign a historic joint declaration with the Chief Rabbis of Israel. This led to a pattern of annual meetings and statements addressing issues of joint concern, a significant development in Anglican relationships with Judaism.

Fifth, and finally, throughout Rowan's time as archbishop, questions of the relationship between Islam and the West and Islam and Christianity have been of greater significance than for any of his predecessors and a particular focus of his own ministry. In addition to the work of the Muslim–Christian Forum noted earlier, he has regularly visited mosques and Muslim community leaders. Significantly he was making such a visit in West Yorkshire on 7 July 2005 at the time of the terrorist attacks on London.

The building up of trust and understanding in and through such meetings has been an important part of his legacy in this area, but two particular forms of his involvement with Muslims and Islam stand out.

On 13 October 2007, a group of 138 Muslim leaders and scholars from around the world (later joined by other individuals and Islamic groups) issued a historic open letter to Christian leaders, including the Archbishop of Canterbury, entitled "A Common Word Between Us and You". This sought to foster dialogue and a way of peace and justice between Muslims and Christians based on love of the one God and love of neighbour. It soon elicited responses from across the Christian world. In June 2008 Rowan hosted an ecumenical consultation at Lambeth to discuss how to progress dialogue with Muslims. The following month he issued, with that consultation's "support and encouragement", one of the most detailed and significant responses to the open letter. This was followed in October by him calling a four-day conference in Cambridge on "A Common Word and Future Christian–Muslim Engagement", which ended in him issuing a joint communiqué with the Grand Mufti of Egypt. As Rowan commented in 2010, the open letter proved "a landmark in Muslim–Christian relations and it has a unique role in stimulating a discussion at the deepest level across the world". He himself played a major part in the positive Christian reaction, both by his own personal response, probably the most substantial theological reply, and through enabling wider dialogue and discussion.

Rowan's commitment and the depth of his engagement with this particular initiative from Muslim leaders arose out of, and was shaped by, his other major contribution to developing relationships and enabling mutual understanding between Christians and Muslims: the Building Bridges Seminar. Begun after 9/11, this was an initiative of Rowan's predecessor, George

Carey, whose chaplain (and Rowan's until 2005), David Marshall, subsequently became its academic director.

From the start, Rowan made this a priority commitment despite it demanding the best part of a week every year in terms of his role as chair for the three-day seminar and the travel involved. Its focus on intellectual questions and dialogue clearly played to his own strengths and interests as it brought together Christian and Muslim academics from across the world for (sometimes public) lectures and small group studies, centred around texts, often from the Bible and the Koran. Nevertheless, many were surprised that, inheriting this initiative after its first meeting, he gave it such significance in his primacy.

The first meeting he attended was in Qatar, not long after his enthronement, in April 2003. His opening remarks captured some of the principles already discussed in his approach to interfaith work. There was no sidestepping of disagreements but an acknowledgment that

> Christians are Christians and Muslims are Muslims
> because they care about truth, and because they believe
> that truth alone gives life. About the nature of that
> absolute and life-giving truth, Christians and Muslims
> are not fully in agreement.[13]

However, shared histories and practices enabled mutual recognizability out of which the gathering sought to listen to each other "to discover more about how each community believes it must listen to God, conscious of how very differently we identify and speak of God's revelation". They were "not seeking an empty formula of convergence or trying to deny our otherness".

His later reflection on that experience captures some of why it became such an important part of his ministry and legacy:

For me, one of the most important such encounters I have ever had was this spring in Qatar, when I was part of an international group of Muslims and Christians meeting to read their scriptures together and discuss them; we Christians were able to benefit enormously from watching Muslims doing what Muslims do with love, intellectual rigour and excitement. It proved a deeper and more truly respectful meeting of minds than any attempt to find a neutral common ground. We met as theologians, committed to exploring the reality of what truthful and holy lives might look like and how they might be talked about. And so we were able not to see each other as competing to answer the same exam paper. At times there was deep convergence, at times monumental disagreement. But I suspect we all emerged with a sharper sense of what our traditions had to deal with, of the complexity of our world and the difference of our questions. My hope for the future of dialogue is for more such exchanges at every level.[14]

Such exchanges continued every year with a specific theme as their focus and leading to a publication based on their work. The issues covered ranged from the more traditionally theological (Scripture, prophecy, revelation, humanity, prayer, death, and human destiny) to the social and political questions facing Christians and Muslims around the world (the common good, justice and rights, science, tradition and modernity). Discussions were also shaped by the locality in which the group met. This has included Sarajevo, Qatar, Singapore, and Georgetown University in Washington. Rowan chaired the seminars and, in addition to his own contributions, also often provided a masterful summing up of the public lectures or the private discussions. He has spoken of the growing trust between participants (about a dozen have attended almost all of the ten during his primacy with others attending only some) and in particular the power of dialogue where you watch each other engaging with the tradition's own sources and "you are looking at someone else's face turned towards God". There have also been the challenging questions such as a Muslim scholar asking what Christians really mean by salvation or grappling with Christian understandings of the Trinity.

One feature of the seminar is that it has not sought a high public profile by making statements but has worked to build relationships and patiently deepen dialogue. The seminar will in future be overseen by Georgetown University and so Rowan's successor will not be required or even expected to play as central a role as he has undertaken. What cannot be doubted, though, is that Rowan's vision, energy, and commitment have helped make this a major distinctive and influential component in Christian–Muslim relations and in the wider inter-faith dialogue.

Conclusion

Much more could be said about specific initiatives, but Rowan's interfaith work is clearly a major part of his legacy as archbishop. Not only has it taken a considerable amount of his time, he has brought to both the theology and the practical task of religious dialogue new insights which grow out of one of his core beliefs:

> God has made us to learn in dialogue… I think that the belief in Jesus' uniqueness and finality allows us… to encounter both the religious and the non-religious *other* with the generous desire to share, and the humble desire to learn, and the patience to let God work out his purpose as is best in his eyes.[15]

He has developed and put into practice a model of Christian engagement with those of other faiths which is unashamedly theological and Christ-centred in both its confession of faith and its commitment to humble, respectful conversation:

> We are very rightly suspicious of proselytism, of manipulative, bullying, insensitive approaches to people of other faith which treat them as if they knew nothing, as if we had nothing to learn and as if the tradition of their reflection and imagination were of no interest to us or God. God save us from that kind of approach. But God save us also from the nervousness about our own conviction which doesn't allow us to say that we speak about Jesus because we believe he matters. We believe he matters because we believe that in him human beings find their peace. Their destinies converge and their dignities are fully honoured. And all the work that we as Christians want to do for the sake of convergent human destiny and fullness of human dignity has its root in that conviction that there is no boundary around Jesus – that what he *is* and *does* and *says* and *suffers* is in principle liberatingly relevant to every human being; past, present and future.[16]

13

The Sharia Lecture and Interactive Pluralism

The prevailing attitude… was one of heavy disagreement with a number of things which the [speaker] had not said. (February 2008, quoting Ronald Knox)[1]

"What a Burkha!" screamed the *Sun* headline. It followed this up by tying the story to sex, the usual issue linked to the church in the tabloids: an extended anti-Rowan campaign called "Bash the Bishop!" with page three models sent to be filmed on a topless bus outside Lambeth Palace.

Of all Rowan's hundreds of speeches given during his ten years, that on Islamic sharia law to almost 1,000 leading legal professionals at the Royal Courts of Justice on 7 February 2008 is undoubtedly the one everyone remembers but very few understand. The incident captures for his critics so many of his weaknesses: bad media management, unwise statements, incomprehensible lectures, academic theorizing detached from the realities of most people's lives, and unhelpfully giving prominence to issues not central to Christian faith and of little wider concern.

The controversy was well underway before he gave the lecture, following an interview with Christopher Landau on Radio 4's *The World At One*. Landau's opening question, trying to capture the heart of the complex lecture, asked whether, if social cohesion required legal accommodation of those with religious faith, "the application of Sharia in certain circumstances... seems unavoidable". Although the lecture only used "unavoidable" to acknowledge that his account of law introduced "what some would see as a 'market' element, a competition for loyalty", Rowan took the bait. He answered with perhaps the three most damaging public words when in office: "It seems unavoidable". He immediately pointed out that "as a matter of fact certain provisions of Sharia are already recognised in our society and under our law; so it's not as if we're bringing in an alien and rival system", but that was air-brushed from the record. The story was now clear: "Archbishop wants Muslim law in UK" was the *Sun*'s subheading. The *Mail*, describing him as a "batty old booby", asked "Who would have guessed that there lurks beneath that genial, bearded exterior a dyed-in-the-wool reactionary who wants to take Britain back to medieval times?" and ran Melanie Phillips calling on him to resign. Few spoke in his defence. Within two days his predecessor, Lord Carey, had written in the *Telegraph* calling the proposal "disastrous".

In fact, the Sharia lecture was a significant contribution to an important debate and flows from Rowan's wide-ranging vision for society, politics, and law already set out in earlier lectures. This chapter sets out that vision which is perhaps his major legacy in relation to Christian social thought and public theology. It then returns to the Sharia lecture in that context.

Church, Society, State, and the Law: Rowan's Vision of "Interactive Pluralism"

Any Christian leader, if they are to engage coherently and consistently with wider social and political debates, must have an understanding of how the church relates to wider society and the role of the state and law within society. Rowan, in a series of lectures, most of them now gathered together in his *Faith in the Public Square*,[2] set out a remarkable vision of these relationships. That vision makes sense of his speech on sharia and his way of addressing other issues explored in the next chapter. He identified and addressed two major challenges: the common understandings of the state as both sovereign and secular and the indisputable plurality of cultures, faiths, communities, and institutions in contemporary British society.

Rowan's approach was shaped by his understanding of Scripture and the Christian tradition of social and political thought but he was particularly influenced by the early twentieth-century Anglican writer from Mirfield, John Neville Figgis. As he told Paul Richardson:

> Figgis was for me one of the most formative influences. When I was at Mirfield they were clearing out the library of the old Hostel of the Resurrection in Leeds and I picked up a complete set of Figgis and started reading him then and thought "Ah, this is important". For my money, Figgis is a far more sophisticated and resourceful thinker than Niebuhr and his work is very relevant to the time we live in. The work of David Nicholls did something to recover his reputation but it is extraordinary that for decades he has been ignored. He is not only a political thinker but a theologian who was trying to hang on to a Catholic identity that was plural and dispersed and yet was also profoundly orthodox.[3]

In a 2005 lecture, in honour of David Nicholls, Rowan gave one of his clearest accounts of his thinking and its theological rationale.[4] He stressed the Christian denial of sacred "givenness" to any political order because "there is, ultimately, only one sovereignty which is theologically grounded, and that is Christ's". Related to this is Christian belief about the church as the body of Christ. Rowan is clear that, although the church often fails to put this into practice,

> the Christian tradition rests upon a strong conviction that no political order other than the Body of Christ can claim the authority of God; and the Body of Christ is not a political order on the same level as others, competing for control, but a community that signifies, that points to a possible healed human world. Thus its effect on the political communities of its environment is bound to be, sooner or later, sceptical and demystifying.[5]

Rowan argues that although the church has this unique calling it is also one of many political communities within wider society alongside such bodies as universities, the British Medical Association, trades unions, and other faith communities. All of these are "'first-level' associations". They take corporate action and define and regulate their own common life alongside one another. The wider political community we often refer to as "the state" is therefore really best understood as a cluster of smaller political communities. These are "negotiating with each other under the umbrella of a system of arbitration recognised by all". State law enables these "first-level" communities to flourish and settles and enforces disputes between them. This is best done by creating conditions to allow each group to pursue what it sees as good and by restraining groups when their conception of the good undermines the good of other groups.

This vision of life together in society is in marked contrast to the dominant view. There the governing authority (also, confusingly, called "the state") is viewed as a single sovereign power which establishes the legitimacy of other groups. In such a situation, the state often becomes unchallengeable as these other political communities lose their significance. People then stand before the state as individual citizens or subjects rather than persons embedded within such first-level associations.

Rowan's vision led him to identify and counter two dangers in contemporary social and political life. The first danger is the dominance of what, following Philip Bobbitt's analysis he called the "market state". He spoke about this in his first lecture as archbishop in 2002 of which, according to Richard Harries, Bobbitt said, "Rowan understood what I was trying to say better than anyone else".[6] The government's role is here seen as clearing space for individuals and groups to negotiate the best deal or value for money given their desires. Here the government sees its function as being "to clear a space for individuals or groups to do their own negotiating, to secure the best deal or the best value for money in pursuing what they want". The problem is, in the words of the lecture's conclusion, that when we ask why we should do what the government tells us the market state's answer is "finally destructive of our liberty" because its structures and priorities "deprive us of the resources we need to make decisions that are properly human decisions, bound up with past and future".

The second danger is that recognizing the plurality of associations, including faith communities, results in them becoming isolated from each other and a general relativism arises which abandons the shared quest for the common good of society as a whole. This leads to what, in another key lecture (in 2007 on multiculturalism), Rowan described as "nothing but a world of unbridled and uncritical social plurality which undermines any possible commitment to overall social cohesion". He warned of simply a "minimal public tolerance for eccentric or exotic private diversities" leading to a managerial and impersonal politics where, despite talking of multiculturalism, in one sense

> we live in probably the least multicultural human
> environment there has even been... It is as universal
> as ever Christianity or Islam aspired to be, but the
> substance of its universality is a set of human functions
> (producing, selling, consuming) rather than any
> sense of innate human capacity and of the unsettling
> mysteriousness that goes with that.[7]

Given these dangers, Rowan set out a better form of multiculturalism which does not keep various convictions about human dignity and destiny out of the public democratic debate but enables interaction, including reasoned criticism, between diverse cultures. This vision Rowan labelled "interactive pluralism", and it shaped his approach to conflict and disagreement in any community. Politically, it means the state has an "arbitrative and balancing function" so as to allow "active partnership and exchange between communities themselves and between communities and state authority". This is not, he insists, a form of relativism, but a commitment to "a properly mutually engaged discussion in public about what is good for corporate human life".

On this understanding what Rowan saw as crucial is that society's various primary or first-level associations, including religious communities, are nurtured. The conclusion of his initial and in many ways programmatic 2002 Dimbleby Lecture was quite explicit and bold: if there is to be a future for "the reasonable citizen", "public debate about what is due to human beings", and "intelligent argument about goals" then this "depends heavily on those perspectives that are offered by religious belief". The public square, if it is to survive as "a realm of political argument about vision and education" needs to take religion much more seriously. Rowan was therefore clear, beginning his primacy, about the enormous opportunities and responsibilities this placed on him and others who, knowing religious involvement in public life has "not always been benign", have also learnt "something of how to engage with the social orders of the modern world":

> It is up to us to articulate with as much energy and
> imagination as we can our understanding of that
> larger story without which the most fundamental and
> challenging human questions won't even get asked, let
> alone answered.[8]

This robust defence of the place of faith, "doing God", in public life clearly raises questions about what it means to be a "secular" society. Rowan responded to these in a number of lectures, most notably his 2006 Rome lecture, "Secularism, Faith and Freedom".[9] He drew a key distinction between two forms of "secularism", which he called "programmatic" and "procedural", crudely "bad" and "good" secularism. Programmatic secularism leads to "the empty public square of a merely instrumental liberalism, which allows maximal private licence". In contrast, procedural secularism welcomes "a crowded and argumentative public square which acknowledges the authority of a legal mediator or broker whose job it is to balance and manage real difference". With the latter, as in India, the state oversees a range of communities of religious conviction and assists them to live in peace and dialogue, favouring none. He argued that Christians can and should have no problem with this. Indeed, he proposes this understanding of the secular arose in Western society because of Christian convictions about the place of political authorities under the lordship of the risen Christ. In contrast, programmatic secularism, often seen as evident in France, excludes religious allegiance from the public sphere and expects clear loyalty to the "neutral" state. Rowan's rejection of this view helps explain, to take just one controversial intervention, his strong protests at decisions obliging Roman Catholic adoption agencies to consider gay couples or to close. Programmatic secularism makes loyalty to one's faith a private preference or emotion. It thus requires people of faith to misrepresent themselves by amputating their religious commitments before presenting any argument in the public square. This in turn prevents them calling the state to account on the basis of their religious convictions and fuels the false conception of the state as an unassailable sovereign power.

This carefully argued framework for Christian witness in contemporary secular society is a major legacy of Rowan's ministry and a significant gift for the ongoing mission of the church. Its wider vision of social and community life also shaped his contribution within the life of the church itself. A form of "interactive pluralism" is evident in his commitment to a "mixed economy" with Fresh Expressions alongside traditional parish churches, his determination to secure strong provision for those opposed to women bishops thus maintaining "two integrities" within the Church of England, his conviction of the need for both a covenant and continuing Indaba within the Communion, and his distinctive pattern of dialogue with other faiths.

Even with only this crude sketch of his vision of church, society, state, and law, it is now possible to see how all the pieces of his thinking were in place well before his 2008 Sharia lecture. Although causing incomprehension and outrage within wider society, the lecture is perfectly consonant with the whole direction of his teaching as archbishop.

How Do You Solve a Problem Like Sharia?

By the time the lecture came to be delivered there was already a firestorm of criticism based on misunderstanding and misinterpretation. Within four hours of the interview the prime minister and other politicians were distancing themselves. The lecture itself could not easily dispel this instant reaction. It is one of Rowan's densest, with over 6,000 words but only 132 sentences, an average of 47 words per sentence.[10] A challenge even for academic legal and Islamic experts in the audience, this was impossible for tabloid and even most broadsheet journalists. In the light of Rowan's wider perspective, however, its central message and concerns are easily set out.

In our pluralist society there are law-abiding communities who relate to more than the British legal system. Muslims with sharia are just one example, but given this was the first lecture in a series on Islam in English law it is one which Rowan's much wider analysis had to consider. Christians too wrestle with such questions given the apostolic confession that they obey God rather than men (Acts 5:29) and Paul's rebuke to Corinthians settling disputes in local non-Christian courts (1 Corinthians 6).

Part of Rowan's problem was that he failed to factor fully into account that, in Tariq Ramadan's words quoted in the lecture, "the idea of *Sharia* calls up all the darkest images of Islam" so "many Muslim intellectuals do not dare even to refer to the concept for fear of frightening people or arousing suspicion of all their work by the mere mention of the word". Attempting to slay such a popular myth was always going to be hard. Most people do not have the dispassionate and questioning intellectual approach Rowan exemplifies ("I think we need to look at this with a clearer eye" as he said to Christopher Landau). Nor can they easily think of sharia as "a method rather than a code of law", a form of scriptural reasoning, interpreting and applying God's will in Islamic law to realities today. Some who did understand the complexities of sharia – notably Bishop Michael Nazir-Ali – offered important critiques of Rowan's proposals, but the media stuck with and fuelled the simple caricature.

Rowan was aware that sharia would be seen as totalitarian and imperialistic and clearly stressed the need for free consent and recognition that the community under sharia was not the same as wider society. The bigger picture here is that Muslims recognize "our social identities are not constituted by one exclusive set of relations or mode of belonging" and might privilege a religious identity. The problem, he argued is when *either* religious *or* secular communities deny this plurality. Indeed perhaps the lecture's central theme is the danger of either a religious community or a secular government being monopolistic.

Here Rowan perhaps touched a raw nerve with his belief that much secular thinking about law and citizenship and politics falls into this monopolistic danger. It insists that citizens be under the rule of the uniform law of a sovereign state in such a way that other commitments and identities are simply a matter of choice to be kept private. The inability to escape the hold of this concept of legal monopoly explains the general incomprehension about his comments which were a serious and prophetic challenge to much secular thinking. People should, he claimed, be allowed to explain their actions in their own terms and related to their different senses of belonging. Indeed, liberal pluralism is actually undermined without this because the religious conscience is neither protected nor understood.

This outworking of his pluralist view raises questions of how existing courts deal with these issues and what it means to live under more than one jurisdiction. Here Rowan addressed most of the objections subsequently raised against his view. He was clear he was not offering blank cheques to religious groups and that any religious courts would need safeguards to prevent reinforcing repressive elements where a minority took away rights which are generally valid (the status of women being the most obvious example). Facing head on the issue of giving up legal monopoly he engaged in another ambitious prophetic challenge and myth-slaying: the Enlightenment focus on equal accountability and accessibility in relation to law actually draws on a longer Judaeo-Christian tradition which affirms the universality and primacy of law. On its own, the Enlightenment understanding "is not adequate to deal with the realities of complex societies". This is because the basis or entirety of social identity and personal motivation is not simply citizenship "as an abstract form of equal access and equal accountability". Indeed, attempts to implement such a reductionist vision have been violent and unjust because in diverse, pluralist societies our identities are formed by "multiple affiliation". These affiliations include religious commitments which cannot be subordinated to and marginalized by a supposedly sovereign authority managing "the abstract level of equal citizenship". The interview highlighted this as central to the argument – "I do want to see a proper way of talking about shared citizenship and that is a major theme of what I am saying in this lecture" – but this too went unreported.

Rowan's argument is that in our complex, plural, multicultural society the role of law is to provide a negative guarantee. It protects against losing certain liberties and gives a right to demand reasons for any infringement of self-determination. Law is, in other words, a way of ensuring dialogue which respects human diversity and human dignity. It thus enables interactive pluralism. Its universal aspect does not supersede specific community (including religious) understandings but rather undergirds these. The fact that the key point here is in a sentence of 146 words didn't help communicate this message.

As so often, Rowan ended the lecture with a provocative theological claim: the standard secular attempt to defend law's monopoly (against religious claims) is not up to the task when faced with a pluralist society. It is actually based on Enlightenment ideas which only really make sense in a theological worldview. This is another part of the problem and explanation for the outcry – the archbishop was saying the Emperor has no clothes and again arguing the need for theology.

The media were only interested in his statements about sharia, but the real problem being addressed was how we understand law. Asked whether people would be surprised that he, as a Christian archbishop, was calling for greater consideration of Islamic law, he made clear that the questions ran deeper:

> People may be surprised but I hope that that
> surprise will be modified when they think about
> the general question of how the law and religious
> community, religious principle are best and fruitfully
> accommodated... How does the law [of the land]
> engage critically and intelligently... with the custom,
> the imperatives, the principles of distinctive religious
> communities? It's a large question, much larger than
> the question about Islam and I think it's a question
> which the Church can quite reasonably be thinking
> about.[11]

Rowan's first big mistake was to believe that the response to being surprised by something he said would be to stop and to think. His second was not to be ready to respond to reactions. The story dominated the news for days, but Lambeth offered no effective defence or clarification to combat distortions and attacks. Nobody had been lined up to explain and support him or his views on television. As his interviewer, Christopher Landau has argued, "it was the subsequent failure to respond to the several criticisms of his views... that caused lasting reputational damage".[12]

The sharia incident clearly reveals several of Rowan's weaknesses, but it also reveals something about wider society, media, politicians, and the church. His main failings were an almost lethal cocktail of naivety in relation to a sound bite on a controversial subject that would be taken from an interview, opacity in relation to the lecture, and a lack of any effective response when the controversy flared. The general reaction was marked by prejudice (including against him), ignorance, and misrepresentation. It revealed the inability of secular society (especially the media) to think seriously about an important issue or to understand the importance of religious commitments and communities in and for public life. The challenge to consider that we need God in order to understand ourselves as a society and discern how we can live together in our diversity of cultures and faiths was met by a refusal to listen, understand, dialogue, or learn. Instead, people reacted instantly with distortion, disbelief, dismissal, and disdain.

In the following days, Rowan described himself privately as "bloodied but unbowed" and when he finally spoke again in his presidential address to Synod four days later he began with the words quoted above: "The prevailing attitude... was one of heavy disagreement with a number of things which the [speaker] had not said." The nearest he came to apology was to say "I must of course take responsibility for any unclarity" in the lecture or interview and "for any misleading choice of words that has helped to cause distress or misunderstanding among the public at large and especially among my fellow Christians". He made clear his strong conviction that the Church of England was often expected to speak for all faith communities and

> if we can attempt to speak for the liberties and
> consciences of others in this country as well as our own,
> we shall I believe be doing something we as a Church

238

are called to do in Christ's name, witnessing to his
Lordship and not compromising it.[13]

The incident undoubtedly did enormous damage to Rowan's media image and public perception of him, but once the furore died down, his lecture's proper significance was acknowledged by some. He would often point out that, a few days after the fuss, the government introduced some sharia-compliant forms of mortgage arrangement for Muslims, which was "absolutely the sort of thing I was talking about". In July, the Lord Chief Justice, Lord Phillips, who had chaired the event, spoke of "a profound lecture and one not readily understood on a single listening". He pointed out that "it was not very radical to advocate embracing Sharia Law in the context of family disputes, for example, and our system already goes a long way towards accommodating the Archbishop's suggestion". By November, Rowan and his family were recovering from the onslaught. He told James MacIntyre of the *New Statesman* that "to quote my son [Pip, aged twelve]: it was a very instructive experience. Very." When the subject came up at a small drinks reception at Lambeth Palace, Jane Williams could even joke "What sharia row?" By the time he announced his retirement he hadn't changed his mind – "I still stand by the argument of it" – although he admitted "It could have been clearer, I am sure. That can always be said, especially of things I write!" His own view, however, was that

> it became a feeding frenzy for a few days. But I didn't
> feel any lasting damage was done. I feel that an
> important point was raised, a point about how the
> single law of the land works with and legitimates other
> kinds of jurisdiction within it, which already happens.[14]

That may be an overly optimistic assessment. Along with Jeffrey

John and the Reading crisis, "Sharia-gate" will remain a symbolic event at the forefront of most people's memories of his primacy. It will sadly take quite some time for the value of the important points he raised to be given the recognition they deserve.

14

"Doing God": Society and Politics

For many of our contemporaries, the Christian message is either a matter of unwelcome moral nagging or a set of appealing but finally irrelevant legends. If it has a place in our public life or our national institutions, it is on the basis of a slightly grudging recognition that "it does a lot of good work" and represents something about continuity with our past. But what if the Christian story offered more than this? What if it proposed a way of understanding some of the most pervasive and dangerous mechanisms in human relationships, interpersonal or international? (March 2008)[1]

In the course of his ten years, Rowan spoke on a very wide range of social and political issues. Space prevents consideration of most of these despite many meriting wider study. For example, re-reading his 2005 lecture "Media: Public Interest and Common Good" in the light of phone-hacking and the Leveson

Inquiry is illuminating. This chapter looks at five key areas. It opens with some of his key interventions in British political life more generally before turning to three areas which stand out because their interconnectedness, their global scope, and their significance in both his own contributions and British life make them central to his legacy. Throughout his time in office, Britain has been involved in the "war on terror" and he has spoken often on matters relating to war and international relationships. There has also been the global financial crash leading to him speaking and writing a considerable amount on economics. Although given less prominence, arguably the most important long-term issue our society has to address is that of global warming and our relationship with the environment generally. Finally, attention is turned to a thread running through almost all his contributions: a commitment to be a public voice for the vulnerable.

British Politics (2002–12)

I'm concerned about these things chiefly because I'm a Christian who believes that the world is to be cherished, the innocent protected and human dignity preserved... The Bible's vision of a properly functioning society is in fact deeply realistic. (March 2005)[2]

During Rowan's primacy Britain had three prime ministers ending in a period of coalition government. He was involved in private meetings and correspondence with party leaders and ministers but also made key public statements most notably in the context of the two general elections.

In March 2005 Rowan wrote an open letter to party leaders as the general election approached. He warned against playing on fears against which people will react and defend themselves without thinking. His letter highlighted and asked questions about four "things that really should make us tremble": the environment, "international economic policies and priorities, which serve to reinforce the instability that feeds violence in poorer nations", the penal system, and alienated youth. He connected these to root causes of the presenting fears and, appealing to the prophet Jeremiah, described his letter as "a plea to see what you think can be built and planted in some of the most vulnerable situations in a vulnerable world". This digging below the surface to raise core questions of those in power and offer a positive vision represents a common pattern of Rowan's engagement with political leadership.

At the 2010 general election he again stepped back from the campaigning frenzy, urging people to "listen again for a moment to the basic questions about what kind of society we want to choose". He called for "a rebirth of civic values and virtues" and a refocusing on the common good and creating a "common wealth" before identifying six key issues arising from church discussion and Christian teaching: equality, stability (especially of home and family life), global responsibility (economically and environmentally), law and justice, children's welfare, and the needs of older people. The crucial question was "what are the outcomes from this election that will give us confidence to move towards a more generous and less anxious society?"

Church leaders usually avoid naming political parties but at the European and local elections in 2009 there were major concerns about the rise of the British National Party (BNP). The archbishops issued an appeal not only for people to vote and "elect those who wish to uphold democratic values and who wish to work for the common good in a spirit of public service" but also to reject "those who would exploit the present situation to advance views that are the very opposite of the values of justice, compassion and human dignity rooted in our Christian heritage".[3] They explicitly condemned the BNP and its abuse of Christian language, a challenge to racism which later led the Church of England to state BNP membership was incompatible with holding office in the church.

This was also the period of the MPs' expenses scandal. Rowan's contribution here was typically against the mainstream, leading some to argue that he was again out of touch. Writing in *The Times* two weeks into the crisis, he acknowledged its seriousness but, doubtless sensing the creation of a mob mentality looking to scapegoat, claimed many thought "the continuing systematic humiliation of politicians itself threatens to carry a heavy price in terms of our ability to salvage some confidence in our democracy". He argued for getting away from rules (keeping or bending them) and regulation and for a return to virtue and cultivation of integrity, pointing to religious ethics which asks "how to encourage us to act in such a way that we can be glad of what we have done – and can also recognise that bad actions diminish us".

In June 2010, shortly after the election, the Church of England issued an important statement, *Living Thankfully Before God*, which drew on the work of Rowan and others to set out an Anglican social and political vision. Like other events during his primacy which gained little or no media attention this, with its account of the common good, may in time also prove a largely unnoticed but important lasting part of his legacy. It was, however, forgotten if not ignored, unlike Rowan's guest editorship of an edition of the *New Statesman* a year later. There he produced a careful, nuanced edition with a range of contributors including Gordon Brown, William Hague, Iain Duncan Smith, Terry Eagleton, Philip Pullman, and A.S. Byatt.

The editorial was another piece of classic social, political, and theological reflection from Rowan, not easily pigeonholed in standard categories but shaped by the vision set out in the previous chapter. It was fundamentally an appeal for debate and discussion about what makes for sustainable community. He pointed to a biblical vision of this and called for a democracy "capable of real argument about shared needs and hopes and real generosity" which asks of any policy:

> how far does it equip a person or group to engage generously and for the long term in building the resourcefulness and well-being of any other person or group, with the state seen as a "community of communities…"?[24]

The media, however, needed to pigeonhole. As the nearest accurate labels ("pluralist" or "syndicalist") would not be understood, it became simply the bearded leftie attacking the non-Labour government. Some sound bite hostages to fortune enabled them to do this: "We're being committed to radical, long-term policies for which no one voted", "Government badly needs to hear just how much plain fear there is around such questions at present". Once again these were lifted and twisted and the archbishop himself became the story. A piece which, if taken as a whole, set in the context of Rowan's wider contributions, and understood on its own terms was not particularly shocking, was reframed (as with sharia) around one or two comments. These made a striking and not wholly inaccurate news story but lost the bigger picture. It was as if lessons had not been learnt or, perhaps more likely, Rowan was determined to say what he wanted to say despite knowing how it would play: an episcopal policy of "publish and be damned".

Finally, two less public developments occurred which are likely to be of longer-term significance. Although most of the archbishop's contributions are very much his own initiative, in conversation with his key advisors, there has developed a much greater level of liaison and co-operation between Lambeth

Palace's work in public affairs and that of the Mission and Public Affairs Division based at Church House. Of particular importance in strengthening the Church of England's role has been the establishment in 2008 of its Parliamentary Unit, based in Church House but with the parliamentary secretary also having a formal role at the Lambeth Principals' staff meeting.

Finally, the "dog that didn't bark" during Rowan's primacy was the issue of the Church of England as the established church. Some thought Rowan would seek to make changes here, but he spoke up for bishops in a reformed House of Lords. The one significant change that did occur (largely unnoticed by the wider public) was Gordon Brown's decision in 2007 to change the convention that the church submitted two names when asked to nominate for a vacant diocese and the prime minister was free to choose either or to ask for others. This change took place when Rowan was on sabbatical in the USA. He left the handling of it with the Archbishop of York, whose acceptance of the proposals led, Tom Sutcliffe claims, to "the incredulity and fury of various senior figures in the church". While presented by some as finally freeing the church from state interference in appointments, this alarmed others as it removed the need for the prime minister's appointments secretary (who must be an Anglican) to be a full-time senior civil servant located in Downing Street, and thus ended a key personal presence linking the church to the corridors of power.

War and International Relationships

Immoral is a short word for a very, very long discussion. (October 2003)[5]

Rowan was famously a short distance from the Twin Towers on 9/11. The repercussions of that day continued to play out throughout his time at Canterbury. His book of reflections, *Writing in the Dust*, appeared before his appointment and shortly after he took office the next phase in the "war on terror" (of which he had always been a critic, favouring a judicial response to a criminal act rather than a military campaign) began with the invasion of Iraq. Although he addressed a number of other important issues such as the proposed renewal of Britain's nuclear deterrent (he remained a strong opponent), the plight of child soldiers, and the conflict in the Middle East (being particularly vocal over the Israeli invasion of Lebanon), it was the "war on terror" which set the context for his most memorable and significant interventions.

As the Iraq war approached, he issued statements jointly with the Roman Catholic Archbishop of Westminster ("doubts still persist about the moral legitimacy as well as the unpredictable humanitarian consequences"), with the Archbishop of York, and with leaders of other faiths, and wrote to Anglican primates. Once war was underway he described the situation as "genuinely tragic" but focused on lessons to be learnt in terms of international relations and on preparing for the post-conflict situation. Identifying the key moral question as "what can mend all the things this war and the processes leading up to it have broken?" he warned prophetically, in a *Times* article in March 2003, that "we must not be caught naked of ideas and clear commitments when a ceasefire arrives".

His own view on the war's legitimacy was thus well known, but he did not continue to argue the case once decisions were made. His awareness of struggling to communicate the complexities of moral arguments through the media was never more starkly revealed than in October 2003. At the end of a difficult *Today* interview about the Primates' Meeting and Gene Robinson, John Humphrys asked him whether he still thought the war in Iraq was immoral. After hearing Rowan sidestep the question by recounting his approach to commenting on the war, Humphrys bluntly asked, "Was it immoral?" There apparently followed a twelve-second pause – an eternity on the radio – before Rowan gave the careful reply:

> It seems to me that the action in Iraq was one around which there were so many questions about long-term results, about legal justification that I would find it very hard to give unqualified support to the rightness of that decision.[6]

When Humphrys commented "You hesitated a very long time before you answered that, Archbishop," Rowan replied – more quickly – "Immoral is a short word for a very, very long discussion." Much to Humphrys's annoyance this whole exchange was never broadcast as Lambeth protested that there had been agreement not to raise the subject of Iraq.

Two fundamental issues raised by the Iraq war surrounded international structures, especially the role of the United Nations, and just war thinking. Rowan offered significant input on both. Within days of the war starting, he described the greatest casualty away from the arena of war as "a coherent approach to international law and to the maintenance of alliances" and sketched proposals for "better methods of working together". He expanded these in a June 2004 speech at the United Nations on "Internationalism and Beyond". The heart of his proposal was a form of global interactive pluralism: to bring NGOs formally into UN structures to enable "global civil society" to be represented alongside nation-states and create more of a transnational body.

On just war theory, in a lecture to the prestigious Royal Institute for International Affairs at Chatham House in October 2003, he argued that Christian tradition had a "presumption against violence" and that "coercion is simply not justified unless it is answerable to a clear account of the common *human* good". In critical dialogue with Roman Catholic George Weigel's work defending pre-emptive action in certain situations, he argued that governments needed to be self-critical and recognize other voices, including the church.

Rowan remained unconvinced by the case for the Iraq war and at various points was attacked in the media for this and his general questioning of the recourse to violence and war. His sermon to mark the end of the conflict in 2009 reflected on generous obedience, making mistakes, and costly sacrifice. It was once again attacked, with parts of the media reporting a "ten-minute tirade" in which he "hijacked a service honouring the sacrifice of British troops in Iraq – to spout an anti-war rant" (the *Sun*).

Rowan hit the headlines again when bin Laden was killed by US special forces in May 2011. At a press conference on "flying bishops" he was asked whether this was "justice for the 9/11 attacks and indeed other attacks" and "morally justified" even though he was unarmed. He replied, "I think that the killing of an unarmed man is always going to leave a very uncomfortable feeling because it doesn't look as if justice is seen to be done, in those circumstances" adding that, although the full details remained confused and bin Laden was "manifestly a 'war criminal'" nevertheless "it is important that justice is seen to be observed". Many again felt his commitment to non-violence, passionate concern for the vulnerable, and his default siding in any situation with the underdog (Mark Santer, his principal at Westcott in the 1980s, remarked of this tendency, "Sometimes the overdog would have liked a bit of sympathy") had led him to speak unwisely. Others, however, were more understanding. Ann Widdecombe admitted in the *Daily Express* that she had cheered the killing but drew attention to the archbishop's calling:

It's the duty of the church to remind us of our
obligations towards wrongdoers because nobody else
will. An Archbishop of Canterbury should put the
gospel first and political expediency second... Rowan
Williams is a representative of Christ not of Barack
Obama and his duty is to remind us of what we would
rather forget: that killing an unarmed man should give
us pause for thought.[7]

As probably one of the most non-military archbishops in
recent decades, Rowan found himself having to preach and give
people "pause for thought" on numerous occasions marking
wars: the sixtieth anniversary of the end of the Second World
War, the ninetieth anniversary of the end of the First World
War, and the death of the last First World War veteran. Rather
than glorying in military triumph or condemning recourse to
violence, he spoke of issues such as vulnerability and suffering
and highlighted virtues displayed and required more widely
than on the battlefield such as truth-telling, courage, and risk-
taking for others. He then was able to point to the God who
fought evil in Christ and "who is discovered in the heart of your
own endurance and pain... the one who holds your deepest self
and makes it possible for you to look out on the world without
loathing and despair".

His witness to peace also occurred in situations of conflict such
as war-torn Sudan where he emphasized the need for honest self-
examination ("Peace is never, never advanced by people incapable
of seeing their own failings") and finding peace with God:

We will only be at peace with one another when we are
at peace with God. And to be at peace with Almighty
God is to know our own hearts and minds; to be
at peace with God is to let go of our suspicion and

struggle. To be at peace with God means to know that we do not have to strive all the time for power over each other. And so it is that when we learn to be at peace with God, we come to be free, to be reconciled with each other.[8]

Economics

Q: What would be your message to corporate business, in the light of the Church's message?
A: I suppose one message might be "repent and believe the gospel". Because, in its original context that is not a word threatening condemnation, it's saying once again, "what are you about, what are your priorities? Where do you want to be?" Repentance, as the biblical scholars say, is changing your mind. (Q&A, February 2008)[9]

In the face of the global economic crisis from 2008 onwards, Rowan Williams became a recognized and respected contributor to the public debate. He spoke not only in church contexts but on the media, at the Trades Union Congress (2009, where he gained many admirers), and at the World Economic Forum at Davos (2010). Although this response dominates his legacy in relation to economics, his engagement with economic issues prior to the crisis and in other areas is also important.

Rowan came to Canterbury with a very positive experience in Wales of credit unions after considering, in the light of active involvement in the Jubilee 2000 campaign, how to address problems of debt locally. Opening a credit union in May 2004, he spoke of credit unions creating three qualities which also later proved important in his analysis of the crash: trust, stability, and skills. Credit unions were also prominent when he initiated a debate in the Lords in April 2008 on "the impact on the family of economic inequality, credit and indebtedness" and he welcomed government action in support of them just three months later.

Rowan was also prominent in addressing issues of economic inequality globally, joining with other Christians to raise concerns with the European Union in December 2008 and writing with leaders of others faiths to G20 leaders in March 2009. One particular initiative was his support for the Anglican Five Talents charity whose microfinance projects he described as bringing "dignity and economic sustainability to some of the poorest communities in the world... working through established church networks". Their approach to solving this economic problem in turn shaped his approach to the crisis: "we believed that you cannot solve problems like debt without changing people's mindset".

His contributions to the public debate about the economic crisis fell into broadly four categories which offer a model for wider Christian engagement with society: analysis of deeper spiritual issues, specific proposals, an alternative vision, and a holistic approach which set economics in relation to other areas. Underlying each of these is the conviction that, as he said at the launch of *Crisis and Recovery*, a 2010 book of articles he co-edited with the *Guardian*'s economics editor Larry Elliott, the economic questions are part of deeper questions:

> What kind of culture have we allowed to develop?
> Not only the subculture of financial institutions and
> money makers, but the culture in which that happens,
> the whole culture of our society. What are the sorts of
> behaviour we reward? What are the kinds of human
> beings we want to see around, that we've encouraged
> to be around?... They are questions about what we
> think is worthwhile in human behaviour. And unless
> we really tackle that kind of question, really revive our

imagination about what human beings might be and
should be, then the whole of our economic structure
will not really change.[10]

The most commonly cited spiritual sickness was obviously greed.
In one of his earliest contributions, for the *Spectator* in September
2008, Rowan succinctly captured the problem: "trading the
debts of others without accountability has been the motor of
astronomical financial gain for many in recent years". However,
he also insisted that

Just to talk about greed is simplistic: it's more that we
are looking at a large-scale system, sophisticated and
normally successful, that can persuade us to imagine
that it is more unquestionably solid and dependable
than it in fact is.[11]

His diagnosis therefore tended to focus elsewhere, highlighting
how we had become blind to and detached from reality and so
needed fresh vision and reconnection with the real world. These
problems were widespread: "we are left with the question of what
it was that skewed the judgement of a whole society as well as of
financial professionals".

Some of the causes were highlighted in a sermon on Matthew
25 (the parable of the talents), where reflecting on a day at
Canary Wharf spent with chief executives he was struck by how
often people spoke about having tried to make profit without
building up relationships of trust and taking time. As he put it in
his major 2009 lecture on the subject ("Ethics, Economics and
Global Justice"):

The search for impregnable security, independent of
the limits of material resource, available labour and
the time-consuming securing of trust by working at

> relationships of transparency and mutual responsibility, has led us to the most radical insecurity imaginable.[12]

Explaining these patterns of behaviour he not only spoke of pride ("which is most clearly evident in *the refusal to acknowledge my lack of control over my environment,* my illusion that I can shape the world according to my will") but more explicitly theological categories such as – in a September 2008 *Spectator* article – idolatry: "ascribing independent reality to what you have in fact made yourself". One memorable intervention was managing briefly to silence Jeremy Paxman on *Newsnight* by offering a theological analysis. When Rowan asked, in a roundtable discussion, why we were seduced by the unreality, the following exchange occurred:

> Jeremy Paxman: Nobody's got an answer to that yet have they?
>
> Rowan Williams: Well I could say "original sin" which is a good start but I'd need to spell that…
>
> JP: I don't think you really believe that do you?
>
> RW: Original sin? Oh yes.
>
> JP: You really believe original sin is the cause of our delusion about this?
>
> RW: I think there is inbuilt into human beings a sort of dangerous taste for unreality.
>
> (2 second pause)
>
> JP: Right, that is far too complex for us all at this time of night… (although he rounded up the conversation with "we shall discuss original sin at some length I think on another occasion…").[13]

Although reticent about claiming the expertise to offer specific proposals, Rowan pointed to the need for a ban on short-selling and, on a number of occasions, the potential of the Tobin, or "Robin Hood", tax. He also set out – in "Ethics, Economics and Global Justice" – five elements in any way forward towards an ethical global economy. First, and most fundamentally, abandoning a model of economics "which simply assumes that it is essentially about the mechanics of generating money" and instead restoring "the role of trust as something which needs time to develop" and accepting the need for risk-taking. Second, considering environmental cost in economic calculations. Third, thinking about governments' role in monitoring and regulating currency exchange and capital flow. Fourth, re-conceiving existing international economic instruments "as both monitors of the global flow of capital and agencies to stimulate local enterprise and provide some safety nets as long as the global playing field is so far from being level". Fifth, considering the level of material and service production "that will provide an anchor of stability against the possible storms of speculative financial practice" while implementing short-term policies to kick-start an economy.

Behind these lay an alternative vision whose theologically based principles were "trustworthiness, realism or humility and the clear sense that we must resist policies or practices which accept the welfare of some at the expense of others". Such a vision seeks, as he argued to the Trade Union Congress (TUC), to think of economic decision-making in terms of creating a habitat, a home in which we can actually live. Here again he insisted that economics cannot be divorced from a wider picture of human flourishing:

> To decide what sort of change we want, we need a
> vigorous sense of what a human life well-lived looks

like. We need to be able to say what kind of human beings we hope to be ourselves and to encourage our children to be.[14]

That holistic approach in Rowan's analysis challenges the standard compartmentalization of different areas of life, something he himself consistently eschewed in speaking on social, economic, and political issues. He would, for example, as at the TUC, relate economic questions to questions of family life ("a culture, especially a working culture, that consistently undermines the family is going to be one that leaves everyone more vulnerable and thus more fearful and defensive"), but one theme in particular would almost always be raised in his discussions of economics. It was summed up in a saying he often quoted: "the economy is a wholly-owned subsidiary of the environment".

Environment

Q: I just wonder what God would think of our custodianship over creation?
A: Well I used to be an academic and I think God might say B minus or worse at the moment, it's not impressive. (October 2009)[15]

Some would argue that, in responding to that question, Rowan was, characteristically, over-generous in his assessment. What cannot be argued with is his commitment to raising questions of our care for the non-human creation, particularly related to global warming, throughout his primacy. He has not held back in emphasizing their importance, claiming that

the biggest challenge that faces us in terms of global policy at the moment is how we are to find ways of

reducing and controlling climate change without
eating into the economic aspirations, the proper
aspirations of our poorest societies towards prosperity,
respect and dignity.[16]

At times he used apocalyptic language, agreeing (in 2004) with those who described climate change as a "weapon of mass destruction" and warning (in 2006) that millions or billions of people could die.

During his time in office he has supported the Church of England's Shrinking the Footprint campaign, urged churches to participate in the Time for God's Creation project, signed Operation Noah's Ash Wednesday Declaration on Climate Change, joined multi-faith statements to governments, and highlighted the environment during general elections. He worked on the basis that, as he told General Synod in 2005, "part of the Church's responsibility… is to hold the corner for certain issues of public and global concern that are never going to make it to the top of an electoral agenda". The 2008 Lambeth Conference had memorable input on the subject – including testimony from the Bishop of Polynesia about how rising sea levels will make some islands uninhabitable within a few years – and Rowan wrote about this for the *Guardian*. It is, therefore, unsurprising that his work in this area was recognized by an award from the Parliamentary Renewable and Sustainable Energy Group.

His teaching on the subject has two distinct strands. At times the emphasis is on demonstrating the connection between environmental concerns and other global issues, warning of the consequences of ignoring the problems. A primary call has been to think through and act on the basis of the connection between the environment and the economy: "The earth itself is what ultimately controls economic activity because it is the source of the materials upon which economic activity works." Again Rowan used stark language about "a steadily darkening situation":

> Social collapse is a real possibility. When we speak about environmental crisis, we are not to think only of spiralling poverty and mortality, but about brutal and uncontainable conflict. An economics that ignores environmental degradation invites social degradation – in plain terms, violence.[17]

Alongside these prophetic challenges there has been Christian teaching and moral exhortation combined with a thorough critique of our default understanding of ourselves as creatures set apart from creation and subjecting it to our will and "rationality". Rowan was an early convert in the recent movement to make Christians aware of our connectedness with creation and call us to care for it:

> I was just finishing my doctorate studies… And one of the writers I was studying at that time, Yannaras, was already writing in Greek journals about the environmental crisis as a Christian issue… I remember translating one or two of his shorter pieces into English and feeling this was really something I needed to get my mind around and my practice around…[18]

It was to Eastern Christian traditions that he particularly appealed in offering a theological rationale, most fully in his July 2004 lecture "Changing the Myths We Live By" and more succinctly in his 2005 foreword to the Church of England's important report "Sharing God's Planet":

> Creation is an act of communication. It is God
> expressing his intelligence through every existing thing.
> The divine logos spoken of at the beginning of St John's
> Gospel is that by which everything comes to be... This
> implies that each thing communicates the character of
> God, by virtue of the eternal Word... God's self-sharing
> love is what animates every object and structure and
> situation in the world. Responses to the world that are
> unaware of this are neither truthful nor sustainable.[19]

Everything in creation is related to God the Creator before it relates to other creatures and within creation humanity is called to fulfil a priestly or liturgical role in which we voice celebration at God's gift of himself in creation. Our sin means we have abandoned this calling and Rowan points out that Russian Orthodox theologian, Alexander Schmemann,

> goes so far as to suggest that the refusal of this calling is
> the very heart of original sin, which is the replacement
> of priestly naming and blessing by the attitude of the
> consumer, who seeks only to dominate and absorb
> things in such a way that it becomes impossible to treat
> them as gift.[20]

Rowan was cautious about claiming authority to offer specific solutions to the environmental questions we face but has spoken for carbon taxation, rewarding environmental responsibility, and other policies. A central argument was that we need, as with international relationships and the economy, to understand the presenting issues as symptoms of deeper problems in how we view and relate to the world. These are problems where Christianity (and other religions) can offer the world wisdom. The issues are ultimately not technological but theological and ethical. In particular, Rowan highlighted these as issues of justice: justice to the non-human creation, justice to the poorest in our contemporary world, and justice to future generations. As manipulating our environment always brings costs and consequences, we need to act in ways that recognize our limits ("we are not and don't have to be God") and acknowledge that "the major issue we need to keep in view is how much injustice is let loose by any given set of economic or manufacturing practices".

To speak of justice points also to the reality of judgment, a subject Rowan was not afraid to talk about, stating that Christians could not disregard the warning signs of the consequences of our actions or simply believe God would step in to prevent catastrophe. On the contrary, at the end of a *Today* interview when asked, "How will God judge those leaders who did not move quickly enough to prevent the deaths of millions – perhaps even billions of deaths that you forecast?" his reply was a sombre one:

> I think if we look at the language of the Bible on this,
> we very often come across a situation where people are
> judged for not responding to warnings. It's very deeply
> built in; there are choices we can make, each one of
> us, to change things now and I think what the Bible
> and the Christian tradition suggests is that those who
> have that challenge put before them, but not only the
> challenge, but the evidence for it, and don't respond,
> bear a very heavy responsibility before God.[21]

Voice for the Vulnerable

**Ethics... is about negotiating conditions in which
the most vulnerable are not abandoned. And we shall
care about this largely to the extent to which we are**

conscious of our own vulnerability and limitedness. (March 2009)[22]

In "Doing God" in and for society, one forum open to the Archbishop of Canterbury is the House of Lords in which he has a seat by right. Although Rowan's contributions have been limited to two or three times a year at most, they have been significant and reveal an important pattern and passion.

Rowan took his seat in March 2003 and within two weeks made his maiden speech in a debate on the role of parents in providing for the needs of the nation's children, presenting the case for more encouragement and support for parents. Exactly a year later he spoke again, this time calling a debate on criminal justice and sentencing, and in 2005 he contributed on Africa, Millennium Development Goals, and causes of conflict. In 2006 he addressed concerns about immigration detention centres, spoke in the debate on the Assisted Dying for the Terminally Ill Bill, and initiated a debate on "the contribution of the role of the churches in the civic life of towns and cities, the churches' partnership with other bodies and the part they play in addressing the problems of deprivation". In 2007 he prioritized opposing "super casinos", while in 2008 he initiated a debate combining two of his concerns – families and economic inequality – and also spoke on the Human Fertilisation and Embryology Bill and criticized the "indefensible" treatment of young offenders. The debate on the Good Childhood Report drew him back to the chamber in 2009, and a year later he concluded a speech in a debate on citizenship and the role of government and civil society in shaping social policy with words of Richard Sennett, which sum up much of his own vision: "a good polity is one in which all citizens believe they are bound together in a common project". A year later he was back to speak on events which signalled this vision was far from reality: the London riots of the summer of

2011. He has also brought global concerns to the House, asking questions on Egypt and Sudan and introducing and closing a five-hour debate (in December 2011) on the plight of Christians in the Middle East.

As this short summary makes clear, the archbishop has used the limited number of his appearances in the corridors of power at Westminster to speak up for the marginalized and the vulnerable and against developments that threatened them further. This hallmark of his Westminster contributions is also a major part of his wider legacy of contributions to public life as he has emphasized the need to respect human dignity and consider the effects of any actions on the weakest and least powerful members of society and parts of the globe. As he said in the House of Lords in April 2008, "Christian morality mandates the defence of the vulnerable. That is central to any society that claims any residual loyalty to our traditional ethic."

Embryos and Euthanasia

It is within the frame of reference of focusing on the vulnerable that it is best to set Rowan's contributions on what might be seen as traditional Christian concerns such as gambling and especially the beginning and end of life. A long-standing opponent of abortion, he is clear that

> If you believe that every organically distinct human individual, from the first moment it exists as such, stands in a unique and unbreakable relation with the creator, even prior to any conscious appropriation of that relation, it is rational to object to abortion and the breeding of embryos for experiment.[23]

In March 2005, on the verge of a general election, he made clear his concerns in *The Sunday Times*, noting a "groundswell of distaste and dis-ease" about the current law and asking where the issue can be addressed given that it is not a party political matter in elections. Two years later, marking the fortieth anniversary of the Abortion Act in the *Observer*, he typically sought to reframe the public debate arguing that "the model of competing rights or liberties (the mother's and the unborn child's) is not the most useful vehicle for a coherent moral grasp of the question". Warning that the implementation of the 1967 abortion legislation is "an object lesson in how slippage can occur between thinking compassionately or flexibly about extreme and exceptional cases and losing the sense of a normative position", he called for society to be better at "keeping our eyes open... for the unintended consequences, the erosion of something once taken for granted which occurs when we do not keep in focus the fundamental convictions about humanity".

Concerns about a similar trajectory in relation to the elderly and terminally ill contributed to his opposition to assisted dying and euthanasia. Again he set the issue in a wider framework, raising concerns about the effect of a change of the law on the vulnerable elderly. Speaking to Friends of the Elderly, of which he is a patron, he was clear:

> The current drift towards a more accepting attitude to assisted suicide and euthanasia in some quarters gives me a great deal of concern. What begins as a compassionate desire to enable those who long for death because of protracted pain, distress or humiliation to have their wish can, with the best will in the world, help to foster an attitude that assumes resources spent on the elderly are a luxury.[24]

He was also clear in telling the Lords that when we think through the network of relationships impacted by such decisions "we jeopardise the security of the vulnerable... by radically changing the relationship between patient and physician". This works both ways: the danger of someone being pressured by relatives or hospitals but also, as he wrote in *The Times*, "the pressure a sick person who is determined to die places on those around them".

Children and Young People

Within British society two groups of vulnerable people were a particular concern. One, unsurprisingly, given Jesus' teaching, was children and young people, about which he had already written (in *Lost Icons*) before becoming archbishop. In addition to highlighting how wider social and economic problems such as homelessness, poverty, asylum seeking, and debt (in 2003 he launched the "Parents, Pennies and Pounds" website) particularly hit children, Rowan warned of the impact of deeper, less obvious problems in our society.

As guest editor of *Today* in December 2006 one of his themes was the need for a balanced childhood and the dangers of a hurried culture including "hurrying to get children into the market, to get children into the adult world rather than giving them the time they need... We want to get children to be consumers as soon as we can get them to be consumers..."

These concerns shaped his contributions on education where he drew not only on the unusual situation of having a child of school age throughout his time as archbishop but also his regular visits to schools which were an important and much-enjoyed part of his regular diary. In addition to calling for the need for "a bit of time to explore the creative, the apparently not very productive, time for human growth", he warned against the emphasis on testing and results.

Perhaps the most significant and long-lasting contribution associated with Rowan in this area was the Children's Society

Good Childhood Report begun in 2007 and completed in 2009. A strong supporter of its work, he wrote the afterword, emphasizing the centrality of love – "long-term commitment to someone else's well-being as something that matters profoundly to one's own well-being" – and being clear that "it will not serve us as a society, and it will not serve the growing generation, if we simply regard marriage as just one option in the marketplace of lifestyles". As always, his commitment and his writing on it was theologically founded as his conclusion made clear, pointing to biblical teaching to argue:

> It is the very powerlessness or vulnerability of the child that is important – important in securing their place of privilege, but also important as reminding the adult that receiving the news of the possibility of change, freedom, love, reconciliation, requires of the adult a degree of vulnerability and spontaneity that is normally overlaid by suspicion and self-defensiveness.[25]

Prisoners

The other significant group on whose behalf Rowan spoke was prisoners. When David Hare interviewed him for the *Guardian* in 2011 and tossed out a succession of quick questions to throw him off balance, his reply to "If you could change one thing about British society, what would it be?" was "a more realistic prison policy". It is, therefore, no surprise that Peter Selby, Bishop to Prisons for the first half of his primacy, is of the view that "There is nobody I would rather have worked under as Archbishop in my capacity as Bishop to Prisons."[26] Rowan's ministry here again combined both the political and the pastoral. Politically, in the House of Lords and through speeches in other places of influence, he addressed the need for reform of the criminal justice system and in particular emphasized the importance of forms of restorative justice. His contributions were not always welcomed or reported favourably in the media. Among the most remarkable headline appearances he made during his primacy was in the *Mail* – "Archbishop backs axe killer" – a reference to his support in January 2011 for prisoners being allowed to retain the right to vote. Pastorally, Selby recalls his gifts, on display after a major lecture on penal affairs at Worcester Cathedral in which he responded to three professionals (one of whom got the biggest laugh by beginning, "The first thing I want to say Archbishop is I've understood everything you said"):

> We went in a car to a nearby prison. Rowan sat down
> and talked with the prisoners. He showed himself –
> as the prisoners' response made clear – an unusual,
> brilliant, attentive pastor who also thinks with great care
> about these difficult issues. That's been an enormous
> contribution.[27]

Tudor Griffiths provides a similar, powerful testimony from an international context, originating in his closing months at Monmouth when he visited Uganda:

> We visited the prison in Luzira, a harsh place in a
> beautiful setting near Lake Victoria. Rowan and the
> team went to the condemned section and addressed
> more than 300 men who had been sentenced to death.
> Rowan spoke on his recent visit to Jerusalem including
> the condemned cells where Jesus may have been held.
> He then preached on the resurrection and assured the
> men that no situation is hopeless. Following the service
> (led entirely by inmates) Rowan was presented with
> a petition to ask him to speak on their behalf to the
> President. The next day Rowan did just that and was

heard graciously. A little postscript to this story is that
I visited Uganda again in 2005 and went to Luzira to
the condemned section. Before going I emailed Rowan
to tell him what I was doing and by return he sent
a personal message that I read out to the men – that
he continued to remember them. This was a great
encouragement to them.[28]

Global Poverty

Finally, as discussed briefly in Chapter 8, in both his national
and international ministry Rowan spoke up for the poorest of
the world's population, seeking to change policies towards them.
International development issues were high on his agenda from
the start with, for example, the ecumenical and international
London Forum in 2005 in advance of the G8 meeting and
the Lambeth Walk of Witness through central London during
the 2008 Lambeth Conference. A particularly strong and
recurrent emphasis has been his advocacy of the Millennium
Development Goals both in secular, political debate and within
the life of the Anglican Communion, often drawing attention
to the important role of the Christian church on the ground in
helping communities wrestling with these issues.

Conclusion: A Missional Politics and Political Mission

For Rowan, all these areas are understood not in terms of political
agendas but as part of God's mission and the church's mission.
The areas discussed in this chapter show the considerable legacy
he leaves in relation to leading and equipping the church in
relation to the last three of the Anglican five marks of mission
(the first two of which were explored in Chapter 4):

- to respond to human need by loving service;

- to seek to transform unjust structures of society;

- to strive to safeguard the integrity of creation and sustain and renew the life of the earth.

His contributions leave the church with a vision of human flourishing and a model of understanding and engaging with secular society confidently and creatively. In the words of Richard Harries,

> It may be that Rowan's main contribution in the public sphere has not been on any single issue, for he has contributed on a very wide range, but the fact that in all his contributions he has kept before the country a Christian understanding that as human beings we essentially belong together, and that the highly individualistic view of what it is to be human, coupled with rampant capitalism, which has characterised our time, betrays a very defective and impoverished view of what it is to be made in the image of God.[29]

The impact of Rowan's speeches, writings, and interviews is impossible to judge. He himself is honest about the limits. When asked on *Today* if people still listen to an Archbishop of Canterbury he replied "occasionally – they don't always agree with him".

A common criticism has been the complexity of his contributions, in large part due to the complexity of the issues he addressed. This has divided people from the start and not always between obvious insiders and outsiders as illustrated by two reports on his 2002 Dimbleby Lecture. Mike Hill, Bishop of Bristol, with the proviso that "my sense is that this was an isolated incident", recalls

> Though mostly I admire him for his understanding
> of, and willingness to communicate complexity, there
> have been times when I think he might have lost
> his audience. I remember early on in his time, his
> Dimbleby lecture. He chose to take on that difficult
> book written by Philip Bobbitt, *The Shield of Achilles*...
> The lecture was televised and with the hand-picked
> audience, the rest of us gathered around our television
> sets in eager anticipation. Ten minutes in to the lecture
> it was clear that Rowan had lost us ordinary mortals.
> The body language had switched from "edge of their
> seats" to something more passive![30]

In contrast, Tony Benn wrote in his diary on Thursday 19 December 2002:

> In the evening I listened to the whole of the Dimbleby
> Lecture by the new Archbishop of Canterbury, Rowan
> Williams. I must say, it was a marvellous lecture...
> a thoughtful analysis of where power had gone and
> the effect of market forces on society... It was a
> tremendously powerful attack upon what he called
> the market state. It illustrated how a religious leader
> can be a teacher, quite unlike Carey or Fisher or any
> of the other archbishops, and I think probably a bit
> more like Archbishop William Temple, though I never
> heard him speak. He was doing what I'm trying to
> do in my lectures – that is to say, look thoughtfully at
> problems, rather than relate them simply to Labour or
> Tory philosophy. It represents a powerful turning of the
> spiritual tide...[31]

It has to be acknowledged that much of what Rowan has said was quickly forgotten by the media. This was shown by the fact that in June 2012 a number of press reports claimed he was about to launch outspoken attacks on various issues in a new book and citing excerpts, without realizing that the volume simply brought together contributions over the previous ten years. It would, however, be a tragedy if his contributions are forgotten by the church for they are a central part of his legacy which have the potential to resource the church and influence wider society for many years to come.

In the words of Peter Selby:

> The most significant thing he has done without any doubt in my mind – this must be speaking in block caps or red – is his commentary on public affairs. This is in a class on its own… I know that you can have a conversation with Rowan and you will be introduced to a consideration you'd not previously had. You will get a tangential position that is not on one of the poles that the press wants to find you on… It's outstanding. There is not anything else to be said about it. It's always difficult to say these things without some kind of "but" which you come to, but on this, without any ifs and buts, I think he is outstanding.[32]

15

Being a Priest and a Bishop

The primary job for me remains what it has long been: I have to go on being a priest and bishop. (July 2002)[1]

Making decisions that will lose you friends, compromise people's perception of your integrity – that's very hard. On the other hand, that is only part of the reality. First and foremost, I'm a priest and a bishop. (June 2007)[2]

This book has traced the ministry of Rowan as archbishop through the mission of the Church of England and its disputes on sexuality and gender (Chapters 3–7), the life of the Anglican Communion (Chapters 8–10), his interactions with other churches (Chapter 11) and other faiths (Chapter 12), and his contributions to public life (Chapters 13 and 14). In all of these can be found part of his legacy, but another key element of his legacy is the model he offers of what the opening quotations show he has consistently seen as his primary calling: being a priest and a bishop. As Ben Myers, author of *Christ the Stranger: The Theology of Rowan Williams*, noted on news of his retirement from the post to serve as Master of Magdalene College, Cambridge:

> What is unique about Rowan Williams is simply the fact that he is a priest. If anything will come to define his new position at Cambridge, it will be that he approaches academic life just as he approaches Church leadership: as a Christian and as a priest.[3]

This concluding chapter therefore examines some of the hallmarks of his priestly and episcopal ministry drawing on his own statements about these callings which give a vision of how Christ is revealed through these vocations in the church and the world. It also draws extensively on reflections received by email and in conversation from those who have worked with him in the course of the last ten years and can testify about key features of his ministry.

The Body of Christ and its Unity

Philip Giddings, the longest-serving member of Archbishops' Council and current chair of General Synod's House of Laity, when asked what he thought people would look back on and say was Rowan's gift to the church, replied, with little hesitation:

> At a basic minimum, and it says something that one needs to say this, both the Church of England and the Anglican Communion are still there. One thing absolutely clear about Rowan's tenure is his over-riding commitment to the vocation of being the focus of unity. He has sought to hold that unity and given that the highest priority in a time when that has been very difficult indeed.[4]

This analysis is one shared by many. Peter Selby, Bishop of Worcester through most of Rowan's time at Canterbury, puts it like this:

> I think in terms of his theological positions that anything Rowan thinks about anything comes more or less second to his conviction that it is God's will that there should be a church and it should not shatter into pieces. I'm not saying there could never be an issue on which he would put himself at variance with what he saw as "the best interests of the church". I do think it would be an extraordinarily rare, major, terrible moment for him. I think Rowan really believes he is in some sort of way the prisoner of the church, that it is that community in which he is held, that it is God's supreme will that there should be a church and that those of us who have responsibilities of oversight within that church have a supreme responsibility not to allow the church to be fractured. I think he believes that. And I think that has trumped every ace of his theological convictions.[5]

Rowan, asked by *The Hindu* about holding together diversity replied, "to the extent that the Communion has not fractured beyond repair and the Church of England is still engaged in shared discussion of these things, I don't think I have yet failed completely. But time will tell." He was, however, sometimes more sanguine. A year earlier, in 2009, when asked by the *Telegraph* if there could ever be a consensus in which biblical traditionalists can be in communion with [practicing] homosexual bishops he paused and said "I'm not holding my breath."

The common criticism levelled at him, particularly by those who might be identified as "liberal" and hoped he would offer reforming and radical leadership, including in relation to the church's response to gay and lesbian Christians, is that he has prioritized unity over truth. This has been said at least since the Reading crisis and his response to the consecration of Gene Robinson.

As early as February 2005, Rowan told General Synod, "I've become very much accustomed to being accused by both sides in this debate of setting unity before truth." He explained his dilemma lay in the fact that "I'm not sure as a Christian that I'm wholly able to separate truth from unity" and set out thinking which shaped his whole ministry:

> For a Christian I believe that unity is what enables
> us to discover truth within the body of Christ, not
> simply truth according to my own preferences, my
> own intelligence, my own resources, but in the richness
> of life an understanding that is shared in the body.
> And part of the agony of the situation we face at the
> moment has to do with those two things beginning to
> pull apart from one another.[6]

His concluding Lambeth Conference address made clear this unity is not simply human loyalty or sentiment but *Christian* unity which is union with Jesus Christ:

> We are one with one another because we are called into
> union with the one Christ and stand in his unique place
> – stand *in* the Way, the Truth and the Life… That's the
> unity which is inseparable from truth. It's broken…
> when we stop being able to see in each other the same
> kind of conviction of being called by an authoritative
> voice into a place where none of us has an automatic
> right to stand.[7]

To understand how his ministry relates to serving that unity the best starting place is a 1982 article written long before he became a bishop,[8] which he himself drew attention to in 2011:

> Thirty years ago, little knowing what fate had in store, I wrote an article about the role of a bishop, saying a bishop is a person who has to make each side of a debate audible to the other. The words "irony" and "prescience" come to mind. And of course you attract the reproach that you lack the courage of leadership and so on. But to me it's a question of what only the archbishop of Canterbury can do.[9]

The article opens with a discussion of the question of authority and develops an understanding focused on Christ – who calls and creates the church – and the sacraments. Quoting the Orthodox theologian John Zizioulas, he points out that in the early church the bishop's "primary function is always to make the catholicity of the Church reveal itself in a certain place". The bishop is "the focal point around which the community gathers, overcoming its divisions, to affirm a single identity governed by the paschal symbol in its Eucharistic shape". The actual limits of the church are discerned by reference to "the single figure in a district set apart to be *himself* a 'symbol' accessible to all, related to all, not representing only a sector of the community". In words which capture much of his own ministry and legacy to the church, he wrote:

> The bishop's authority is an authority to unify; not an authority to abolish or minimize conflict within the community, but the task of referring all sides of a debate to the unifying symbol over whose ritual recollection he presides, in such a way to show the face of strangers or opponents in the Church as Christ's face for each other.[10]

That authority operates positively in the church when a bishop tells a group he recognizes their opponents as in communion with him and they need to listen to each other and not rupture their fellowship. Negatively, he sees it exercised when "a bishop says to the community at large: 'Such-and-such a group has broken the fellowship of Christ's table by its attitudes, and I cannot see how it confesses Christ.'"

A bishop's authoritative role is to realize in the community of the church those patterns by which the body of believers as a whole is meant to be characterized: mutuality, gift, "the rejection of rejection", acceptance. A bishop's ministry should therefore help the church be the church and in being the church be a sign in the world of God's call to everyone: "His exercise of authority, in manner and context, must serve the creation and growth of that community of gift which is God's purpose for the humanity made in his image." This also means that any bishop – particularly the Archbishop of Canterbury – must transcend the local because "the local church's representative must be actively and regularly engaged in interpreting his church to other churches, and vice versa".

During his primacy Rowan offered the church his own form of that pattern of ministry. Seven characteristics particularly stand out in relation to his commitment to serve the church and its unity in Christ.

A Listening and Learning Linguist

A common, although not universal, assessment of Rowan is that he is a gifted listener who leaves people feeling they have been valued and heard. Phil Groves, Director of the Listening Process, comments:

> Rowan is a great listener; in some ways infuriatingly good. He is so soft he falls for sob stories and hard luck cases. He is partially deaf, perhaps that helps as he has

to actively listen and in doing so you feel listened to because you are. He puts effort into listening and values what he hears. Of course everyone then thinks you are an ally.[11]

Giles Goddard of Inclusive Church writes, "Rowan had a tremendous ability to give people the impression that he was listening to them. Meetings with him usually ended with a sense of positivity, that he was hearing our concerns and could understand them."[12] Part of this reflects his own desire, despite what all acknowledge to be his great intellect and breadth of knowledge, to learn more of Christ. Philip Giddings' assessment after watching him work in the councils of the church is "the one thing you can say about Rowan is that there are very few issues on which he has a *closed* mind, very few issues indeed".[13]

His Lambeth Conference retreat addresses, focused on the calling of the bishop, explore this listening – and then speaking in response – in terms of being a linguist. As with learning a language, so in listening there needs to be a form of obedience:

> listening for the nuances, listening for the hidden music
> in what someone says or does, listening sometimes
> for what's beneath the surface as well as what is
> immediately in front of us. It's a tough experience, and
> it doesn't happen quickly.[14]

It is, therefore, unsurprising that within the Communion, part of his legacy is the Listening Process, the reconfiguring of the Lambeth Conference as Indaba and the Continuing Indaba Project which followed.

Part of the bishop's role is then to interpret people to one another, and this is even more the case in his role at Canterbury as he acknowledged in an interview just before taking office:

"I suppose what I've sometimes said about the role of a bishop – someone who assists communication to happen between congregations... that applies with knobs on, really."

He has particularly sought to listen to those on the margins, as he told the bishops on retreat, with reference to the Rule of St Benedict, "St Benedict is telling us to listen to the marginal communities because they are as likely to present the imperatives of justice and truth as anyone else." This approach has, some believe, been part of the problem when the margins to whom he listened were unrepresentative. Kenneth Kearon, secretary general of the Communion, qualifies his high assessment of Rowan's primacy – "he has remodelled what the Archbishopric of Canterbury can be, restated it for the modern world in a very helpful way" – by expressing a concern in this area:

> He doesn't lead from the centre, he leads from the edge and that isn't always helpful in his role. He actually listens to the extremes and then tries to represent those voices which he sees to be marginalised, which runs the danger of making the whole thing quite unbalanced. While it's necessary to have those voices there, the safer role is to speak from the centre, articulate the centre and discern where the centre is – it's not halfway between the two extremes. I think that's sometimes why he fails.[15]

The commitment to listen and interpret people to each other gives rise, in turn, to a pattern of enabling and engaging in patient conversation.

Patient Conversation

Rowan's passion for and his commitment to conversation, perhaps reflecting his Oxbridge academic background and love of the seminar, is evident across all the spheres of his ministry: his engagement with wider society in mission, his commitment to Building Bridges and dialogue with Islam, and his ministry in both the Church of England and Anglican Communion faced with potential fractures. It is also a central element in his vision of "interactive pluralism", bringing different communities into conversation with each other to discern the common good.

The combination of listening and facilitating conversation was often evident when he chaired meetings. He was seen as always eager to enable people to join in the conversation (even, sometimes, those whom others thought had little to add). Here, and in other contexts, he was often able to offer a masterly summing up of discussions. Bishop Andrew Burnham, reflecting on Rowan's ministry, describes him "professor-like, magisterially summing up and moving on the discussion when he was working with the House of Bishops, whether as chairman or contributor",[16] while another bishop writes:

> I recall, particularly, one House of Bishops meeting when there was a long, complex and controversial discussion of some issue or other – I forget what – at the end of which he gave a five-minute summary of how things stood which had us all breathless with its accuracy, clarity and brevity. When he finished, Richard Harries, sitting next to me (and I think the longest-serving bishop still in office at that point), turned to me and said "That's why he's Archbishop of Canterbury."[17]

The determination not to bring conversation to a premature end has, however, created its own tensions and problems. Some of these were evident in his handling of legislation for women bishops and in relation to homosexuality. The importance of enabling patient conversation played a large part in his decision in relation to Reading. As he told Melvyn Bragg:

> It had to do with weighing up a whole lot of factors
> about how… the Church could hang together
> in the continuing conversation about this rather
> than simply splitting into bits that weren't going to
> communicate with each other. And that continues to
> be the difficulty we face world-wide. But that I think
> in itself is a theological thing. If… St. Paul is right in
> saying that in the body of Christ and the Church we
> all need one another's perspectives, then shepherding,
> trying to broker and facilitate relationships and keep
> a conversation going even when people want to walk
> out of the room, has something to do with witnessing
> to how the Church ought to behave… The particular
> responsibility I have… in virtue of the Office, is to
> do all I can to hold the conversation together with
> integrity. I don't pretend that there may not come a
> point where that's not possible. But I hope and pray
> that we carry on with it… that's I think the particular
> job that an Archbishop of Canterbury has to exercise in
> that world-wide context now.[18]

Although in relation to Reading the desire to continue conversation upset those on his left, the determination to continue conversation subsequently led to frustrations on his right, most notably from 2007 among those associated with GAFCON, but also more widely. They looked not for constant conversation but for clearer direction and action, particularly in response to the American church's disregard for the moratoria. His commitment to conversation thus was not without its problems. In the words of Mike Hill, Bishop of Bristol: "I think we will remember Rowan as a man of great patience. In the minds of some it was a patience that frustrated them. I think he really does prefer 'jaw-jaw to war-war'."[19]

Christopher Rowland, New Testament scholar and contemporary of Rowan as an undergraduate at Christ's, describes how he came to understand Rowan's time as archbishop better through an article Rowan wrote on William Blake. In it Rowan discussed Blake's distinction between contraries and negations and as a result Rowland saw his ministry "has been to try to keep opposites together… you need to keep both poles in play and leave it to God at the Last Judgment".[20]

This approach has been warmly received in many parts of the Communion although their thanks are not heard as often as those unhappy with Rowan's stance. Sarah Rowland Jones writes (from experience of the Church in Wales and now the Anglican Church of Southern Africa and work on Communion commissions) of how Rowan's waiting on God gives him the courage seen in

> his refusing to act when he believes it would be to "close down" (a frequent phrase) some situation too early, and so halt the ongoing working of grace, redemption within it. This is most visible of all within the Anglican Communion, where I think his "doing so little" (as some see it) will in the end turn out to have been the right thing. He has not forced, or allowed the premature forcing of, "a solution" which would have required everyone to "pick sides", thus ensuring and entrenching polarisation and division. Whereas this may have been very frustrating for those who attempted to get him to back this or that decisive stance, it has meant that for the great fuzzy central bulk of the Communion, where this is not seen as either a defining or church-dividing issue, we can carry on with focusing on our primary

callings. It also means that provinces like Southern Africa, where there is a huge range of views, have been able to continue working through them slowly, and not come to artificially early conclusions when there is still more to be unpacked and explored. 2 Pet 3:9 ["The Lord is… patient with you, not wanting anyone to perish, but everyone to come to repentance"] comes to mind – an ability to live in the patience of God which is not a slowness to act, but a desire to keep working with redemptive grace for as long as it takes.[21]

Phil Groves' assessment is similar: "If there was an inflexible leader the Anglican Communion would fall apart. Such strength would be brittle. What was needed was a strong leader who could walk with all and not end conflict with demands for uniformity, but enable harmony where conflict could be part of the reality of the Anglican Communion."[22]

Rowan's legacy is one of maintaining unity by keeping conversations going in the midst of conflict as a means of learning the truth together. But this of course requires that people are willing to accept they do not already possess the truth. As he explained back in 2002 there are contrasting approaches which will shape the nature of any conversation:

If what I basically am is a fixed identity with lots of needs and priorities, then when I enter into public dialogue I do so on the assumption that it's a boxing ring. I've got to find my corner, and ideally, I've got to defeat an opponent, or at least make it clear which bit of the rings belongs to me, and what belongs to him… If we enter into conversation with some awareness that where I'm speaking from is not fixed and final. That we haven't yet discovered who we are, and the conversation helps us find that out – then I think we move a bit away from the idea that conversation is all about competing for territory.[23]

The crucial question is whether the different groupings within the Communion and perhaps even the Church of England are losing patience and have slipped too far towards the former approach. If so, and particularly if the covenant fails to gain widespread support as a means of structuring and facilitating such conversation, his successor may find it impossible, even if he wishes, to continue Rowan's almost unqualified commitment to ongoing conversation as part of keeping united.

An Unreliable Ally

One of Rowan's most telling descriptions of the bishop in his Lambeth retreat addresses is related to these commitments to listen and to learn and to discover truth in conversation. Bishops, he said, are "deeply unreliable allies":

> Many groups, many individuals, many causes will want us on their side. And as bishops, we always have to say that there is more than just being on your side... At some point, we are going to have to say, "There's more to this than just your interest. I have to let you down in the name of Jesus, because for the sake of the health and the fullness of the body, everyone in this situation needs to change, to be converted and to grow." And once again, if you are like me as a bishop, you will find that appallingly difficult. And you will look back on your ministry, as I look back on mine, conscious of the many times when I have tried to avoid saying just that. We would all like to be good and reliable allies, and yet God says, "You're never just

the prisoner of one person, one agenda, one cause, one nation, one political perspective. You are always the person who has that 'something more' to add in the name of the body of the Christ who gathers."[24]

Undoubtedly one of the difficulties with Rowan's style of leadership was that people easily concluded from the fact he was listening carefully to them that he was actually agreeing with them, could fix things, and would act accordingly. As a result, he sometimes left people feeling let down and disappointed. In the words of one person who worked closely with him, "He has a lot of ways of implying he agrees with you, without actually committing himself."[25]

Some of the perplexity, pain, and anger he generated, particularly in North America, is related to this aspect of his ministry, combined with a sense, on the part of the American leadership, of not being listened to by Rowan. Privately, leaders on both sides of the American divisions expressed their frustration in the same terms of looking for the leadership of a Churchill and finding instead that of Chamberlain. Probably the starkest public expression of this came in early 2007 from Bishop Paul Marshall of Bethlehem, Pennsylvania:

[The] situation of alienation was regrettably worsened by his remarkable distancing of himself from a church that has followed his own carefully thought-through teachings on sexuality... The situation of the shunning of North American bishops would be painful under any circumstances. The pain is more intense here because it comes from the withdrawal of a human who was friend, teacher, and colleague to many in this church – with no notice that either his opinions or commitments were in flux... Our relationship to the one who is expected to be first in a world-wide college of bishops is distant, confused, and multiply-triangulated... This ought not to be... Can the Archbishop of Canterbury not come to meet us just once...?[26]

The criticism was clearly taken to heart by Rowan who visited the American House of Bishops in September 2007 and General Convention in 2009. Many, however, remained unhappy and confused, particularly among gay and lesbian Anglicans in America as vividly captured by Gene Robinson's comments in 2010:

We were dancing in the streets when Rowan Williams was made Archbishop of Canterbury. We just thought it was a wonderful choice. And we are so perplexed here in the American Church about what he has done, what he has said... I have clergy friends in England who literally studied at Archbishop Williams' feet when he was teaching and who have said to me it is almost as if aliens have come and taken Rowan away from us and they have left something here that looks like him but we don't recognise him any more. And that's from people who know him very, very well.[27]

Louie Crew, the founder of *Integrity*, remained very unhappy in September 2012:

He spent an enormous amount of time with those attacking us in the Communion, but almost no time with TEC leaders. He waited a long time before his first meeting with Bishop Gene... He made almost no efforts to understand how TEC and General Convention try to speak the truth to power in this country... Nor does Rowan seem to have any knowledge of or respect for the role of laity and clergy

in the polity of TEC... Rowan has spent next to no
time with LGBTQ leadership in the USA... Given the
huge chunk of his time devoted to the Communion's
response to homosexual persons, I just cannot wrap
my mind around how he could possibly have allowed
himself to have so little personal contact with us. He
should have been seeking us out, not trying to avoid us
on the few occasions when we sought him out.[28]

It is perhaps because this perspective is still quite widespread
that, shortly before retirement, Rowan admitted that

I don't think I've got it right over the last 10 years, it
might have helped a lot if I'd gone sooner to the United
States when things began to get difficult about the
ordination of gay bishops, and engaged more directly.[29]

He later told Vatican Radio that not inviting certain bishops
to Lambeth "felt like both an inevitable thing, to honour
commitments we had declared together, and also a very, very
hard and un-kingdom-like thing to be doing. It's those things
that are the tough memories."

It wasn't, however, only Robinson sympathizers who came to
see him as a deeply unreliable ally. Those who thought he was
committed to enabling the Instruments to develop and implement
a coherent response, supportive of Windsor and its supporters
in the American church, were also bitterly disappointed. In the
words of one who had hoped he would deliver:

One by one he has allowed and at times participated
in the systematic destruction of the credibility of the
Instruments. Much of the Communion now thinks
they are not worth the bother. A charitable view is that
he is someone of almost inconceivable administrative

incompetence – an Archbishop Clouseau. Another more sinister view is that he was really Archbishop Machiavelli. I incline to the former; either way the structures of the Communion have been destroyed and will have to be re-built, if that is even possible.[30]

Having to be an unreliable ally leads, inevitably, particularly if one is an empathetic listener, to leaving people with a sense of betrayal. Distinguishing instances of the virtue and examples of the vice is, at times, hard. It brings with it its own difficult dynamic, summed up by one bishop who wrote how, after Reading and then New Hampshire:

> From that point, neither friends nor foes quite knew where they were, were not quite prepared to trust him, were quickly disappointable by him – and it seems to me that we have seen this get steadily more complex over the years, not least as it has "internationalised".[31]

For conservatives, a large part of the problem with Rowan is how he implemented another crucial element in his understanding of the bishop's role and his own approach:

No Condemnation

Tom Wright recalls an incident when they were colleagues in Oxford and Rowan was asked to be the Anglican observer at a big international Methodist conference held in Oxford:

> Rowan gave his closing reflections on the conference and said, at the end, that he was disappointed with them for not singing, at any point, the great Methodist hymn "And Can it Be". He made them stand up and sing it right then and there. I heard about this and the next time I was with Rowan I

teased him about his teasing of the Methodists. At
once he became excited about the hymn, and quoted
energetically and enthusiastically "No condemnation
now I dread – Jesus and all in him is mine!" That's
what it's all about, he said.[32]

That emphasis on this central gospel message of freedom from
God's condemnation decisively shapes his pattern of priestly and
episcopal ministry. Tom Wright comments "I wish some of his
evangelical critics could realise that that is at the deep centre
of the man he is", and Sarah Rowland Jones describes it in the
following way:

I see in him courage to be able to look at anything
without bringing a prior judgement to bear, and so to
try only to see as God sees; to focus on the potential
for Christ and his love and redemption to be known,
experienced, and received. For he truly believes
within himself, and reflects in his external attitude,
that Christ's salvation is offered for all the world, and
so every situation, circumstance, and issue can be
approached with hope. His task is to help this hope
be found. It is far more creative (in all senses) than
beginning by juddging or condemning whatever is
awry: one which echoes the dynamic of, for example,
John 3:17, James 2:13.[33]

In his Lambeth retreat addresses he appealed to the Desert
Fathers to explain and justify this pattern of ministry. They were,
he points out, rigorous towards themselves but

at the same time they look upon each other with a
deep and principled reluctance to condemn. There
are many stories of fathers in the desert summoned to

councils where they are invited to condemn someone
and they say, "I carry my water in a broken pitcher
and it runs out as fast as I can walk; what am I doing,
gathered to condemn?"... They... challenge the ease
and the attractiveness with which we sometimes turn
to condemn. And in our Church today, I think, the
Desert Fathers turn a cool eye on both the left and the
right, and turn a warm eye towards the Lord of truth
and mercy.[34]

That quality is seen in his handling of disputes within the church
where he frequently warned against portraying opponents
negatively, condemning and scapegoating. It also marked – to
the frustration of some – his contributions to public life. A *New
Statesman* profile spoke of "a principle that sets Williams apart
from his predecessors: a refusal to condemn" and recalled an early
interview in which he had said he would not condemn or attack,
say, an unmarried couple living in a flat in Kilburn. Rowan's
response sums up this significant characteristic of his primacy:

What I'm deeply uncomfortable with, I think, is
saying things that really don't change anything, that
don't move things on... So much of the language that
we use about scapegoats – whether it's the couple
in Kilburn or whatever – doesn't change anything.
It makes people feel safer, but it doesn't make the
vulnerable feel any safer. And I am very worried
about the morality of simply sounding off. Now I
realise that's not very popular in all quarters. People
feel, you know, "Why don't you give a clear defence
of Christian moral standards?" There are contexts in
which you can do that – and I am actually rather old-
fashioned about some of these issues – but saying it

loudly and aggressively in public doesn't change it. The only effect it has is to increase suspicion and fear of people who already have enough problems… When I first went to train in a parish in the 1970s, I went to one of the worst council estates in Liverpool for a bit as part of my student experience, and the vicar said to me something I've never forgotten: "The people here have doors slammed in their face every day of the week. I want to make sure they don't have another one slammed on the seventh." That's a very central vision for me and that's what I try to work with.[35]

The Vulnerable One Who Gathers

Rowan found his Lambeth retreat reflections on Paul's statement in Galatians 1:16 that Christ is revealed in us. Given that this is true of all disciples, he asks in what sense it is distinctively true of bishops. His answer is that, "In us as bishops, what is distinctive is that the aspect of God's Son that is revealed is the gathering Christ – the Christ upon whom all reality converges, comes together." This again relates to mission and unity: this is "a missionary matter for us as bishops, because that is the mission of God, to draw together the scattered children into one family". He then refers to Paul's words in 2 Corinthians 11:28–29 to highlight how this makes the bishop vulnerable:

> The only way, it seems, of being a "successful" apostle, is to be an apostle who is quite unable to distance him or herself from the weakness of everybody else… If God's Son is to be revealed in us, God's Son is revealed in our vulnerability not the toughness of our defences, the fluency of our solutions or the success of our schemes, but in our freedom (and I choose the word very carefully) to let the grief and the struggle of others come in to us. Why

is this so? It's not because being an apostle is something reserved for people in love with suffering; not because being a bishop is something reserved for those who have a taste for misery. It is because the new humanity that is in Jesus Christ and into which we seek to live is a humanity in which we bear one another's burdens so as to fulfil the law of Christ. The new humanity is a vulnerable place, where if any one loses, is hurt or is held back, everyone loses, is hurt, or is held back.[36]

There is little question that Rowan has left the church a legacy of vulnerable leadership. He has often painfully embodied this vision of apostolic ministry. For some this is one of his most significant and important gifts to the church: offering a Christ-like pattern of power in weakness in marked contrast to worldly patterns of leadership often replicated within the church. For others, his way of expressing this has been part of the problem of his time in office. Giles Goddard, critiquing some of his handling of sexuality and women bishops, points to this element as unhealthy:

> Underlying this is a deeper issue, which is the downside of Rowan's profound and humbling spirituality. It feels as though he saw the role of Archbishop of Canterbury as one which is defined by the suffering caused by division and disagreement. The impression was given that he, and the role, are the focus of the pain of divergence – he as the suffering servant of the church. Rowan's pain was always very near the surface. I think that as a church we internalised the suffering which he projected.[37]

The vulnerability and pain involved in seeking to fulfil the calling to gather was most obvious in the meetings of the Instruments. At the Primates' Meeting it was initially evident in the inability to gather together around the Lord's Table. As Bishop Geoffrey Rowell says on Rowan's approach to the Communion, "Rowan is trying to get people to listen to each other, being prepared to be humiliated when people won't receive communion which is deeply painful."[38] In 2008 it was seen in the many bishops not attending Lambeth (whom Rowan mentioned several times during his addresses) and in 2011 the vulnerability and the difficulties were again evident in the absences from the Primates' Meeting. That inability to gather fellow bishops and primates represents perhaps the most damaging feature of the legacy he leaves his successor and the biggest threat to the future unity of the Communion. Its importance lies in part in the next key element in his vision of the calling of the bishop.

Being a Bishop in Communion

Rowan's fourth Lambeth retreat address highlighted the importance of bishops exercising ministry together, in communion as a worldwide fellowship of bishops. This explains why, from the start, he gave the 1998 Lambeth sexuality resolution such authority and why he opposed Gene Robinson's consecration. John Humphrys, on the *Today* programme, after the Emergency Primates' Meeting, asked Rowan whether he believed Gene Robinson should become a bishop. His answer referred not to Scripture or Christian ethical teaching but to this need to be in communion:

> No I don't because I believe that on a major issue of
> this kind the Church has to make a decision together
> and one of the things that has emerged most painfully
> and with such difficulty in the last couple of days in our

conversations is the large number – the very, very large number – of Anglican provinces who feel that, quite simply, a decision has been made which commits them or involves them in some way and yet in which they have had no part at all.[39]

A commitment to being bishops in communion also explains why Rowan was so keen to reconfigure Lambeth 2008 to enable listening, conversation and relationship-building rather than resolution-forming. Once again, however, his inability to gather many bishops severely weakened this as he acknowledged – the importance of communion is

why the breach of communion also matters, and why it hurts and is felt as a *wound* for us all. In this conference, historically, part of the agenda has been to celebrate our communion... But on this particular occasion we are bound to be aware that we are not only celebrating communion, but working and praying for its restoration and its deepening.[40]

Within the Church of England, many bishops shared the view of Mike Hill that "as time passed under his leadership I felt that the atmosphere in the House of Bishops improved dramatically".[41] Another diocesan wrote that "most of the House of Bishops' meetings I was at were basically good, and when Rowan was taking the lead very good".[42]

Despite Rowan's strong emphasis on collegiality and commitment to listening, many bishops and others shared a concern about his leadership style memorably expressed by Peter Selby:

I think Rowan basically made decisions alone, by going into Lambeth Palace chapel for two hours and emerging and making the decision. I would rather someone who did go into the chapel for two hours than not but it is of some interest to me that you can talk again and again and again to people whom you might judge to have been his friends and find they have never been sounded out or consulted on anything.[43]

Similar sentiments were expressed by others who worked alongside him, reflecting a range of churchmanship. One wrote about how he "often wondered who his [Rowan's] friends are, who he tends to consult, having learned on a number of occasions and issues that people whom I had imagined had advised him or been consulted by him had not done so and were as perplexed, and outside the circle, as I was myself";[44] another recalled a conversation with a fellow bishop about who Rowan consulted in which he himself had to confess "I've never known Rowan ring up to ask advice";[45] while a third can only recall Rowan phoning him up once and concludes on his style, similar to Peter Selby: "He is in that sense a 'charismatic', believing that the proper response to a question or situation is for the leader (i.e. him) to pray, search the scriptures, the tradition, and his own heart, think it through, and go for it."[46] Whatever the reasons – his introvert personality, his academic tendency to work things out in his head on his own, his desire not to have a favoured inner team of consultants – this pattern meant that in practice his acting as a bishop in communion was expressed through formal meetings of the House without less formal, personal consultation with episcopal colleagues.

What is not in doubt is that Rowan's leadership and his determination to seek the unity of the church was rooted in the seventh and final characteristic of his leadership to which Peter Selby pointed in his reference to Lambeth Palace chapel: prayer and silence.

Prayer and Silence

Rowan's fundamental conviction that even the highest office in the church is one which has to be led by the Spirit of Christ and discern the work of Christ means that all these other elements in his leadership are rooted in the prayer, silence, and meditation central to his ministry. Sarah Rowland Jones, asked about what marked his time as archbishop, was clear:

> Prayer! Absolutely the number one element, from which all else flows. Those who have eyes to see can tell it is the bedrock of his life, even if they have not seen (as I have) how each day begins with him semi-prostrated on the floor of the Lambeth Palace crypt chapel for some time, prior to the arrival of staff for the daily Eucharist. And it is the quality and attitude of this prayer: the true humility of laying himself open to whatever God has for him, and his deep trust that whatever God purposes are, they are better than anything else can be. Despite knowing that what God has in store may be painful, dire, and humiliating before the world, he nonetheless remains committed to coming before God with no preconditions. I find this hugely courageous. Most of us let ourselves off the hook, or create ways of engaging with God while keeping God safely in a box to some degree – but he wrestles with himself to try to give God carte blanche, always and everywhere, again and again and again, no matter what the cost.[47]

As he explained to Mark Tully who asked in a BBC interview what he was doing when he was praying:

> As a Christian, my understanding is that what I'm doing is allowing the life of Jesus to come alive in me with the Holy Spirit, which means that from

the depth of my being as a believer there rises up a
kind of welling-up of life and love directed towards
that mysterious source of Jesus' being, which we call
God the Father. So when I pray I'm trying to make
room for that. I'm not trying to fill up the space, I'm
not trying to *do* something, but I'm trying almost
to be *carried* on that "rising water"… but for that to
happen you have to let go of a lot. You have to still your
body and your imagination and let something flower,
let something happen, and sooner or later your mind
and your feelings have to get out of the way. So prayer
is *communion*, it's that allowing the depth *within* and
the depth *outside* to come together.[48]

A significant element in such prayer is silence. His retreat
addresses reminded the bishops of words of Ignatius of Antioch
– "bishops are pleasing to God when they are silent" – and drew
out the importance of this for episcopal service:

The bishop whose ministry is centered on the Eucharist,
performed with the wholeness of the Church in mind,
will be a bishop who is silent in respect of many of the
claims and pressures that are around, holding still so
that God's word – not the bishop's – can come through.
Open, therefore to the differences, the difficulties
in letting God's word through, but also beginning,
maturing, ending in the quiet that allows God to be
God and doesn't impose the agenda of the individual
and their fleshly nature.[49]

His next address offered a practical suggestion to the bishops. He
proposed they find another bishop "about whom you feel fearful
or nervous": "Go and ask him or her to pray with you. Don't

discuss, don't negotiate, just ask to pray: you never know what might happen... See what God can do."

His own pattern, in a busy schedule, he described to Tully:

> It's a matter of trying to make time early in the morning to put the whole day in perspective and have enough space then to frame the rest of the day. And also it's simply making the most of those rare moments when nothing much is going on, to settle physically, breathe from the pit of your stomach for a few minutes, perhaps let a word or two – *come Jesus,* or *God* – just *be* there.[50]

He pointed to this pattern of disciplined prayer and Scripture meditation when asked the source of his strength and how he coped with the demands of being archbishop:

> Turn to Psalm 121. Funnily enough, the first two psalms I ever learned were Psalm 121 and Psalm 84 and so they still have a particular meaning for me. And it's important to me to begin everyday with enough silence with God to give me some resource for the day, to make sure that the pattern of the daily offices is kept up, the Holy Communion nearly every day, these are the things that sustain me. But also very simply, things like making sure I have time to listen to music occasionally and some time to spend with my wife and my children, especially my 11-year old son who is a great source of inspiration to me.[51]

Often criticized for not providing strong leadership, from his perspective he was offering a different sort of leadership, marked by these characteristics and seeking to serve and build the church. As he explained when asked early in his ministry about expectations on his leadership:

What does leadership mean in the context of the Church? It involves a great deal of listening, trying to make sense of people to each other, and out of that trying to find what's possible, in your own prayer and discernment, as to how to nudge things forward. So it can be a slow process, it can be a frustrating process but I think that's partly the way Christian leadership anyway is set up and very much the way in which Anglicans have tended to do the job [laughs].[52]

Being an Anglican

In speaking of an Anglican way, Rowan here points to another feature of his leadership which sheds light on the way he sought to keep the church together and will be a lasting legacy: his vision of what it means to be Anglican and his enactment and embodiment of that during his archiepiscopacy. Politically, Malcolm Brown explains this in terms of viewing Anglicanism as a coalition which requires a certain form of leadership:

We could actually teach the government a thing or two about how you run a coalition. Anglicanism is a lot more complex and difficult world. If they think it's frustrating, talk to Rowan. If you look at his task as managing a coalition, because he believes in the Anglican Settlement in some sense, then an awful lot of criticism of him falls into place. It becomes pointless because it's misunderstood the task. People who are deeply frustrated that they can't make their writ run then bash Rowan about the head for not making his writ run. But I think he's understood at a profound level, probably for most of his life, that's actually not how it works. And so people who complain that he's kept it all together at the expense of direction and action have misunderstood.[53]

The nature of that Anglican Settlement or coalition is described in various terms: evangelical, catholic, and liberal; giving priority to Scripture, tradition, or reason and experience; commitment to complete the Reformation, Counter-Reformation, or Enlightenment. Rowan's articulation was most clearly set out in his 2006 reflection on the challenge and hope of being an Anglican today.[54] He was clear that "There is no way in which the Anglican Communion can remain unchanged by what is happening at the moment" and set out his understanding of the "distinctive historic tradition" that he sought to uphold and preserve in changing times. As usual in such Anglican schema, Rowan's description identified three elements:

- "a reformed commitment to the absolute priority of the Bible for deciding doctrine";

- "a catholic loyalty to the sacraments and the threefold ministry of bishops, priests and deacons"; and

- "a habit of cultural sensitivity and intellectual flexibility that does not seek to close down unexpected questions too quickly".

He was clear that "the different components in our heritage can, up to a point, flourish in isolation from each other" but warned that "any one of them pursued on its own would lead in a direction ultimately outside historic Anglicanism". He set out the dangers in each should it become separated from the others:

- "The reformed concern may lead towards a looser form of ministerial order and a stronger emphasis on the sole, unmediated authority of the Bible."

- "The catholic concern may lead to a high doctrine of visible and structural unification of the ordained ministry around a focal point."

- "The cultural and intellectual concern may lead to a style of Christian life aimed at giving spiritual depth to the general shape of the culture around and de-emphasising revelation and history."

In short, "pursued far enough in isolation, each of these would lead to a different place – to strict evangelical Protestantism, to Roman Catholicism, to religious liberalism". Anglicanism therefore requires an acceptance that "each of these has a place in the church's life and that they need each other". This in turn means that "the enthusiasts for each aspect have to be prepared to live with certain tensions or even sacrifices". Again he succinctly spelt out what he saw as the main challenges a fully rounded Anglicanism presents to each grouping within it:

- living "with a tradition of being positive about a responsible critical approach to Scripture";

- living "with the anomalies of a historic ministry not universally recognised in the Catholic world";

- living "with limits on the degree of adjustment to the culture and its habits that is thought possible or acceptable".

Rowan himself probably identified most with the catholic tradition. As he explained to Charles Moore early in office, "I would describe myself as a Catholic Christian, meaning by that someone whose Christian discipleship is shaped by belonging in a sacramental community and consciously inheriting a certain set of disciplines of prayer." Parts of that tradition have been among his strongest supporters, as one of their leaders, David Houlding, makes clear: "Archbishop Rowan is held to this day in the highest regard by traditional anglo-catholics in the Church of England, which is a lot more than can be said of other constituencies. He has always enjoyed our full support, because actually he has always supported us."[55]

Rowan himself arrived at Canterbury associated not with Houlding's form of Anglo-Catholicism but with Affirming Catholicism, a movement which could be said to have tried to bring together the second and third of his groupings. It is the third grouping, perhaps in part because he arrived with a "liberal" label and then opposed American actions in relation to sexuality, that have found his primacy most difficult. Few, however, could dispute that he has himself shown and sought to encourage "a habit of cultural sensitivity and intellectual flexibility that does not seek to close down unexpected questions too quickly".

On coming into office the part of the Anglican world he probably knew least well was that of the first – Reformed or evangelical – grouping. Unsurprisingly, elements within that were most opposed to his appointment. Rather than react against them, Rowan sought to learn and many evangelicals feel his initial comparative ignorance has changed. He has even quoted Tim Keller and pointed to his agreement with the Archbishop of Sydney in General Synod presidential addresses. This development is in part because of his greater experience of this tradition in the wider Communion and in part because of his commitment to mission and Fresh Expressions where evangelicals were so prominent. In the words of David Hilborn:

> He's much more attuned than he was at the beginning
> of his archiepiscopate to the thoughtful practices
> of evangelical missiology. I think he's read and
> he's listened. I can testify personally he's been very
> respectful of evangelicals and that he's been much

301

more able to process the dialects of evangelicalism than he perhaps used to be. I think he's done his homework. I know he's spoken more to evangelical theologians. I've been impressed at how his ear has become more attuned to an evangelical approach.[56]

Despite being related in different ways to these three constituent elements of Anglicanism, what marked out Rowan's time as archbishop is that he embodied and sought to nurture what needs to be widespread across the three components of the Anglican heritage for the coalition to hold together: seeing what is authentic, genuine, and good and true in others' point of view.

Rowan's articulation and exemplification of what it means to be Anglican are a major element of his legacy as archbishop but what is less clear – as in many areas – is the extent to which his influence has gone beyond the personal and become in some sense embedded and structural. His 2006 reflection was clear that for traditional Anglicanism to survive intact "we need closer and more visible formal commitments to each other". Indeed,

> If we are to continue to be any sort of "Catholic' church, if we believe that we are answerable to something more than our immediate environment and its priorities and are held in unity by something more than just the consensus of the moment, we have some very hard work to do to embody this more clearly.[57]

The heart of that hard work for Rowan was the Anglican Covenant and a major question he leaves his successor both in the Church of England and the Anglican Communion is how to either revive its fortunes or to develop some alternative means of holding the coalition together. This uncertainty points to one aspect of his ministry which has been the subject of common criticism: the lack of strategy.

Refusing Strategy

Rowan's 2003 *New Directions* article on the Communion begins "I don't want in this brief article to try and shape a full scale strategy, even supposing I could", and in 2006 he admitted to the *Guardian*, asking about his media strategy, "I know that I'm not the world's greatest strategist for thinking forward." In fact, it often seemed as if "strategy" was something deliberately rejected, a dirty word in Lambeth Palace. Giles Goddard recalls, "At one meeting Inclusive Church had at Lambeth Palace, I asked him what his strategy was regarding questions of inclusion. He looked out of the window and laughed, and said, 'We don't have a strategy'."[58] Tom Wright, in his appreciation, describes Rowan's style as "private and unstrategic", recounting how "once, questioned about strategy, he responded crossly 'I believe in the Holy Spirit!', seemingly oblivious to the possibility that the Spirit might work through long-term planning". Rowan's response shows that while undoubtedly his temperament and gifting was a factor in this, it was also related to the theological vision of leadership sketched earlier:

> My job is like that of a bishop in any diocese… to create an atmosphere of prayer in which it's possible to make a discernment which isn't just a reaction to prejudice or whatever, and to see how the Church moves forward. I know that it sounds like a very modest description of the Archbishop's job and in that sense I have to be a servant of the churches and put into the discussion whatever I can of qualification, alternative perspective, which can of course look like

time-wasting, but in God's timetable, isn't. I say that in faith.[59]

Such lack of concern, even antipathy to strategy, was undoubtedly another reason why Americans – on all sides of the sexuality debate – found him so difficult to work with or understand.

It would be wrong to suggest that he was never strategic. On becoming archbishop he set out clear priorities including the exploration of a strategic approach to church planting for the Church of England, which became Fresh Expressions. Ian Douglas also points to his reshaping of the Lambeth Conference, and his subsequent sponsorship of Continuing Indaba would be a further example of longer-term strategic thinking.[60] Nevertheless, a strategic approach to leadership and the problems facing the church is clearly not part of Rowan's legacy. In particular, as Wright points out, he has not showed any great concern with the structures of the Church of England. Asked by David Hare in the *Guardian* in 2011 what he would change if he could change one thing about the church his instant response was "rethink the General Synod". Yet, despite others sharing this unhappiness, nothing has been done in terms of strategic thinking. Wright's assessment, reflecting on the pattern of leadership described above, concludes with praise but also critique, setting an agenda for the future in the light of Rowan's approach: "Maybe that's what we needed then. Certainly nobody doubts that he leads by example in his life of prayer and self-discipline. But we now need consultation, collaboration, and, yes, strategy."

Pastor, Teacher, and Servant

Rather than understand his role in terms of strategy, management, or being CEO, Rowan's ministry focused on Paul's exhortations in Ephesians 4 – "be patient, bearing with one another in love. Make every effort to keep the unity of the Spirit through the bond of peace" – and he lived out his calling as a pastor, a teacher, and a servant.

Pastor

Chris Rowland explains the shift in his view which enabled him to be more understanding of Rowan's primacy as "I had thought and hoped Rowan would be a prophet but he turned out to be much more of a pastor – that is the heart of what he is about".[61] The pattern of leadership explored above is part of that pastoral approach to being archbishop but most of his pastoral care went unseen and unreported. It was regularly experienced in his ministry within the diocese of Canterbury through his time sharing the retreat with those he would ordain deacon, his commitment to the Easter Monday youth pilgrimage every year, and particularly his visits to parishes. Early on in his time in Canterbury diocese he took a morning service at St Martin's, Maidstone, whose priest, Clive Tomkins, had just been diagnosed with terminal cancer. The Bishop of Maidstone, Graham Cray, recalls how, after the service, he and Rowan went to the vicarage for lunch:

> During the meal there was a ring at the doorbell. The
> church warden arrived and said "Really sorry, vicar, the
> retired priest who'd agreed to cover the baptism has
> not arrived and the family are here". I started to get up.
> Rowan said, "Don't you move, I won't be a moment",
> disappeared, and went and took the service. He didn't say
> who he was, came back afterwards and said "That was
> really good, they didn't know me from Adam" and carried
> on with the meal. That story went like wildfire as to who
> we had pastorally. He hugely valued being able to come
> and do those parish visits. It's the bit of "bishopping"

he really missed. He was enormously loved through the diocese for many reasons but that's one of them.[62]

Bishops were also recipients of his pastoral support as a pastor to the pastors. Mike Hill recalls:

> Given the weight of responsibility upon him I was amazed by his ability to respond to individual pastoral need. On October 1st 2006 when my wife and I had an horrific car crash, I remember taking a concerned call from a gentle pastor. His voice and his words were more important to me in that moment when my wife was so critically injured than he will ever know.[63]

The pastoral care was also provided in correspondence and personal meetings. Clare Herbert, asked to comment on Rowan as archbishop, cited none of the big issues which are normally viewed as someone's legacy but her own personal experience:

> My main reason for thanks is the way he takes each and every one of us so seriously if we approach him pastorally. He has met with me when needed, and always, but always, answered my letters. That is astonishing when you think about it as I must be so much a lesser fish in the solar sea of the C of E and yet he bothers and knows his encouragement of me is as important in the greater scheme of God's mercy as mine of him. Personally, as a busy and somewhat irritable pastor when over-stretched, I find that breathtaking.[64]

Teacher and Preacher

More obvious, because more public, is Rowan's lasting impact through his teaching (both spoken and written) and his preaching. His communication skills have often been criticized with concerns that he can be incomprehensible and also naive about the media's reporting of what he says. Both of these have, at times, been valid concerns. He himself has admitted that

> I really have to struggle on some levels to say just what I want to say, and yes, I know, I know, I know it's very clotted and when it is, it's partly having to try and formulate something quickly and partly that sometimes the subject matter isn't wrestled to the ground very easily.[65]

One problem is created by his own intellectual capacity as Philip Giddings notes: "Part of the difficulty for him is that he can immediately think of the 51 most powerful objections to what he's about to say never mind what he's just said and that can make for difficulties."[66] Rowan finds it hardest speaking to the general public rather than a specific, concrete audience as he confessed in 2004:

> When you're speaking in the public register, and nuance is difficult to get, you get self-conscious and it's as if you're always speaking to that imagined, undifferentiated audience, or at least that's the temptation. And I'm still struggling with that.[67]

He is undoubtedly at his best simply addressing a gathered group of people, especially when he speaks without notes. Hence his frustration at complaints about his ivory-tower convoluted style of communication: "If I'm being really whingeing, the biggest misconception is that I am incapable of talking to the person in the pew. Yet ninety per cent of my public speaking is unscripted talking to people in the pew."

It is not just when talking to people in the pew that he adopts this approach. Major lectures were often unscripted and even delivered without a single note in front of him. The published text is therefore frequently produced subsequently by a member of the Lambeth Palace staff who transcribes Rowan's addresses from recordings. Some of this pattern arises simply because of the sheer workload and variety of occasions at which he is called upon to speak, often in quick succession on the same day, but the more informal, often conversational, style is also how he communicates best.

Mike Hill, Bishop of Bristol, comments that "Fellow bishops will remember with awe his unique ability to stand at the Eucharist with an open Bible and hold us spellbound with profound thoughts simply and beautifully crafted without a note in sight!"[68] Confirming this, the bishop quoted earlier recalling his masterful summing up of a complex discussion in the House of Bishops remembers what happened next:

> We then trooped through to the Chapel for the
> midday Eucharist at which, within about five minutes,
> Rowan was himself presiding, and at which he gave
> one of his masterly seven-minute homilies, weaving
> together the readings for the day, the Saint whose feast
> it happened to be, and some of our current anxieties,
> all with a deft humour and many a wry phrase. All
> without notes, of course.[69]

Alastair Cutting captures the experience of many in his observation that Rowan "really comes into his own, theologically, in the public context, in giving his brief homilies, for example at General Synod, when there are early morning eucharists. Nearly always Rowan had something new, yet accessible, out of the most frequently heard and preached passages."[70] As pro-prolocutor occasionally at the confirmation of election of a diocesan bishop, Cutting describes how Rowan reads the formal legal charge then

> He metaphorically rolls it up and puts it under his arm, says "And now…" whilst catching the new bishop's eye. He opens up an intensely personal encounter that I'm sure each new bishop will never forget. Sometimes picking up the relevant saint's day, or an aspect of the diocese they are appointed to, thoroughly biblical and imaginative. Under these circumstances he is such an excellent communicator.[71]

This ability enables him to step in to speak and teach even at short notice when under great pressure. Graham Tomlin, Dean of St Mellitus, recalls one such occasion:

> We were looking for a speaker to stand in for our students on the split between the East and the West. The speaker we had booked had dropped out at the last minute. Jane Williams [on the staff at St Mellitus] rang me a few days beforehand to ask if I would be interested in getting Rowan to give the session. I asked how on earth he could fit this into his diary, to which the answer was that his flight to an important Primates' Meeting had been delayed which meant that he had the morning free. I asked Jane whether he wouldn't prefer to relax during that time, and she said this was his way of relaxing, he simply loves teaching and would enjoy the opportunity to explain this issue to students. He turned up on the Monday morning, armed simply with a Greek New Testament and little else, and delivered a crystal-clear and brilliant lecture on the historical origins and current meaning of the split between the East and the West![72]

As that example illustrates, part of the power in his teaching and preaching derives from his own personal character and in particular his humility and willingness to serve.

Servant Leader

The calling of the Christian, particularly the priest and bishop, is to be someone in and through whom Christ makes himself known to others. Given the self-emptying, kenotic humility of God revealed in Jesus, a primary pattern of discipleship, ministry, and mission will therefore be coming alongside others in self-giving service. That is part of the underlying theological rationale for Rowan's listening, prayerful, conversational rather than commanding and directional approach to leadership in the service of the church's unity. It is evident too in other ways.

Rowan's leadership during the Lambeth Conference itself was such that the bishops of one African province reflected together afterwards on this as a model of how a bishop should be in his diocese: he was mainly one of the bishops, joining in lines for food, sitting in the congregation at every act of worship and not giving announcements or being on a platform, except on three occasions when he stepped forward from his seat among the bishops to address them as "first among equals". Tom Wright recollects a similar pattern at the ACC in Nottingham: "I recall seeing him praying quietly with a delegate in the margins of an ACC meeting and wondering how many Archbishops would have been sufficiently informal to do that."[73]

Kenneth Kearon recalls another particularly striking example at the end of the Lambeth Conference:

> There were volunteer stewards, all under the age of 30, from every province of the Communion, some clergy, some lay, a really dynamic crowd. After it was all over there was a clear-up day and then they were going to do a retreat for

two days. The big thing we didn't tell them was that Rowan had agreed to lead the retreat. Of all people, he'd have been entitled to say, "The Conference is over, I'm going", but he went and led the retreat that morning for them and I understand he actually spoke on – perfect, typical Rowan – – the role of a steward and guiding people. He used that as an analogy for the church – guiding, stewarding, not telling people what to do, and exploring the boundary between that and steering. The following day they were going to get a coach to visit sites around the capital and they were completely thrown by the fact that Rowan jumped on the coach with his own bag of lunch and spent the day with them, sitting with different people on the coach. That's truly memorable. It really captures him.[74]

A similar example of how this pattern of ministry away from the media spotlight and church politics has left a lasting legacy, particularly among young people, is offered by Mark Russell of Church Army:

My passion is young people, and the Church of England is losing young people, isn't connecting to young people. Rowan has been a real supporter to me in voicing my angst in this. I came up with a mad idea (the March 2011 Regeneration Summit in Sheffield) to put a bishop from every diocese in a room with 200 young people and 30 youth workers to ask the question "How can we tell the story of Jesus again in this generation?" From day one, Rowan signed up to come. It meant we got bishops from practically all the dioceses. He was there from the start and was just part of a small group of young people, working alongside them, praying alongside them. My favourite moment was when he came back with a tray of glasses of orange juice. One of the young people couldn't believe the Archbishop of Canterbury had gone to make them orange… she said to me "now I know how the disciples felt when Jesus washed their feet!"[75]

This personal impact fed into difficult political contexts. It is interesting that his harshest critics are often people who have not had time with him. One person recalls his impact on a Nigerian bishop:

In 2009 I saw him in a meeting speak with a Nigerian bishop-elect who had, prior to the encounter, been fulminating at great length according to the "received wisdom" of his Province. But he was totally bowled over by Rowan, first by the straightforwardness with which he addressed the group, and then by a wholly open and natural conversation with him over coffee, which ended with Rowan placing a hand on his shoulder and praying with him informally, and then giving him a pectoral cross. He went away singing Rowan's praises (though still condemning various other aspects of Euro-Atlantic Anglicanism unabated!). There was total honesty, a complete lack of guile, in how Rowan spoke, and everything burst into flower! [76]

Another Nigerian bishop, Martyn Minns, offers a memorable example of this self-effacing service in Rowan's ministry and also captures his sense of humour:

I was at Lambeth Palace for a meeting. Rowan came out of his study looking his usually slightly bedraggled self and carrying a tray with teacups and a tea pot, from a previous visitor. I said "The new tea boy…" Folks around me looked shocked. Rowan, not missing a beat, said, "At least this is a job that I can do!" Classic Rowan.[77]

Conclusion: Rowan's Legacy?

Rowan is often criticized for not offering leadership and on standard models of leadership it is easy to see why that is the case. He has not, for example, been particularly concerned to establish his own legacy. Indeed, his pattern of leadership described here and the Christ-centred, kenotic theology which shapes it would suggest that part of his legacy should be a questioning of the whole concern to identify anyone's legacy. It is too allied to the autonomous, possessive, controlling individualism which Rowan has sought to critique in both church and world throughout his primacy. Its emphasis on achievement and success also sits uncomfortably with an insight in his 1997 *Church Times* review of Tom Wright's book, *Jesus and the Victory of God*: "the victory sought must be God's alone, and thus the Messiah must suffer, not conquer".

The story of Rowan's time as archbishop is one of battle, suffering, and sometimes defeat on various fronts as he sought to live out a vision of faithfulness to Christ in church and world. It is, by definition, impossible to tell which of his many initiatives and contributions will last as part of his legacy. What cannot be doubted is that his personal ministry as a priest and bishop in the office of Archbishop of Canterbury has already left a legacy in the lives of many. This was constantly witnessed to by those who contributed to the writing of this book but perhaps summed up best by David Hilborn:

> I believe that as time rolls on his reputation, his stature will grow. One thing that really hit me, having written

313

a critical article a while ago about his work, not having properly met him, is this: the most important quality in an Archbishop and in any leader in the church is their holiness, their integrity and their Christ-likeness. Those things are palpable when you sit around the table with Rowan. That he's listening to God as he's listening to you. The intellectual formation, the prayer all feed that but ultimately one goes away feeling "this is a holy man; I met Christ through meeting this man; I know more about my faith and the gospel through meeting this man". I think he has borne the pressures with exemplary Christian humility. Church leadership needs to be godly before it is strategic. God's strategy, we know, time and again from Scripture, is not always immediately evident. Rowan's legacy will not be one that is remembered as strategic but it will be remembered as godly. In the end, that's more important than pretty much anything else.[78]

Notes

1 The Making of an Archbishop

1. I am grateful to Stephen Williams, Geraint Williams' nephew, for information about his uncle.
2. Email correspondence with Dominic Walker, August 2012.
3. Email correspondence with Tudor Griffiths, September 2012.
4. *Ibid.*
5. Email correspondence with Bob and Mary Hopkins, October 2012.
6. Tom Sutcliffe, "Lost in the Wilderness" online at www.thinkinganglicans.org.uk/archives/005486.html
7. Interview with Geoffrey Rowell, August 2012.
8. Peter Mullen, "Tales of Canterbury's Future?: A terror apologist may soon lead the Church of England", *Wall Street Journal*, 12 July 2002.
9. Quoted at http://www.surefish.co.uk/news/features/2003/rowan2.htm
10. Introduction to *Speaking Love's Name; Homosexuality: Some Catholic and Socialist Perspectives.*
11. The lecture, from which the quotations which follow are taken, can be found online and has been published in various places including Eugene Rogers (ed.), *Theology and Sexuality: Classic and Contemporary Readings* (Blackwell, 2002).
12. Interview with Peter Selby, August 2012.
13. Quoted online at http://changingattitude.org.uk/archives/1311
14. "Anglican Media Sydney's exclusive interview with Archbishop Rowan Williams, Primate of Wales", Anglican Communion New Service, online at http://www.anglicancommunion.org/acns/news.cfm/2002/6/17/ ACNS3022
15. This and following quotations from Rowan Williams, "Our Differences Need Not Destroy Us", *The Tablet*, 8 April 2000, online at http://trushare. com/60may00/my00rowa.htm

2 A New Archbishop of Canterbury

1. Rowan Williams, "Statement at First Press Conference", 23 July 2002, online at http://www.archbishopofcanterbury.org/articles.php/1809/ statement-at-first-press-conference
2. "Contenders for the Succession", *Guardian*, 7 January 2002, online at http://www.guardian.co.uk/uk/2002/jan/07/religion.world1
3. Interview with Peter Selby, August 2012.
4. The excerpts that follow are taken from Rupert Shortt, *Rowan's Rule: The Biography of the Archbishop* (Hodder & Stoughton, 2009), pp. 242–43.

5. This and following quotations are taken from Rowan Williams, "Statement at First Press Conference", 23 July 2002, online at http://www.archbishopofcanterbury.org/articles.php/1809/statement-at-first-press-conference

6. Rowan Williams, "Letter to Primates, 23 July 2002", online at http://www.churchinwales.org.uk/structure/bishops/sermonsr/r15.php

3 Mission-Shaped Church and Fresh Expressions

1. "Rowan Williams on being remembered", interview on Fresh Expressions website at http://www.freshexpressions.org.uk/ondemand/rowanwilliams-beingremembered

2. Rowan Williams, Talk at Order of the Black Sheep, September 2011, transcribed from YouTube video.

3. Email correspondence with Mark Broomhead, October 2012.

4. Rowan Williams, "Looking, Listening, Respect", *Expressions,* Autumn 2005, p. 10.

5. Email correspondence with Tudor Griffiths, September 2012.

6. *Good News in Wales*, p. 3.

7. Email correspondence with Bob and Mary Hopkins, October 2012.

8. Interview with Graham Cray, September 2012.

9. Rowan Williams, "Foreword", *Mission-Shaped Church: Church planting and fresh expressions of church in a changing context* (Church House Publishing, 2004).

10. Rowan Williams in *Mixed Economy*, Autumn/Winter 2008/09, p. 13.

11. Rowan Williams speaking at Springfield Church, Surrey, March 2012, online at http://www.archbishopofcanterbury.org/articles.php/2413/archbishop-speaks-at-springfield-church-surrey

12. Interview with Steven Croft, September 2012.

13. Rowan Williams, General Synod, February 2007, online at http://www.archbishopofcanterbury.org/articles.php/1745/fresh-expressions-the-life-blood-of-who-we-are-general-synod-february-2007

14. Email correspondence with Andy Lines, August 2012.

15. John Milbank, After Rowan: Priorities for the Anglican Communion at http://www.abc.net.au/religion/articles/2012/09/28/3599887.htm

16. Interview with Malcolm Brown, September 2012.

17. Rowan Williams, "Faith in the Future Q&A", February 2008, online at http://www.archbishopofcanterbury.org/articles.php/1377/faith-in-the-future

4 Leader in Mission

1. "Called to Live and Proclaim the Good News", Lambeth Conference 1998, Section Two Report.

2. Rowan Williams in Mick Gordon and Chris Wilkinson (eds), *Conversations on Religion* (Continuum, 2008), p 33.

3. *Ibid.*
4. Email correspondence with Michael Green, August 2012.
5. Email correspondence with Phil Groves, September 2012.
6. Email correspondence with Phil Groves, reporting Jon Groves, September 2012.
7. The letter appeared in an article by Alex Renton in *The Times* on Good Friday, 2011, online at http://www.archbishopofcanterbury.org/articles. php/2389/the-archbishop-writes-to-lulu-aged-6-about-god
8. Rowan Williams, Address at al-Azhar al-Sharif, Cairo, September 2004, online at http://www.archbishopofcanterbury.org/articles.php/1299/ archbishops-address-at-al-azhar-al-sharif-cairo
9. Rowan Williams, "What is Christianity?", *Islam and Christian–Muslim Relations*, xix (2008), pp. 323–63; online at http://www. archbishopofcanterbury.org/articles.php/1087/what-is-christianity (November 2005).
10. Rowan Williams, Q&A at Westminster School, April 2008, online at http://www.archbishopofcanterbury.org/articles.php/698/archbishop-answers-stimulating-questions-at-westminster-school
11. *Ibid.*

5 Capturing the Imagination

1. Rowan Williams, "Statement at First Press Conference", 23 July 2002, online at http://www.archbishopofcanterbury.org/articles.php/1809/ statement-at-first-press-conference
2. Rowan Williams, "Belief, Unbelief and Religious Education", March 2004, online at http://www.archbishopofcanterbury.org/articles.php/1838/belief-unbelief-and-religious-education
3. Rowan Williams, "Analysing atheism", *Faith in the Public Square* (Bloomsbury, 2012), pp. 381–91.
4. Rowan Williams, "How Religion is Misunderstood", October 2007, online at http://www.archbishopofcanterbury.org/articles.php/1751/how-religion-is-misunderstood
5. Rowan Williams, "The spiritual and the religious: is the territory changing?", *Faith in the Public Square* (Bloomsbury, 2012), pp. 85–98.
6. Rowan Williams, "Preface" in Adrian Whittaker (ed.), *Be Glad: An Incredible String Band Compendium* (Helter Skelter Publishing, 2003).
7. Tom Wright, "Rowan Williams: An Appreciation", *The Times*, 17 March 2012, online at http://www.fulcrum-anglican.org.uk/page.cfm?ID=710
8. Rowan Williams, "Religious lives", *Faith in the Public Square* (Bloomsbury, 2012), pp. 313–27.
9. Rowan Williams, Greeting to European Youth Meeting promoted by the Ecumenical Community of Taizé, December 2007.

10. Rowan Williams, "Sharing the Story", Hereford Diocesan Conference, June 2008, online at http://www.archbishopofcanterbury.org/articles. php/1207/the-archbishop-addresses-the-hereford-diocesan-conference-sharing-the-story

11. *Ibid.*

12. Robert Webb, "As a 'Four-Episodes-Of-The-West-Wing' Christian, I'll miss Rowan", *New Statesman*, 26 March 2012.

13. Email correspondence with Mark Russell, September 2012.

6 The Reading Crisis and Sexuality Debates

1. Rowan Williams, Letter to Bishops, 23 June 2003.

2. Rowan Williams, Presidential Address at ACC-13, Nottingham, June 2004, online at http://www.archbishopofcanterbury.org/articles. php/1678/archbishops-presidential-address-13th-meeting-of-the-anglican-consultative-council

3. Reported by Ruth Gledhill in "Archbishop fuels row with message of comfort to gays", *The Times*, 10 June 2003.

4. Email correspondence with Colin Coward, September 2012.

5. Email correspondence with Louie Crew, August 2012.

6. Interview with Philip Giddings, September 2012.

7. Philip Giddings, reported in "Stand aside, or church splits", 30 June 2003, online at http://www.getreading.co.uk/news/s/7127_stand_aside_or_church_splits

8. Rowan Williams, Letter to Bishops, 23 June 2003.

9. Interview with Peter Selby, August 2012.

10. *Ibid.*

11. Interview with Philip Giddings, September 2012.

12. Editorial, *The Times*, 19 June 2003.

13. Rowan Williams, Letter to Bishops, 23 June 2003.

14. Rowan Williams, Statement on Jeffrey John's Withdrawal, 5 July 2003.

15. Rowan Williams, Presidential Address, General Synod, July 2003, online at http://www.archbishopofcanterbury.org/articles.php/1826/archbishops-presidential-address-general-synod-york-july-2003

16. Interview with Peter Selby, August 2012.

7 Women Bishops

1. Rowan Williams, "Help, my friends think I'm mad!", June 2012, online at http://www.archbishopofcanterbury.org/articles.php/2537/help-my-friends-think-im-mad-youth-day-at-lambeth-palace

2. Rowan Williams, Archbishop Dismisses Newspaper Reports on Female Ordination as "Wilful Misinterpretation", 16 November 2006, online at http://www.archbishopofcanterbury.org/articles.php/1461/

archbishop-dismisses-newspaper-reports-on-female-ordination-as-wilful-misinterpretation

3. Rowan Williams, Introduction to the Transformations Report, online at http://www.archbishopofcanterbury.org/articles.php/2186/archbishop-hosts-conference-on-womens-ministry

4. Rowan Williams, The Archbishop's Concluding Remarks, *Transformations Report*, p. 36.

5. Rowan Williams, Opening and Closing Speeches at General Synod Debate on Women in the Episcopate, July 2006, online at http://www.archbishopofcanterbury.org/articles.php/1775/women-in-the-episcopate-general-synod-debate-july-2006

6. Rowan Williams, "General Synod: Speech Moving Motion on Women in the Episcopate", 16 February 2005, online at http://www.archbishopofcanterbury.org/articles.php/1805/general-synod-speech-moving-motion-on-women-in-the-episcopate

7. Rowan Williams, General Synod Speech, 9 February 2006, online at http://www.archbishopofcanterbury.org/articles.php/1782/speeches-to-general-synod-on-women-bishops

8. Key texts relating to Cardinal Kasper's contribution are gathered together in *Women in the Episcopate*, GS Misc 885, April 2008.

9. Rowan Williams, Speech at General Synod, July 2008.

10. *Ibid.*

11. *Ibid.*

12. Rowan Williams, Presidential Address, General Synod February 2009, online at http://www.archbishopofcanterbury.org/articles.php/831/the-archbishops-presidential-address-general-synod-february-2009

13. Rowan Williams, Presidential Address, General Synod, February 2010, online at http://www.archbishopofcanterbury.org/articles.php/590/the-archbishops-presidential-address-general-synod-february-2010

14. Archbishops of Canterbury and York, General Synod Draft Legislation: Women in the Episcopate, June 2010, online at http://www.archbishopofcanterbury.org/articles.php/993/general-synod-draft-legislation-women-in-the-episcopate

15. *Ibid.*

16. Email correspondence with Andrew Burnham, August 2012.

17. Rowan Williams, "Help, my friends think I'm mad!", June 2012, online at http://www.archbishopofcanterbury.org/articles.php/2537/help-my-friends-think-im-mad-youth-day-at-lambeth-palace

18. Rowan Williams, Presidential Address, General Synod, November 2012, online at http://www.archbishopofcanterbury.org/articles.php/2716/archbishop-tells-synod-we-must-care-for-those-feeling-unwanted-and-unsure-after-women-bishops-vote

19. *Ibid.*

8 Canterbury and the Anglican Communion

1. Rowan Williams, Letter to the Primates, 23 July 2003.

2. "The Communion" (capital C) refers to the body of Anglican churches around the world known as the Anglican Communion, "communion" (small c) refers to the pattern of relationship or fellowship between churches or individual Christians.

3. Rowan Williams, First Presidential Address, Lambeth Conference 2008, online at http://www.archbishopofcanterbury.org/articles.php/1353/archbishops-first-presidential-address-at-lambeth-conference

4. Rowan Williams, "The Structures of Unity", *New Directions*, September 2003 at http://trushare.com/0100Sep03/Rowan%20Williams%20Structures%20of%20Unity/Rowan%20Williams%20020903%20structures%20of%20Unity.htm

5. Rowan Williams, "Communion, Covenant and our Anglican Future", 27 July 2009, online at http://www.archbishopofcanterbury.org/articles.php/1505/communion-covenant-and-our-anglican-future

6. Rowan Williams, Easter Message to the Anglican Communion, March 2005, online at http://www.archbishopofcanterbury.org/articles.php/646/an-easter-message-to-the-anglican-communion

7. Rowan Williams, Advent Letter to Primates, November 2011, online at http://www.archbishopofcanterbury.org/articles.php/2268/archbishops-advent-letter-to-anglican-primates

8. Rowan Williams, Interview with Simon Mayo, December 2005, online at http://www.archbishopofcanterbury.org/articles.php/761/simon-mayo-interview-on-bbc-radio-5-live

9. Rowan Williams, Interview with Dan Damon, March 2007, online at http://www.archbishopofcanterbury.org/articles.php/1523/reflections-on-angola-africa-and-the-communion

10. Rowan Williams, "No-one can be forgotten in God's kingdom", *Anvil*, xxv (2008), pp. 117–28.

11. Interview with Kenneth Kearon, September 2012.

12. Rowan Williams, Presidential Address at ACC-13, Nottingham, June 2004, online at http://www.archbishopofcanterbury.org/articles.php/1678/archbishops-presidential-address-13th-meeting-of-the-anglican-consultative-council

13. Primates' Meeting Communiqué, October 2003, online at http://www.archbishopofcanterbury.org/articles.php/653/primates-meeting-2003-final-statement

14. *Ibid.*

15. Greg Venables quoted in Pat Ashworth, "Primates speak of 'miraculous' unanimity", *Church Times*, 25 February 2005.

16. Email correspondence with Mark Russell, September 2012.

9 Cracking Communion? 1. The Windsor Path

1. Rowan Williams, First Presidential Address, Lambeth Conference 2008, online at http://www.archbishopofcanterbury.org/articles.php/1353/archbishops-first-presidential-address-at-lambeth-conference

2. Rowan Williams, General Synod Speech, February 2005, online at http://www.archbishopofcanterbury.org/articles.php/1680/general-synod-speech-in-debate-on-the-windsor-report

3. *Windsor Report*, para. 157 (Anglican Communion Office, 2004), online at http://www.anglicancommunion.org/windsor2004/

4. Rowan Williams, Statement on Los Angeles Episcopal Elections, December 2009, online at http://www.archbishopofcanterbury.org/articles.php/1000/archbishop-of-canterburys-statement-on-los-angeles-episcopal-elections

5. Email correspondence with John Chane, August 2012.

6. Primates' Communiqué, February 2007, online at http://www.anglicancommunion.org/communion/primates/resources/downloads/communique2007_english.pdf

7. Rowan Williams, Advent Letter to Primates, December 2007, online at http://www.archbishopofcanterbury.org/articles.php/631/the-archbishops-advent-letter-to-primates-2007

8. Rowan Williams, Video Address to Fourth Global South to South Encounter, April 2010, online at http://www.archbishopofcanterbury.org/articles.php/1479/archbishop-there-are-no-quick-solutions-for-the-wounds-of-the-body-of-christ

9. Rowan Williams, Answer at Final Press Conference at Tanzania Primates' Meeting, February 2007, online at http://www.archbishopofcanterbury.org/articles.php/1742/final-press-conference-at-tanzania-primates-meeting

10. Geoff Chapman, Memo of 23 December 2003, online at http://www.thinkinganglicans.org.uk/ss/archives/000405.html

11. Mark Harris, Update of "What's In A Name?", September 2004, online at http://www.rci.rutgers.edu/~lcrew/dojusticc/j190.html#corrected

12. Rowan Williams, BBC Interview with Sir David Frost, March 2006, online at http://www.archbishopofcanterbury.org/articles.php/758/transcript-of-archbishops-bbc-interview-with-sir-david-frost-in-sudan

13. Quoted in Wim Houtman, "The Church is not inclusive", Nederlands Dagblat, 19 August 2006.

14. Email correspondence with Philip Turner, August 2012.

15. Rowan Williams, Q&A from the launch of the Lambeth Conference, January 2008, online at http://www.archbishopofcanterbury.org/articles.php/1332/questions-and-answers-from-the-launch-of-lambeth-conference

16. Email correspondence with Phil Groves, September 2012.

17. Rowan Williams, Second Presidential Address, Lambeth Conference 2008, online at http://www.archbishopofcanterbury.org/articles.php/1352/archbishops-second-presidential-address-at-lambeth-conference

18. Rowan Williams, "The Challenge and Hope of Being an Anglican Today", June 2006, online at http://www.archbishopofcanterbury.org/articles.php/1478/the-challenge-and-hope-of-being-an-anglican-today-a-reflection-for-the-bishops-clergy-and-faithful-o

19. Interview with Philip Giddings, September 2012.

20. What follows is taken from "Towards an Anglican Covenant", online at http://www.anglicancommunion.org/commission/covenant/consultation/index.cfm

21. Rowan Williams, "The Challenge and Hope of Being an Anglican Today", June 2006, online at http://www.archbishopofcanterbury.org/articles.php/1478/the-challenge-and-hope-of-being-an-anglican-today-a-reflection-for-the-bishops-clergy-and-faithful-o

22. Rowan Williams, "Why the Covenant Matters", March 2012, online at http://www.archbishopofcanterbury.org/articles.php/2380/archbishop-why-the-covenant-matters

23. Rowan Williams, "A Message on the Anglican Communion Covenant", December 2009, online at http://www.archbishopofcanterbury.org/articles.php/1504/a-message-from-the-archbishop-of-canterbury-on-the-anglican-communion-covenant

24. Rowan Williams, Speech at General Synod, February 2009, online at http://www.archbishopofcanterbury.org/articles.php/828/archbishop-what-kind-of-global-communion-do-we-want-to-be

25. Rowan Williams, "The Challenge and Hope of Being An Anglican Today", June 2006, online at http://www.archbishopofcanterbury.org/articles.php/1478/the-challenge-and-hope-of-being-an-anglican-today-a-reflection-for-the-bishops-clergy-and-faithful-o

26. *Ibid.*

10 Cracking Communion? 2. Lambeth, Indaba, and the Future

1. Rowan Williams, Video Address to Fourth Global South to South Encounter, April 2010, online at http://www.archbishopofcanterbury.org/articles.php/1479/archbishop-there-are-no-quick-solutions-for-the-wounds-of-the-body-of-christ

2. Rowan William, Advent Letter to Primates, December 2007, online at http://www.archbishopofcanterbury.org/articles.php/631/the-archbishops-advent-letter-to-primates-2007

3. Rowan Williams, Pastoral Letter to Bishops of the Anglican Communion, August 2008, online at http://www.archbishopofcanterbury.org/articles.php/1225/archbishops-pastoral-letter-to-bishops-of-the-anglican-communion

4. Email correspondence with Phil Groves, September 2012.

5. Email correspondence with Colin Fletcher, September 2012.

6. Interview with Ian Douglas, August 2012.

7. Rowan Williams, First Presidential Address, Lambeth Conference 2008, online at http://www.archbishopofcanterbury.org/articles.php/1353/archbishops-first-presidential-address-at-lambeth-conference

8. Rowan Williams, Concluding Presidential Address, Lambeth Conference 2008, online at http://www.archbishopofcanterbury.org/articles.php/1350/concluding-presidential-address-to-the-lambeth-conference

9. Tom Wright, "Rowan Williams: An Appreciation", *The Times*, 17 March 2012 at http://www.fulcrum-anglican.org.uk/page.cfm?ID=710

10. Rowan Williams, Presidential Address, General Synod, November 2010 online at http://www.archbishopofcanterbury.org/articles.php/919/archbishops-presidential-address-general-synod-november-2010

11. Email correspondence.

12. Rowan Williams, "St Benedict and the Future of Europe" (lecture, St Anselmo, Rome, 21 November 2006) as "Saint for Europe and Our Age", *Tablet* (25 November 2006), and online at http://www.archbishopofcanterbury.org/articles.php/1770/benedict-and-the-future-of-europe-speech-at-st-anselmo-in-rome

13. Rowan Williams, BBC Interview with Sir David Frost, March 2006, online at http://www.archbishopofcanterbury.org/articles.php/758/transcript-of-archbishops-bbc-interview-with-sir-david-frost-in-sudan

14. Rowan Williams, "The *Guardian* Interview" with Alan Rusbridger, March 2006, online at http://www.archbishopofcanterbury.org/articles.php/757/the-guardian-interview

11 Anglicanism and Other Churches

1. Rowan Williams, Greeting to Pope Benedict, November 2006, online at http://www.archbishopofcanterbury.org/articles.php/1772/rome-archbishops-greeting-to-pope-benedict

2. Rowan Williams, Interview with Vatican Radio, November 2010, online at http://www.archbishopofcanterbury.org/articles.php/550/archbishops-interview-with-vatican-radio-in-rome

3. Rowan Williams, Address at 50th Anniversary of PCPCU, November 2010, online at http://www.archbishopofcanterbury.org/articles.php/803/archbishops-address-at-50th-anniversary-of-pcpcu

4. Cardinal Kasper, Letter to Rowan Williams, December 2004, online at http://www.vatican.va/roman_curia/pontifical_councils/chrstuni/card-kasper-docs/rc_pc_chrstuni_doc_20041217_kasper-arch-canterbury_en.html

5. Rowan Williams, Sermon at Vespers, Westminster Cathedral, January 2009, online at http://www.archbishopofcanterbury.org/articles.php/955/sermon-at-vespers-in-westminster-cathedral-during-the-week-of-prayer-for-christian-unity

6. Rowan Williams, Address at the Signing of an Anglican–Methodist Covenant, November 2003, online at http://www.anglican-methodist.org.uk/cofesermon.htm

7. Rowan Williams, Sermon at a Service of Reconciliation, Healing of Memories and Mutual Commitment, Westminster Abbey, February 2012, online at http://www.archbishopofcanterbury.org/articles.php/2346/joint-

church-of-england-and-united-reformed-church-service-of-reconciliation-and-commitment

8. Interview with Geoffrey Rowell, August 2012.

9. Interview with Kenneth Kearon, September 2012.

10. Rowan Williams, Speech on "The Church of the Triune God", General Synod, July 2008, online at http://www.archbishopofcanterbury.org/articles.php/1206/general-synod-york-2008-the-church-of-the-triune-god

11. Rowan Williams, Interview with Paul Handley – "Less a Roman holiday, more an Italian job", *Church Times*, 16 November 2006, online at http://www.churchtimes.co.uk/articles/2006/17-november/news/less-a-roman-holiday,-more-an-italian-job

12. Email correspondence with Andrew Burnham, August 2012.

13. George Pitcher, "Taking a Break from Canterbury Travails", *Daily Telegraph*, December 2009, online at http://www.archbishopofcanterbury.org/articles.php/2037/dr-rowan-williams-taking-a-break-from-canterbury-travails-daily-telegraph-article

14. Email correspondence with Andrew Burnham, August 2012.

15. Interview with Geoffrey Rowell, August 2012.

16. Email correspondence with Christopher Wells, August 2012.

17. *Ibid.*

18. Mark Langham, "Vatican II, 1982 and now: the Ecumenical Relationship", Paper for a Symposium held on 30 March 2012 and organized by the British Embassy to the Holy See. I am grateful to Monsignor Langham for providing me with the text of this as yet unpublished paper.

19. Rowan Williams, BBC West Midlands Interview with Andrew Peach, November 2010, online at http://www.archbishopofcanterbury.org/articles.php/1978/archbishops-bbc-west-midlands-interview

20. Rowan Williams, Interview with Paul Handley – "Less a Roman holiday, more an Italian job", *Church Times*, 16 November 2006, online at http://www.churchtimes.co.uk/articles/2006/17-november/news/less-a-roman-holiday,-more-an-italian-job

21. Rowan Williams in Conversation with Frank Skinner, October 2011, online at http://www.archbishopofcanterbury.org/articles.php/2179/archbishop-rowan-and-frank-skinner-in-conversation

12 Anglicanism and Other Faiths

1. Rowan Williams, "The Finality of Christ in a Pluralist World", March 2010, online at http://www.archbishopofcanterbury.org/articles.php/585/the-finality-of-christ-in-a-pluralist-world

2. Rowan Williams, Q&A at Westminster School, April 2008, online at http://www.archbishopofcanterbury.org/articles.php/698/archbishop-answers-stimulating-questions-at-westminster-school

3. Rowan Williams, "Christian theology and other faiths", in M. Ipgrave (ed.), *Scriptures in Dialogue: Christians and Muslims Studying the Bible and*

the Qur'an Together (Church House Publishing, 2004, 2/2007), pp. 131–43.

4. Ibid.

5. Ibid.

6. Rowan Williams, "The Finality of Christ in a Pluralist World", March 2010, online at http://www.archbishopofcanterbury.org/articles.php/585/ the-finality-of-christ-in-a-pluralist-world

7. Rowan Williams, "Christian Identity and Religious Plurality", Ecumenical Review, lviii (2006), pp. 69–75; also Christian Century, cxxiii (2006) pp. 29–33.

8. Ibid.

9. Rowan Williams, "The Finality of Christ in a Pluralist World", March 2010, online at http://www.archbishopofcanterbury.org/articles.php/585/ the-finality-of-christ-in-a-pluralist-world

10. Rowan Williams, "Dialogue for Me is Recognition of the Serious", Interview with P. Jacob, The Hindu, October 2010, online at http:// www.archbishopofcanterbury.org/articles.php/553/the-hindu-interview-dialogue-for-me-is-recognition-of-the-serious

11. Interview with Steven Croft, September 2012.

12. Rowan Williams, "The Place of the Covenant in Judaism, Christianity and Jewish-Christian Relations", December 2004, online at http://www. archbishopofcanterbury.org/articles.php/2103/a-lecture-given-at-a-conference-on-the-place-of-covenant-in-judaism-christianity-and-jewish-christia

13. Rowan Williams, Opening Remarks at the Second Building Bridges Seminar, April 2003, online at http://www.archbishopofcanterbury.org/ articles.php/1300/archbishops-opening-remarks

14. Rowan Williams, "Christian Theology and Other Faiths", June 2003, online at http://www.archbishopofcanterbury.org/articles.php/1825/ christian-theology-and-other-faiths

15. Rowan Williams, "The Finality of Christ in a Pluralist World", March 2010, online at http://www.archbishopofcanterbury.org/articles.php/585/ the-finality-of-christ-in-a-pluralist-world

16. Ibid.

13 The Sharia Lecture and Interactive Pluralism

1. Rowan Williams, Presidential Address to General Synod, February 2008, online at http://www.archbishopofcanterbury.org/articles.php/1326/ presidential-address-to-the-opening-of-general-synod-february-2008

2. Rowan Williams, Faith in the Public Square (Bloomsbury, 2012).

3. Rowan Williams, "A Higher Responsibility", Interview with Paul Richardson, Church of England Newspaper, 8 May 2008, online at http:// www.archbishopofcanterbury.org/articles.php/694/a-higher-responsibility-interview-with-paul-richardson

4. Rowan Williams, "Law, Power and Peace: Christian Perspectives on Sovereignty", David Nicholls Memorial Lecture, September 2005, online at http://www.archbishopofcanterbury.org/articles.php/1181/david-nicholls-memorial-lecture-law-power-and-peace-christian-perspectives-on-sovereignty

5. *Ibid.*

6. Email correspondence with Richard Harries, September 2012.

7. Rowan Williams, "Multiculturalism – friend or foe?", *Faith in the Public Square* (Bloomsbury, 2012), pp. 99–112.

8. Rowan Williams, The Richard Dimbleby Lecture, December 2002, online at http://www.archbishopofcanterbury.org/articles.php/1808/the-richard-dimbleby-lecure-2002

9. Rowan Williams, "Secularism, faith and freedom", *Faith in the Public Square* (Bloomsbury, 2012), pp. 23–36; also included in G. Ward and M. Hoelzl: *The New Visibility of Religion: Studies in Religion and Cultural Hermeneutics* (Continuum, 2008), pp. 45–58.

9. Rowan Williams, "Secularism, Faith and Freedom", Rome Lecture, November 2006, online at http://www.archbishopofcanterbury.org/articles.php/1175/rome-lecture-secularism-faith-and-freedom

10. Rowan Williams, "Civil and Religious Law in England: A Religious Perspective", February 2008, online at http://www.archbishopofcanterbury.org/articles.php/1137/archbishops-lecture-civil-and-religious-law-in-england-a-religious-perspective

11. Rowan Williams, Radio 4 Interview with Christopher Landau, 7 February 2008, online at http://www.archbishopofcanterbury.org/articles.php/707/archbishop-on-radio-4-world-at-one-uk-law-needs-to-find-accommodation-with-religious-law-codes

12. Christopher Landau, "What the Media thinks about Religion: A Broadcast Perspective", in Jolyon Mitchell and Owen Gower (eds), *Religion and the News* (Ashgate, 2012).

13. Rowan Williams, Presidential Address to General Synod, February 2008, online at http://www.archbishopofcanterbury.org/articles.php/1326/presidential-address-to-the-opening-of-general-synod-february-2008

14. Rowan Williams, Interview with Press Association, March 2012, online at http://www.archbishopofcanterbury.org/articles.php/2409/archbishops-interview-with-press-association

14 "Doing God": Society and Politics

1. Rowan Williams, "We live in a culture of blame – but there is another way", *Observer*, 23 March 2008, online at http://www.archbishopofcanterbury.org/articles.php/618/we-live-in-a-culture-of-blame-but-there-is-another-way

2. Rowan Williams, Open Letter to Party Leaders, March 2005, online at http://www.archbishopofcanterbury.org/articles.php/1178/archbishop-issues-letter-to-party-leaders

3. Archbishops of York and Canterbury, Joint statement on the European Parliamentary and local elections, 24 May 2009, online at http://www. archbishopofcanterbury.org/articles.php/1050/joint-statement-from-the-archbishop-of-york-and-archbishop-of-canterbury

4. Rowan Williams, Editorial in *New Statesman*, 13 June 2011, p. 5.

5. Rowan Williams, Unbroadcast *Today* interview with John Humphrys, October 2003, reported at http://www.guardian.co.uk/media/2003/oct/18/bbc.Iraqandthemedia

6. *Ibid.*

7. Quoted in Rowland Jones, "Doing God in Public: An Anglican Interpretation of MacIntyre's tradition-based reasoning as a Christian praxis for a pluralist world", Unpublished PhD thesis, p. 253.

8. Rowan Williams, "Religions of Peace Have to Show Trust in Each Other", February 2006, online at http://www.archbishopofcanterbury.org/articles. php/1278/archbishop-in-sudan-religions-of-peace-have-to-show-trust-in-each-other

9. Rowan Williams, "Faith in the Future Q&A", February 2008, online at http://www.archbishopofcanterbury.org/articles.php/1377/faith-in-the-future

10. From the book launch for Rowan Williams and Larry Elliott, (eds), *Crisis and Recovery: Ethics, Economics and Justice* (Palgrave Macmillan, 2010) – which includes the Archbishop's "Knowing our Limits", pp. 19–34; see http://www.archbishopofcanterbury.org/articles.php/941/crisis-and-recovery-book-launch-28th-september

11. Rowan Williams, Speech at Lord Mayor's Banquet, November 2008, online at http://www.archbishopofcanterbury.org/articles.php/1347/archbishops-speech-at-lord-mayors-banquet-2008

12. Rowan Williams, "Ethics, economics and global justice", *Faith in the Public Square* (Bloomsbury, 2012), pp. 211–24.

13. BBC *Newsnight*, 15 September 2009, video at http://news.bbc.co.uk/1/hi/programmes/newsnight/8259172.stm

14. Rowan Williams, "Human Well-Being and Economic Decision-Making", November 2009, online at http://www.archbishopofcanterbury.org/articles.php/767/human-well-being-and-economic-decision-making

15. Rowan Williams, Interview for BBC *One Planet*, October 2009, online at http://www.archbishopofcanterbury.org/articles.php/1755/one-planet-archbishop-on-bbc-world-service

16. Rowan Williams, from a video message to the religious leaders' gathering at the UN Bali Climate Change summit: "Climate Change Action a Moral Imperative for Justice", December 2007, online at http://www. archbishopofcanterbury.org/articles.php/1706/climate-change-action-a-moral-imperative-for-justice

17. Rowan Williams, "Ecology and Economy", March 2005, online at http:// www.archbishopofcanterbury.org/articles.php/1550/ecology-and-economy-archbishop-calls-for-action-on-environment-to-head-off-social-crisis

18. Rowan Williams, Interview with Martin Wright for *Green Futures*, April 2008, online at http://www.archbishopofcanterbury.org/articles.php/1996/archbishops-environment-interview-green-futures-magazine

19. Rowan Williams, "Foreword" to *Sharing God's Planet*, online at http://www.archbishopofcanterbury.org/articles.php/2008/the-archbishops-foreword-to-sharing-gods-planet

20. Rowan Williams, "Changing the myths we live by", *Faith in the Public Square* (Bloomsbury, 2012), pp. 175–84.

21. Rowan Williams, Interview on Climate Change for *Today* programme on Radio 4, March 2006, online at http://www.archbishopofcanterbury.org/articles.php/756/climate-change-interview-for-the-bbc-radio-4-today-programme

22. Rowan Williams, "Ethics, economics and global justice", *Faith in the Public Square* (Bloomsbury, 2012), pp. 211–24.

23. Rowan Williams, "Belief, Unbelief and Religious Education", March 2004, online at http://www.archbishopofcanterbury.org/articles.php/1838/belief-unbelief-and-religious-education.

24. Rowan Williams, "The gifts reserved for age: perceptions of the elderly", *Faith in the Public Square* (Bloomsbury, 2012), pp. 243–51.

25. Rowan Williams, "Afterword", *Good Childhood Report*, February 2009, online at http://www.archbishopofcanterbury.org/articles.php/1153/full-text-of-the-good-childhood-report-afterword

26. Interview with Peter Selby, August 2012.

27. *Ibid.*

28. Email correspondence with Tudor Griffiths, September 2012.

29. Email correspondence with Richard Harries, September 2012.

30. Email correspondence with Mike Hill, September 2012.

31. Tony Benn, *More Time for Politics: Diaries 2001–7* (Hutchinson, 2007), pp. 74–75.

32. Interview with Peter Selby, August 2012.

15 Being a Priest and a Bishop

1. Rowan Williams, "Statement at First Press Conference", 23 July 2002, online at http://www.archbishopofcanterbury.org/articles.php/1809/statement-at-first-press-conference

2. Rowan Williams, *Time* Magazine Interview, June 2007, online at http://www.archbishopofcanterbury.org/articles.php/725/time-magazine-interview

3. Ben Myers, "An Inclusive Mission", 22 March 2012, *Times Higher Education* at http://www.timeshighereducation.co.uk/story.asp?storycode=419416

4. Interview with Philip Giddings, September 2012.

5. Interview with Peter Selby, August 2012.

6. Rowan Williams, Speech on the *Windsor Report*, General Synod, February 2005, online at http://www.archbishopofcanterbury.org/articles.php/1680/general-synod-speech-in-debate-on-the-windsor-report

7. Rowan Williams, Concluding Presidential Address, Lambeth Conference,

August 2008, online at http://www.archbishopofcanterbury.org/articles.
php/1350/concluding-presidential-address-to-the-lambeth-conference

8. Rowan Williams, "Authority and the Bishop in the Church", in Mark
    Santer (ed.), *Their Lord and Ours: Approaches to Authority, Community, and
    the Unity of the Church* (SPCK, 1982), pp. 90–112.

9. Rowan Williams in David Hare, "Rowan Williams: God's Boxer",
    Guardian, 8 July 2011, online at http://www.guardian.co.uk/uk/2011/
    jul/08/rowan-williams-interview-david-hare?INTCMP=SRCH

10. Rowan Williams, "Authority and the Bishop in the Church", in Mark
    Santer (ed.), *Their Lord and Ours: Approaches to Authority, Community, and
    the Unity of the Church* (SPCK, 1982), p. 99.

11. Email correspondence with Phil Groves, September 2012.

12. Email correspondence with Giles Goddard, September 2012.

13. Interview with Philip Giddings, September 2012.

14. Rowan Williams, "God's Mission and a Bishop's Discipleship",
    Third Lambeth Retreat Address, July 2008, online at http://www.
    archbishopofcanterbury.org/articles.php/1739/the-archbishops-retreat-
    addresses-parts-iii-iv-v

15. Interview with Kenneth Kearon, September 2012.

16. Email correspondence with Andrew Burnham, August 2012.

17. Email correspondence.

18. Rowan Williams, Interview with Melvyn Bragg, 19 June 2005, online at
    http://www.sarmiento.plus.com/cofe/bragginterview1.html

19. Email correspondence with Mike Hill, September 2012.

20. Interview with Chris Rowland, August 2012.

21. Email correspondence with Sarah Rowland Jones, August 2012.

22. Email correspondence with Phil Groves, September 2012.

23. Rowan Williams, The Social Edge interview with Gerry McCarthy, 2002,
    online at http://web.archive.org/web/20050311042825/http://www.
    thesocialedge.com/archives/gerrymccarthy/1articles-mar2002.htm

24. Rowan Williams, "God's Mission and a Bishop's Discipleship", Third
    Lambeth Retreat Address, July 2008, online at http://www.archbishopof
    canterbury.org/articles.php/1355/the-archbishops-retreat-addresses-parts-i-ii

25. Interview, September 2012.

26. Paul Marshall, January 2007, online at http://www.bbc.co.uk/blogs/
    ni/2007/01/the_abc_of_invisibility.html

27. Gene Robinson, interview with Ruth Gledhill, online at http://www.
    youtube.com/watch?v=z9D1GFS2HqE

28. Email correspondence with Louie Crew, September 2012.

29. Rowan Williams, reported in *Telegraph*, 7 September 2012, online at
    http://www.telegraph.co.uk/news/religion/9528915/My-job-is-too-big-for-
    one-man-says-Archbishop-of-Canterbury.html

30. Email correspondence, September 2012.

31. Email correspondence.

32. Email correspondence with Tom Wright, August 2012.

33. Email correspondence with Sarah Rowland Jones, August 2012.

34. Rowan Williams, "God's Mission and a Bishop's Discipleship", Fourth Lambeth Retreat Address, July 2008, online at http://www. archbishopofcanterbury.org/articles.php/1739/the-archbishops-retreat-addresses-parts-iii-iv-v

35. Rowan Williams, Interview with James MacIntyre, *New Statesman*, 22 December 2008, online at http://www.archbishopofcanterbury.org/articles. php/609/archbishops-new-statesman-magazine-interview

36. Rowan Williams, "God's Mission and a Bishop's Discipleship", Second Lambeth Retreat Address, July 2008, online at http://www. archbishopofcanterbury.org/articles.php/1355/the-archbishops-retreat-addresses-parts-i-ii

37. Email correspondence with Giles Goddard, September 2012.

38. Interview with Geoffrey Rowell, August 2012.

39. Rowan Williams, Interview on *Today* with John Humphrys, Anglican Communion News Service, ACNS 3640, 18 October 2003, online at http://www.anglicancommunion.org/acns/news.cfm/2003/10/18/ ACNS3640

40. Rowan Williams, "God's Mission and a Bishop's Discipleship", Fourth Lambeth Retreat Address, July 2008, online at http://www. archbishopofcanterbury.org/articles.php/1739/the-archbishops-retreat-addresses-parts-iii-iv-v

41. Email correspondence with Mike Hill, September 2012.

42. Email correspondence.

43. Interview with Peter Selby, August 2012.

44. Email correspondence.

45. Interview.

46. Email correspondence.

47. Email correspondence with Sarah Rowland Jones, August 2012.

48. Rowan Williams, Interview with Mark Tully for "Something Understood", September 2009, online at http://www.archbishopofcanterbury.org/ articles.php/660/the-archbishop-on-understanding-prayer

49. Rowan Williams, "God's Mission and a Bishop's Discipleship", Third Lambeth Retreat Address, July 2008, online at http://www. archbishopofcanterbury.org/articles.php/1739/the-archbishops-retreat-addresses-parts-iii-iv-v

50. Rowan Williams, Interview with Mark Tully for "Something Understood", September 2009, online at http://www.archbishopofcanterbury.org/ articles.php/660/the-archbishop-on-understanding-prayer

51. Rowan Williams, "Stop doing that which is pulling us apart", Interview, May 2007, online at www.globalsouthanglican.org/index.php/comments/ stop_doing_that_which_is_pulling_us_apart_archbishop_of_canterbury_ appeals/

52. Rowan Williams, Interview with Mary Ann Sieghart, *The Times*, 26 May 2004.

53. Interview with Malcolm Brown, September 2012.

54. Quotations below come from Rowan Williams, "The Challenge and Hope of Being an Anglican Today", July 2006, online at http://www.archbishopofcanterbury.org/articles.php/1478/the-challenge-and-hope-of-being-an-anglican-today-a-reflection-for-the-bishops-clergy-and-faithful-o

55. Email correspondence with David Houlding, September 2012.

56. Interview with David Hilborn, October 2012.

57. Rowan Williams, "The Challenge and Hope of Being an Anglican Today", July 2006, online at http://www.archbishopofcanterbury.org/articles.php/1478/the-challenge-and-hope-of-being-an-anglican-today-a-reflection-for-the-bishops-clergy-and-faithful-o

58. Email correspondence with Giles Goddard, September 2012.

59. Rowan Williams at Press Conference with Church of Canada, April 2007, online at http://www.archbishopofcanterbury.org/articles.php/732/press-conference-with-church-of-canada

60. Interview with Ian Douglas, August 2012.

61. Interview with Chris Rowland, August 2012.

62. Interview with Graham Cray, September 2012.

63. Email correspondence with Mike Hill, September 2012.

64. Email correspondence with Clare Herbert, August 2012.

65. Rowan Williams, Interview with Mary Ann Sieghart, *The Times*, 26 May 2004.

66. Interview with Philip Giddings, September 2012.

67. Rowan Williams, Interview with Mary Ann Sieghart, *The Times*, 26 May 2004.

68. Email correspondence with Mike Hill, September 2012.

69. Email correspondence.

70. Email correspondence with Alastair Cutting, September 2012.

71. *Ibid.*

72. Email correspondence with Graham Tomlin, August 2012.

73. Email correspondence with Tom Wright, August 2012.

74. Interview with Kenneth Kearon, September 2012.

75. Email correspondence with Mark Russell, September 2012.

76. Email correspondence.

77. Email correspondence with Martyn Minns, October 2012.

78. Interview with David Hilborn, October 2012.

Index